Contents

S0-CKA-892

Lesson Eleven
Critique Writing

Lesson Twelve
Research Writing

Preface

Writing Progressions is a textbook designed to help college students develop a range of writing skills. In each of twelve lessons, you write a different type of essay emphasizing a particular writing skill. These skills, whether providing descriptive detail, a compelling illustration, strong factual evidence, or relevant comparisons, carry over from essay to essay and can also be applied to any writing that you may do in or out of school.

Essay writing goes well beyond the artificial confines of the classroom. In the "real world," essays can take the form of online and periodical articles, newspaper editorials, "letters to the editor," e-mail letters to particular reading audiences (e.g. state legislators, the school administration, the city council), collections of readings in anthologies, private letters to individuals, and even job applications. Undoubtedly you will find occasion to write essays in various forms throughout your life.

Writing Process

Writing Progressions is a process-oriented text that recognizes both the similarities that characterize the writing process for most writers and the differences that make each individual's writing process unique. While the text takes all writers through the process of prewriting preparation, drafting, revision, and editing for each essay, it also provides the flexibility within each step that allows for individual differences in how writers write. From the suggestions provided in the text and the writing experience that you bring to the course, you will develop and refine an individualized writing process that works best for you.

Communicating with Readers

Writing is a form of communication, and most essays are written to be read. The text strives to make your essay-writing experience as "real" as possible, and throughout the text, you will write essays for specific reading audiences of your choice and when possible, get feedback from them.

Sometimes your reading audience may be quite narrow - college women interested in nursing career options - and other times more general - anyone voting in the upcoming state general election. You will write each essay with a specific reading audience in mind and for particular purpose: to inform, to change readers' minds, to move them to action, to give them a different perspective, or to share something that you learned. The essays that you write and share with readers may have an impact on their lives, whether changing the way they think about something, broadening their knowledge or interests, or even altering their behavior.

Writing Progression

Lessons in the text are organized so that each writing skill that is emphasized in one lesson carries over to subsequent essays. For example, you can apply what you learn about writing effective description in Lesson One and providing relevant examples in Lesson Two to most of your writing. By the end of the lessons, you will be able to apply the writing skills you have developed to any essay writing, including providing vivid description, effective examples, strong illustrations, relevant comparisons, clear explanations, compelling factual evidence, insightful causal analysis, and viable solutions to problems. Each lesson builds on the writing skills emphasized in previous lessons, and cumulatively, these skills give you a variety of effective ways to develop your essays.

Reading-Writing Connection

Much of what you learn about writing in the text will come from reading and analyzing the sample essays included in each lesson. You will read the essays to learn more about a variety of topics and see how other writers have applied the skills that you are working on to their writing, how they have organized and developed their topics, how they have expressed their ideas, how they have revised their essays to improve them, to what purposes they have written the essays, and what impact their writing has on you as a reader. There is no doubt that writers improve their writing through reading, and the text provides you with a range of reading experiences relevant to the type of writing you are doing in each lesson.

Writing Variety

While the writing emphasis in the text is on the non-fiction essay, you will write a number of different types of essays during the course including narrative, biographical, illustrative, process, comparative, persuasive, causal analysis, and critique, along with a final research paper. Writing different types of essays will help you develop a range of writing skills, expose you to the types of writing you may do in the "real world,"and hopefully, engage your interest throughout the course.

Writing Correctness

All college students should be able to write "correctly," without any distracting errors impinging on the effectiveness of their writing. To that end, the text provides instruction in grammar usage and punctuation in each lesson, offers suggestions for effective proofreading and error detection, and encourages students to identify and work on eliminating the types of errors they are most prone to make. By the end of course, the goal of writing error-free final essays is within every student's reach.

Lesson One: Descriptive Writing

Objective: To write a personal-experience narrative essay with an emphasis on description.

Purpose: To bring to life a personal experience by providing descriptive details that capture the experience, including sights, sounds, action, thoughts, and feelings.

Audience: Classmates

Descriptive Writing

The most interesting writing of any kind - essays, novels, poems, short stories, biographies - is often filled with description. Descriptive writing helps readers see, hear, feel, and understand what the writer is conveying. For example, in the following paragraph, writer Candice Millard describes the conditions in Chicago at the time of the great fire of 1871.

> At the time of the fire, Chicago had been a tinderbox. A hundred days had passed with little more than an inch of rain. The buildings were made of wood, wooden planks covered the streets and sidewalks, and, in anticipation of the coming winter, cords of wood, gallons of kerosene, and mounds of hay had been stockpiled throughout the city. The fire, which had started in a cow barn on the city's west side, raged for almost two days, destroying thousands of buildings and more than seventy miles of street, killing at least three hundred people, and leaving a hundred thousand homeless.

The ominous details in the paragraph reveal a Chicago ripe for a fiery disaster: a hundred days with little rain, a city built of wood, highly combustible substances "stockpiled" everywhere. Readers anticipate the impending doom, and the devastating results of the fire are detailed in the final sentence. The paragraph is filled with images that readers can visualize: wooden-planked sidewalks and streets, cords of wood and mounds of hay piled everywhere, a cow barn where it all started, a fire that "raged" for two days through the "tinderbox" of a city.

While visual details are a vital part of descriptive writing, readers are also interested in the workings of the human mind. For example, when a president is elected to office, we assume that a sense of elation and great satisfaction comes with the victory. However, when James Garfield was elected President of the United States, Millard describes a very different mind-set in the following paragraph.

In the days that followed, surrounded by celebrations and frantic plans for his administration, Garfield could not shake the feeling that the presidency would bring him only loneliness and sorrow. As he watched everything that he treasured - his time with his children, his books, and his farm - abruptly disappear, he understood that the life he had known was gone. The presidency seemed to him not a great accomplishment but a "bleak mountain" he was obliged to ascend. Sitting down at his desk at a rare moment to himself, he tried to explain in a letter to a friend the strange sense of loss he had felt since the election. "There is a tone of sadness running through this triumph," he wrote, "which I can hardly explain."

The paragraph describes the surprising, and somewhat disturbing, state of mind of president-elect Garfield, who viewed the presidency as a "'bleak mountain' he was obliged to ascend." Garfield had been a reluctant presidential candidate who never sought the Republican nomination; given that context, his feelings are more understandable. The paragraph clearly captures the depressed state of mind that plagued Garfield throughout his adult life. It provides readers with a startling and revealing glimpse into the thoughts and feelings of a great man at the apex of his political career. Just months into office, Garfield was assassinated by a crazed killer.

In this first lesson, you will write a personal-experience essay with an emphasis on descriptive detail. Your descriptive writing skills will be of benefit for most writing that you do.

What to Describe

Writing involves a constant series of choices: what to write about, how to begin or end a paper, how to word a particular thought, when to start a new paragraph, how best to order your ideas. With descriptive writing, the choices involve what in particular to describe in an essay and how best to describe it. Writers often include the following types of description in their writings:

1. **Place.** Describing the place or "setting" where something occurs enables readers to visualize the scene:

   Our playground was nothing more than a large country lot owned by the neighbors living next to it. The soil was sandy, so the lot was pitted with large "foxholes" that we dug to play war. There were some old rabbit hutches in the front of the lot where we kept our prisoners and a huge eucalyptus tree in the back where we ate our rations under its leafy shade. We considered the lot our property, and young trespassers were greeted with a barrage of dirt clods. The hot summer sun and stifling humidity drove nearby strawberry pickers from the fields by noon, but we played on, oblivious to everything but overrunning the enemy in the next foxhole.

2. **Person.** Describing the people who are important to a story helps bring them to life for readers:

Ms. Haber stood five-feet tall at most and wore large, black sleeveless moo moos to class which covered everything but her hamhock arms and sandaled feet. Her large, unlined face, sitting on a short stump of a neck, was framed with hair resembling black cotton candy. She had a bright red gash of a mouth and dark, piercing eyes. She paced back and forth as she lectured, her sandals squeaking plaintively with every step.

3. **Action.** Describing things that happen - from a summer electrical storm to a child's response to getting her first doll - captures the readers' interest:

Sarah walked stiffly to the piano, a frightened look on her face, and I knew there could be problems. With the audience quietly attentive, she began her recital piece, "Country Gardens." It didn't sound bad, but she seemed to move her fingers robotically, her hands disengaged from her mind. Suddenly she stopped, and I knew in her panic that she had completely lost her place in the song. She sat at the piano frozen, and her teacher walked up, put her hand on Sarah's shoulder, and whispered something in her ear. Sarah started again, playing in a rapid frenzy, and this time she got farther into the song before stopping again, and the audience began applauding. On that cue, Sarah walked - half ran - from the room, exiting the first and last piano recital of her brief career. Outside the hall, I gave her a hug and said, "You did fine." "I just want to go home," she sobbed. And we left.

4. **Sounds and smells**. Writers engage all of the readers' senses in bringing their writing to life. If sounds or smells are a distinctive part of a particular experience, include them in your writing:

Aromas of cotton candy, corn dogs, and barbecued chicken wafted from the enticing food booths, sparkling colored lights lit the ferris wheel and roller coaster, and blood-curdling screams filled the throats of the Giant Parachute riders as they dropped precipitously from the dark sky. The fair surrounded us in all its garish glory, and we wanted to try everything.

5. **Thoughts and feelings.** A runner writes of stumbling just yards from the finish line, ending her quest for Olympic glory. A high school student writes of being arrested for possessing marijuana that his arch enemy had planted in his car. A partially paralyzed accident victim writes of taking her first halting steps after months of grueling rehabilitation. For readers, such revelations beg the obvious questions: "What did it feel like?" "What was going through your mind?" "How did you react?" Writers share their thoughts and feelings to create interest for readers, to help them relate to different experiences, to reveal something of themselves or other people they are writing about, and to allow readers to ponder,

"How might I have reacted in that situation?":

It was late at night, I was in a part of town I shouldn't have been in, and a car began following me. I turned down a street, hoping it would lead to a freeway entrance, but instead saw a dead-end in front of me. I turned around quickly to get out, but the car that had followed me blocked my path, its high beams blinding my eyes.

I just sat there, stunned and frightened, and saw the silhouettes of four heads in the car. After a few seconds, two car doors opened and I saw two large figures get out and approach my car. Scared for my life, I made the split-second decision to get out any way I could. I gunned the car and headed towards the sidewalk, jumping the curb and driving with two wheels on the sidewalk and two on the street. I skirted the other car and bounced back on the street, turning the corner with tires screeching and my heart pounding out of my chest.

I raced down the street, passing intersection after intersection, never looking back. I finally saw a freeway sign, turned the corner and flew towards the entrance lane. Once on the freeway and out of harm's way, I noticed my face and shirt were covered in sweat. I had never been so frightened in my life, and I vowed never to venture to the westside at night again.

Writing Activity 1.1

For practice incorporating descriptive detail in your writing, write three descriptive paragraphs. In the first paragraph, describe a place that you find particularly interesting, attractive, or unappealing to the eye. Describe it in a way that will help readers visualize the place. In the second paragraph, describe a particular person to provide readers a visual image of the person. In the third paragraph, describe briefly something that happened to you recently, including your thoughts and feelings as it occurred.

Examples:

Describing a place:

The most popular gathering place for students at school is the large central square surrounded by two-story classroom buildings. A raised circular fountain dominates the center of the square, shooting spray 30 feet into the air, and students sit on its broad concrete rim. They also fill the benches around the square on a nice day, shaded by sycamore trees planted in cut-out spaces. On one side of the square colorful national flags fly, signifying the different countries where our many foreign students come from. Two sides of the square are lined with green student booths where a variety of clubs publicize events, sell fund-raising food and paraphernalia, advocate for political causes, and recruit prospective members. Music and conversation hum throughout the square; it's a great place to watch people and hang out with friends.

Describing a person:

Malcolm's sheer size stunned people who saw him at the gym for the first time. There were a lot of buff weight lifters who worked out, but Malcolm was in a different class. Every part of his 6' 5" body was huge: his bulging arms, tree-trunk legs, massive chest, broad shoulders, and thick neck. His body glistening with sweat, he would effortlessly dead lift 400 pounds above his head as everyone watched in awe. With that huge, muscular body, Malcolm could have been a menacing presence, but he always wore a broad grin and helped out anyone who needed a spot, truly a friendly giant.

Describing something that happened, including thoughts and feelings:

I picked up my niece at her elementary school and made a U-turn to head towards her house. Immediately a police car appeared and pulled me over, which shocked me. A young, burly policeman approached the car and said, "Didn't you see that No U-turn Sign?" "Sorry," I said. "I didn't see it." "Is this the first time you've ever driven?" he asked sarcastically," and I said rather heatedly, "No, but it's the first time I've picked up my niece." "That's no excuse," he snapped. Then I lost my temper. "Look," I said. "I made a mistake. But I don't need your sarcasm and attitude. I want your name and badge number." He just looked at me a second, a bit stunned, and said, "I'll be back," and went back to his car. A couple minutes later he returned and said, "Look, I'm sorry. It's been a rough day. Make sure you don't miss that sign again." "You bet," I said. My anger drained and I just felt relief for not getting a ticket. I felt bad for my young niece sitting in the back seat, wide-eyed and mouth agape.

Descriptive Words

Word choice obviously plays a big role in descriptive writing. Choosing the best combinations of words to describe something most vividly for readers is a great challenge. Of course, the more words at your disposal, the better your chances of selecting the most appropriate words to describe a particular image or thought. Broadening your vocabulary through reading and word study and using a thesaurus can help you enhance your descriptive powers.

The Power of Verbs

Verbs are the most powerful words for describing action, thoughts, and feelings. Consider how the italicized verbs in the following sentences provide action images for readers.

The drunken man *staggered* from the bar and *collapsed* on the sidewalk.
The hummingbirds *flitted* from flower to flower.
Irene *agonized* over what field to major in.
The losing coach was *inundated* by e-mails from frustrated fans.

The extreme fighting champion *pummeled* his opponent into unconsciousness.
The student's behavior *perplexed* her teacher, who couldn't *fathom* the reason for her sudden lackadaisical attitude.
Miriam's little brother *mimicked* her every word.
The Kentucky Derby favorite *bolted* from the starting gate and *shot* into the lead.

Consider how the following italicized verbs change the action and visual image of the sentence:

The young boys *ambled* down the hillside.
The young boys *careened* down the hillside.
The young boys *tumbled* down the hillside.
The young boys *trudged* down the hillside.
The young boys *scrambled* down the hillside.
The young boys *meandered* down the hillside.
The young boys *flew* down the hillside.

As you can see, there are a variety of verbs available to describe different types of action, each providing a different visual image. In descriptive writing, the challenge is to select the best verb for describing each particular action you are conveying.

To use verbs most effectively in your writing, consider these suggestions:

1. **Select verbs that most accurately describe the action for readers, and consider different options.** For example, what might be an appropriate verb for describing how a cat moves towards her prey, an unsuspecting bird? The cat *snuck up* on the robin? The cat *crept* slowly towards the robin? The cat *stalked* the robin? The cat *tiptoed* towards the robin?

2. **Avoid using the same verbs too often.** For example, in describing the running events at a track meet, the verb "raced" could be used frequently: The runners *raced* down the track. The milers *raced* around the curve. The 100 meter winner *raced* to the finish line and broke the tape. Instead of overusing the verb "raced," a writer could use other verbs with similar meaning such as "sprinted," "dashed," "sped," "tore," "jetted," or "flew."

3. **If you can't put your finger on the best verb to express an action or thought, check a thesaurus to consider some options.** For example, let's say a math instructor didn't say specifically that there would be a quiz on Friday, but he hinted at it. You want to express that idea without using the verb "hinted." In looking up "hinted," a thesaurus would provide you with some verbs to consider such as "implied," "insinuated," and "inferred," one which might best suit your need.

Thesaurus Tips

    Writers often use a thesaurus to find the best words to express themselves and to learn new, useful words. However, when you look up a particular word in a thesaurus, you may find under "synonyms" a list of synonyms and related words without distinction.

    For example, for the word "rankle," some of the listed words are appropriate alternatives: "annoy," "irritate," "aggravate," "exasperate." Others are clearly not synonymous: "embitter," "mortify," "obsess," "inflame," "fester."

    To find a synonym to use in your writing, don't just select any word from a thesaurus list. Some of the words may work well; others will not. Find the best word for your purpose, and look up the meaning of any word you are unsure of.

    For practice, find an appropriate replacement among the following words listed in a thesaurus for the underlined word as it is used in the following sentence: The young girl's smile <u>belied</u> her growing anxiety. Thesaurus list: denied, exploded, repudiated, contradicted, opposed.

Writing Activity 1.2

Fill in the following sentences with verbs that best convey the image that you have in mind.

Example:

Julian <u>rejoiced</u> upon hearing the news that he had been accepted into the physical therapy program at Minter State College.

1. The spectators _____ the efforts of the marathon runner who _____ himself across the finish line.

2. Juanita's success in college _____ hope to her younger siblings that they too could succeed.

3. Felix _____ to the fear of flying that had _____ him for weeks and cancelled his flight.

4. Her classmates were _____ when Michelle abruptly _____ from the race for student body president.

5. The stock market _____ dramatically on Thursday, and
   investors _____ even more bad news on Friday.

6. The once mighty waterfall _____ weakly down the mountainside,
   _____ in flow by the dry winter.

7. The rocket _____ slowly into the sky, its massive size and gravity
   _____ its gradual ascent.

8. We were all _____ by the sight of thousands of pelicans diving
   into the ocean in unison, which _____ the
   surfers to abandon the water.

9. The smell that _____ from the garbage bin _____
   of rotting food and dirty diapers.

10. The explosion _____ the tall building and
    _____ people on its top floors.

The Power of Adjectives and Adverbs

Adjectives and adverbs provide much of the detail of descriptive writing, helping readers to see, hear, feel and understand most accurately what the writer is conveying. Note how the italicized adjectives in the following sentences help to create both an image and a mood for readers:

The *languid* stream cut a *sinuous* path thrown the *lush* jungle growth.
A *palpable* cloud of despair hung over the campaign headquarters where *dejected* Hernandez loyalists gathered the night of the *ill-fated* election.
The *dark, ominous* clouds gathering in the west could bring *drenching* rain to our campsite by evening.

Adverbs work in tandem with both verbs and adjectives to modify and enhance their meaning:

Nellie *futilely* tried to gather up her manuscript pages scattered by the sudden whirlwind.
(The adverb "futilely" modifies the verb "tried.")
We were *terrifyingly* close to going over the waterfall in our pontoon boat.
(The adverb "terrifyingly" modifies the adjective "close.")
The eagle soared *majestically* across the canyon.
(The adverb "majestically" describes how the eagle "soared.")
The violin solo by the first-year orchestra student was *excrutiatingly* bad.
(The adverb "excruciatingly" modifies the adjective "bad.")

Notice how in each sentence, the italicized adverb provides critical descriptive detail that sets the mood, creates an image, or describes a person's efforts clearly for readers.

To use adjectives and adverbs most effectively in your writing, consider the following suggestions:

1. **Use adjectives and adverbs to provide the clearest, most accurate picture for readers**: what the incoming clouds looked like, how the college debate winner felt, how Chicago's winter wind affected ill-prepared tourists, the pace of commuter traffic on Los Angeles' I-5 freeway, how spectators reacted to the plane crash at the air show.

2. **Vary your choice of adjectives and adverbs rather than relying on a few common words**. For example, the adjective "great" can be overused to describe how someone felt after pain-ending knee surgery, after losing 20 pounds, after winning the lottery, or after returning to college after years in the workforce. To vary her adjectives rather than overuse the word "great," a writer might consider using adjectives such as "exhilarated," "thrilled," "fantastic," "joyful," "rapturous," "ebullient," or "terrific."

3. **Avoid weighing down a sentence with too many adjectives and adverbs.** A sentence over-laden with modifiers can slow down and distract readers and weaken the descriptive impact. For example, the sentence "The *short, stout, balding* man in the *green, rumpled, overly large* sweat suit surprised marathon spectators with his *brisk, constant, rapid, unrelenting* pace through the 26 miles of the *hot, grueling, crowded, competitive* Philadelphia Marathon" has readers more focused on the multitude of modifiers than the meaning of the sentence. A stripped-down version of the sentence reads more effectively: "The *short, stout* man in the *rumpled* sweat suit surprised marathon spectators with his *brisk, unrelenting* pace through the 26 miles of the *grueling* Philadelphia Marathon." A few well-chosen modifiers usually best serve a writer's purpose.

4. **Through overuse, some adjectives become cliched and lose much of their descriptive power.** For example, words such as "amazing" and "awesome" have become so commonplace that their meanings have been devalued. Other overused adjectives fall within the realm of "slang:" informal words more suited to speech than writing. Adjectives such as "cool," "neat," "gnarly," "bad" (meaning "good"), or "sweet" (meaning "really good"), are best suited for cafeteria conversation or e-mail exchanges. As a general rule, avoid cliches and slang in your descriptive writing, neither of which has the power of more original, authentic description.

Writing Activity 1.3

Fill in the following blanks with adjectives and adverbs that best describe the sights, sounds, smells, or feelings that you want to convey in each sentence. Feel free to use a thesaurus to consider possible word choices.

Examples:

Felipe was <u>exultant</u> after receiving an "A" on the <u>most</u> <u>challenging</u> calculus test of the semester.

The young children were playing <u>dangerously</u> close to the landfill area, <u>oblivious</u> to the danger it posed.

1. _____ pain shot through Mary Ann's shoulder whenever she tried _____ to lift her right arm.

2. The _____ lights of the boardwalk played upon the _____ ocean waves crashing against the pier.

3. Feeling _____ and _____, I left the concert early and went straight to bed.

4. _____, the _____ contestant in the judo competition was among the _____, _____ flipping his opponents and winning matches.

5. _____ by all of the attention, our fox terrier hid under the sofa, out of the _____ hands of the _____ children.

6. The _____ movie was one of the most _____ and _____I've seen in a long time.

7. Gwendolyn's _____ disposition contradicted her _____ behavior when she was defending a client in court.

8. The _____monkey hurled a banana peel at the _____ teenage girl in front of his cage.

9. It was _____ _____ for anyone to climb the fence into the stadium, _____ guarded by the _____ security patrol.

10. No one looked more _____ at the movie premiere than the leading actress, who astonished everyone with her _____ attire.

Writing Assignment

This lesson's assignment is to write a *narrative* essay - a first-person account - of a personal experience with an emphasis on description. Select an experience from your distant or more recent past that you remember clearly and that made some impact on your life at the time. Consider a number of different experiences and select the one that you are most interested in writing about and that you would like to share with classmates.

    Narrative essays are among the most interesting for readers because they relate eventful "real life" experiences which readers may relate to or learn from. For writers, narrative essays allow them to share compelling experiences and analyze their impact, often helping them understand the experience better. As you consider different experiences to write about, ask yourself, "What experience(s) is most memorable and had the most lasting or profound effect on me?"

Sample Topic: My playground accident in elementary school

Preparation

Writers do different things to help prepare them to write an essay, from thinking deeply about their topic to writing out a detailed plan. No doubt you have used different prewriting strategies in the past that have worked well for you, and you may find some helpful new strategies in the text. Each "Preparation" section provides you with some prewriting techniques to apply in ways that you find most useful.

    For your upcoming narrative essay, consider using one or more of the following prewriting strategies in preparation for writing the first draft of your essay.

1. **Free writing.** Write freely for ten minutes or so on your personal experience, writing down anything that comes to mind about what happened. Free writing can help you recall details of the experience, reveal how much you remember about it, jog your memory and increase your recall, and rekindle the emotions that you felt.

2. **Replaying the experience.** Close your eyes and visually replay the experience in your mind, like viewing a movie. Try to visualize and hear everything that occurred. Mentally replaying an experience can bring back memories, recapture your thoughts and feelings at the time, and help you visualize the "moving picture" that you want to describe for readers.

3. **Answering questions.** Answering questions about the experience will help you decide on the most important elements to include in your essay. Answer questions such as the following: When and where did the experience take place? Who and/or what was involved? What exactly happened? Why did it happen? What were your thoughts and feelings? What happened as a result? Why was it so memorable?

4. **Telling the story**. Relate your experience orally to someone. Encourage them to interrupt you with questions to see what you may be leaving out, to discover what readers may be most interested in, and to help you decide what to include in your essay.

Writing Activity 1.4

Use one or more of the prewriting strategies suggested in preparation for writing the first draft of your essay.

Example:

Free writing

I remember it was a warm, sunny day and I was playing on the ocean wave on the playground. One or two other kids were also on it. Somehow I got my finger caught between the bench that rocked back and forth and the metal pole, and I smashed my finger. It really scared me with all the blood, and a yard duty teacher took me to the office where the nurse bandaged it. Mom came and took me to the doctor's office and I was in a lot of pain by then. He gave me a shot beneath the finger nail to numb it before he pulled the nail off. Mom fainted. She cut her forehead. The doctor had to bandage up both of us. I still have a funny-looking finger nail and mom has a scar on her forehead to remind us of that day.

Drafting

When you write the first draft of your narrative essay, your goal is to get your experience on paper as clearly as you remember it. There is no pressure when writing a first draft to be "perfect," and you will have time to change and improve whatever you want during the "revision" process.

Writing and revising drafts is typical for most writers, no matter how experienced. Few writers, including professionals, can get their thoughts on paper "perfectly" the first time. As they read through a draft, writers often find sentences that can be improved, details or examples that can be added, a paragraph that needs further development, another paragraph that needs dividing, or an ending that seems incomplete. The first draft provides you with a great start, and the revision process helps you shape and develop the essay in the most effective ways.

In writing your first draft, consider these suggestions:

1. **To begin the draft, provide an opening that "sets the stage" for the experience.** Your opening may include some details of setting and time, the introduction of people involved, and conclude with some foreshadowing of what is to come: "Never did I realize that this routine check-up with my doctor would change my life," or "I had looked forward to my first school chess tournament for months."

2. **Write about the experience *chronologically*, relating different aspects of the experience in the time order that they occurred.** Generally, narrative essays unfold most effectively in time order, which readers can follow most easily.

3. **As you write, provide the descriptive details that you feel are most important to helping readers visualize and understand the experience**. What do readers need to see, hear, and feel to bring the experience to life for them?

4. **If conversation is an important part of the experience, include some dialogue in the essay.** Dialogue is interesting for readers, helps bring people to life, and creates a dramatic effect.

5. **Include your thoughts and feelings during the experience.** Readers are often as interested in what you were thinking and feeling as in what was actually happening. Try to capture your thoughts and feelings as you remember them.

6. **Conclude the essay by relating the impact of the experience**. What happened as a result? Why it was memorable for you? What did you learn, gain, or lose from the experience? Reflect on the experience from your current perspective, which may be different from when you actually experienced it.

7. **To paragraph the essay, change paragraphs as you move to something new in the**

experience: a different time, place, or part of the experience. Most experiences are made up of a series of occurrences which usually fit naturally in different paragraphs.

Dialogue Tips

To include dialogue most effectively in your writing, use it sparingly. Include just the most crucial dialogue at the most important times in your experience. In other words, use dialogue for dramatic effect. For example, a direct quote like, "I am going to tear your head off, Farley," the class bully hissed in my face, has a greater impact than writing, The class bully said that he was going to tear my head off.

When you quote people, make sure to put quotation marks (" ") around the spoken words and identify the speaker: Lucinda grimaced, "One more day of eating salmon loaf in the cafeteria and I'm going to puke!" "Yeah, and the mystery meat they serve on Mondays is just as bad," I offered in support.

Writing Activity 1.5

Write the first draft of your narrative essay. You may first want to read the following sample draft to see how the writer opened her paper, related her experience, included descriptive detail throughout the experience, concluded her draft, and paragraphed the essay.

Sample first draft:

The Playground Accident

On a warm spring day when I was in the first grade, I was on the playground at recess and headed for my favorite piece of play equipment: the ocean wave. The ocean wave was composed of a circular bench attached to a center pole by several iron rods. When riders were on the ocean wave, it would rock back and forth and spin around as we pulled and pushed on the rods to make the circular bench move.

As the bench rocked back and forth, it made a clanging sound as it hit against the center pole, a sound you could hear across the playground. It was great fun to rock as high as possible and make the loudest clanging noise as the bench crashed into the pole and then shot back out again. We riders would make whooping sounds - "woooop, wooooo, woooop, wooooo" - with each up-and-down motion of the bench.

Thinking back on it, it was a pretty dangerous apparatus, an accident just waiting to happen, and I was the unlucky recipient. While I had always kept my hands on the rods to help move the bench, for some reason I gripped the front of the bench with one hand and held a rod with the other. When the bench came clanging down into the pole, my hand was in the unfortunate position of being between the two. When the bench hit the pole, the top of my ring finger was smashed between the bench and the pole, and I let out a sharp cry. The ocean wave stopped, and I looked down at the smashed nail on my finger, blood running down my hand. While I sat on the bench stunned, someone ran to get the on-duty teacher, and she immediately walked me to the principal's office.

The next few minutes were a blur, and I think I was in shock because I didn't feel any pain. The school nurse wrapped my finger and my mother showed up a few minutes later to take me to the doctor. On the way to the doctor, I remember the pain finally hit, and I had never felt anything like it. My whole finger was throbbing, and I started to sob. Luckily, the doctor's office was nearby, and I was whisked into the doctor in front of other people in the waiting room. I lay down on the table and he took a look at my finger. "Boy, you sure did a number on that nail," he said calmly. "We need to take it off so your finger can heal." I had never heard anything as frightening.

Before he pulled the mangled nail off my finger, he needed to numb the area with a shot, and out came a long needle. He stuck the needle into the bloody flesh behind the nail, and I screamed in pain. "That's the last pain you'll feel," he assured me as the finger started getting numb. Then I heard a loud thud on the floor. My mom had passed out and hit her head on the floor. Now the doctor had one patient on the table and another bleeding from the head.

The doctor helped my mom into a chair, had her hold a towel to her forehead, and then proceeded to pull my nail off with some tweezers. I didn't feel a thing. He put some salve on my finger and then wrapped it with gauze, and then my mom and I traded places. Now she was the one to get the numbing shot along with seven stitches in her forehead. I remember my mom seemed more embarrassed from fainting than anything else, and I was so engrossed in my own situation that I had little pity left for her. Finally, we walked out of the doctor's office hand in hand, all bandaged up. The waiting patients must have wondered what had gone on inside that room.

The doctor gave mom a pain medication prescription for my finger, and I took pills for the next few days when I felt the pain coming. My finger nail started slowly growing back, but strangely, it grew back as a weird-looking double nail, which still causes people to ask, "What happened to your finger?" My mom sports a diagonal scar across her forehead which she sometimes covers with bangs, so we both have our life-long reminders of what happened long ago on that nice spring day. The ocean wave was removed from the playground, and from every other playground in the school district. I guess the only good thing that came from my accident was that no other kid ever got a mangled finger from the ocean wave.

Revision

Most writers, including those who write for a living, find things that they can improve in a first draft. That is not surprising since the first time you put your thoughts on paper, you are feeling your way through the essay, deciding what to write next, often using the first words that come to mind, and uncertain of how well everything is fitting together.

When you set aside your draft for a while and then read it over, you often see more clearly what you have done well, what doesn't sound quite right to you, what doesn't fit as well as you'd like, what you might add, or what you might delete. While you may not make wholesale changes in the draft, the changes you do make - adding some description, emphasizing an important point, deleting some irrelevant information, improving some sentence wording - can improve your paper significantly.

In this lesson, the revision emphasis is on improving your descriptive detail and "balancing" the parts of your essay to make sure you are emphasizing its most important elements. While in later lessons your revision emphasis shifts to other considerations, you will continue to scrutinize your drafts for effective description and balance, which are important to most writing.

Descriptive Detail

As you read your draft and consider how you might improve its descriptive power, ask yourself the following questions:

1. **What details might I add to help readers visualize the experience?**
   Are there places in the essay where some added description would help readers see or hear more clearly what happened? In the sample draft "Playground Accident," for example, the writer described in detail the playground apparatus, where her hand was placed, and how the bench clanged into the pole so readers could visualize the accident. Consider adding any details that would help readers "watch" what happened.

2. **Where might I improve my descriptive wording?** As you read your draft, check your descriptive verbs, adjectives, and adverbs to see whether some better word choices would sharpen your images or more accurately depict what was happening.

3. **Are there places where I should add my thoughts or feelings, or those of other people involved in the experience?** For example, in the "Playground Accident" essay, the writer detailed her feelings throughout the experience. However, we learn nothing of how her mother felt about what her daughter was going through. Would this have been of interest to readers?   As you consider adding a thought or feeling at a particular time in the experience, ask yourself, "Was I feeling or thinking anything at this point in the experience, and would readers be interested?" For example, in the "Playground Accident," when the writer's finger smashed against the pole, readers

undoubtedly wanted to know how that must have felt, which the writer provided.

4. **Is there any irrelevant description that I can delete?** Sometimes in first drafts, writers can "over-describe" in an attempt to leave nothing out. For example, in "Playground Accident," the writer could have gone into detail describing the playground where the accident occurred, what the on-duty teacher looked like, or what kind of car the writer drove in to the doctor's office. However, none of this detail would have been significant to the experience or help readers visualize or understand it. In evaluating your descriptions, ask yourself, "Is this detail relevant to the experience or to how readers will view it?"

Writing Activity 1.6

Read the descriptive revisions below that the writer made in one paragraph of the "Playground Accident" draft. Then keeping in mind the four suggestions in the text, read your draft and make any changes in description that you feel will improve the essay.

Revisions in one paragraph of the "Playground Accident" draft

(Deleted words crossed out, added words in bold print)

Before he pulled the mangled nail off my **bloody** finger, ~~he~~ **the doctor** needed to numb the ~~area~~ **upper finger** with a shot, and out came a long, **frightening-looking** needle. **I closed my eyes, and** he stuck the needle into the bloody flesh ~~behind~~ **beneath** the nail. ~~and~~ I screamed in pain. "That's the last pain you'll feel," he assured me as the finger started getting numb. Then I heard a loud thud on the floor. My mom, **who had been standing next to me,** had passed out and hit her head on the floor. Now the doctor had one patient on the table and another bleeding from the head.

Balancing Your Essay

When writers reread the first draft of an essay, they sometimes discover some imbalances among its different parts: an overly long opening, a brief, forgettable conclusion, or descriptive detail limited to certain parts. Such imbalances are often not evident as you are writing the first draft but become obvious when you reread the draft as a whole.

In narrative essays, certain imbalances tend to occur within first drafts. As you read your draft, consider these suggestions.

1. **Make sure your opening isn't overly long.** Sometimes in the opening - where you provide information leading to the heart of the experience - a writer starts back too far in time or provides so much detail that the opening dominates the essay. Keep in mind that your lead-in is just that: information that "sets the stage" for the main

incident. If an opening drags on too long, readers can lose interest before they get to the actual experience.

2. **Make sure your essay focuses on the "main event."** For readers, the most important part of the essay is *what actually happened*: the main incident or event that you are writing about. Make sure you have given this part of the essay the attention it deserves by describing it clearly, providing your thoughts and feelings at the time, and charging it with the right dramatic feel. In the "Playground Accident" draft, the essay details two main events - the accident itself and the writer's ensuing visit to the doctor's office - each central to her experience.

3. **Conclude with an ending worth reading.** Of final interest to readers is what happened as a result of the experience, which is usually revealed in the ending. The ending might include the impact the experience had on the writer, what happened to others involved, or what the writer learned or gained from the experience. A short, abrupt wrap-up generally isn't that satisfying for readers and creates an imbalance with the other parts of the essay. Keep in mind that the ending provides the final impression that readers are left with.

Writing Activity 1.7

Read the following first draft. With a friend or a group of classmates, identify any imbalances in the essay and the effect they have on readers. Discuss how the writer could eliminate the imbalances and improve the essay by adding more detail and providing more information in some parts and deleting some content in others.

A Frightening Night

When I was eleven years old and my sister was thirteen, we were at home alone one evening when our parents went out with friends. They had gone to a dance because my mom loved dancing and dragged dad along. My dad really didn't like dancing, but once every couple of months he'd go dancing with mom so that she couldn't complain when he had his poker nights. That was their trade-off. They were going to be out until after midnight, but that wasn't a problem for us. We had stayed home alone before and were too old for a babysitter. Nothing bad ever happened.

   A night alone at the house was not a bad thing at all, even if I had to hang out with my sister. We could eat anything we wanted, watch anything on T.V., or call our friends and talk as long as we wanted. We were sitting on the sofa around 10:00 with a large bowl of buttery popcorn between us and tall glasses of Pepsi with lots of ice, watching a horror flick on T.V. Zombies were walking out of their graves and terrorizing the town, but the zombies were more funny looking than scary and we were laughing at them and stuffing huge handfuls of popcorn in our mouths.

   My sister and I liked watching scary movies when our parents were gone because they didn't really like us watching them. The problem was that sometimes I would have nightmares after watching a scary movie and would wake up my parents in the middle of the night. I wouldn't really be scared during the movie, but I couldn't control having the nightmares. So they would say, "We don't want you watching movies that give you nightmares."

As we sat watching the zombie movie, all of a sudden we heard what sounded like footsteps on the roof. That scared us a lot more than the zombie movie. Then we heard scratching noises on a window. We ran down to the basement and hid under the staircase. Then we could hear footsteps above us in the house.

It turned out that my sister's boyfriend and two of his buddies were just trying to scare us. They did a good job. That was a night I'll never forget.

Writing Activity 1.8

Read your first draft to see if there are any imbalances among different parts that weaken the essay. Eliminate any imbalances by adding more information or description to some parts or by deleting any unnecessary or irrelevant content in others.

Reader Feedback

Writers often get feedback from others to help improve their writing. Seldom is any writing published without being scrutinized by editing experts, who usually offer revision suggestions.

With a narrative essay, a writer is so familiar with the experience that he may leave "holes" in the narrative that readers are unable to fill. For example, if the writer of the "Playground Accident" essay had assumed her readers knew what the Ocean Wave was and didn't describe it in detail, most readers couldn't have visualized the apparatus or the accident itself. Writers also can't predict what will interest readers the most about a particular experience or anticipate questions they may have. For these reasons, getting feedback from readers can be a valuable part of the revision process.

Evaluating a Draft

Since you have a classroom of "readers" available, exchanging drafts with a classmate or two can provide some valuable feedback. When reading a classmate's draft, the following suggestions will help you provide some useful feedback:

1. **Are there sentences in the draft that you don't understand?** If the meaning of a particular sentence is unclear to you, it would probably be unclear to other readers. Bring such sentences to the writer's attention.

2. **Is there anything in the draft that you are uncertain why the writer included it?** Writers can get off on tangents or fail to show how some information is relevant to the experience You can simply ask, "Why did you include this in your draft?"

3. **Does the draft raise questions that you would like answered?** You might wonder how the writer reacted to something that happened, how she felt at a particular point in the experience, what something or someone looked like, or why, for example, the writer did something so risky. As questions come to your mind, raise them with the writer.

4. **Are there any suggestions you can provide that would make the essay more interesting for readers?** Perhaps the main incident hasn't received adequate attention. Perhaps the ending is too abrupt and leaves unanswered questions. Perhaps the writer's thoughts and feelings are seldom revealed. Perhaps the opening doesn't "set the scene" clearly enough for readers to visualize it. Some general suggestions may help the writer make some worthwhile revisions that add interest for readers.

Writing Activity 1.9

Read the following first draft. With a classmate, evaluate the draft by applying the previous four questions. Decide what suggestions you would make and questions you would raise to help the writer revise his draft.

Shop Class

When I was in seventh grade, I enrolled in a fifth-period wood shop class. I didn't know anything about making things out of wood, but I figured it would be an easy class and an easy grade.

I was a pretty good student, and I noticed a lot of the guys in the class weren't among the best students. I soon learned, however, that being good in school had little to do with being good in shop class. Some of the guys already had experience with power saws and sanders, and I had hardly ever hammered a nail.

I decided that my first project would be a small one, so I set about making a belt holder. I worked on it for a couple weeks, but I could never get the two sides of the holder balanced. It turned out to be worthless piece of junk that I threw away after I took it home. The shop teacher, Mr. Aguilera, gave me a "C" on the project and said, "That was just your first project. You'll get better."

Christmas was nearing and I decided I wanted to make my mother something. I looked in the project book and found something that looked simple to make but very nice: a wooden candy bowl. It wouldn't require any sawing, nailing, or assembling, none of which I was good at. Basically, all I needed were some chisels and sandpaper, so I was set.

While I attacked a piece of wood with a chisel, other guys were busy using a variety of power saws, hand saws, hammers, screw drivers, and power sanders to create gun racks, footstools, and even chests of drawers. I was amazed by their skill and embarrassed by my own inability. However, I was determined to make the best candy bowl I could, and although it didn't rival my tablemate's lacquered bookshelf, I thought my mom would like it.

I just kept chiseling and sanding, chiseling and sanding, and the candy bowl started taking shape. Mr. Aguilera would drop by the table occasionally, spending most of his time checking on the bigger projects. "As you get nearer the bottom of the bowl, use a finer chisel and sandpaper," he recommended. "You bet," I said. I could imagine the finished product in my mind and my mom's surprise when she unwrapped it.

It was getting near Christmas break and guys were starting to finish their projects. It was taking me a long time to finish a candy bowl, but as unskilled as I was, I took twice as long as anyone else would. "You've got to finish it up, Flores," Mr. Aguilera said somewhat sharply, wondering how one student could spend so much time on a little candy bowl. "I'm just about there," I said, and kept on chiseling.

Rushing to finish, however, was the worst thing I could have done. I was in the most delicate stage, chiseling and sanding out the very bottom of the bowl, and with one clumsy thrust of the chisel, I gouged a hole through the bottom.

I ended up getting a "D" on the project, a "C-" in the class, and some final words from Mr. Aguilera: "Wood working may not be for you, Flores." What an understatement.

Writing Activity 1.10

Exchange drafts with a classmate or two, read each other's drafts, and make suggestions or raise questions that could improve the essay from your perspective. Keeping your classmate's suggestions in mind, make any further revisions to your draft that you feel will improve it.

Writing Activity 1.11

Set your revised draft aside for awhile, and then give it a final evaluation. Check your paragraphing to make sure you have changed paragraphs as you moved to different parts of the experience. Reread your draft to see whether there is anything else you would like to add. Reread your sentences to make sure you are satisfied with the wording of each sentence. Make any changes that you feel would improve the paragraphing, sentence wording, or content.

As you reread your draft and make a few revisions, you probably realize what most writers discover: you can always find something to change in a paper. The question is, "At what point do I quit revising?" The obvious answer is, "When you are completely satisfied with your paper." However, even the best writers are seldom "completely satisfied" with their writing. A sensible time to stop is when you reach a point of diminishing returns: the meager, or questionable, gains you make don't justify the continued time and effort. In other words, when your revising veers towards nitpicking and second-guessing yourself, it's time to move on.

Editing

During the final "editing" phase of the writing process, you proofread your paper for errors and make the necessary corrections to produce the "cleanest" final draft you can. Errors can distract readers from an essay's content and weaken its impact, so producing an "error-free" final draft is a worthwhile goal for any writer.

Writers generally proofread their papers at the end of the writing process, after all content, wording, and organizational revisions have been made. To proofread for errors while an essay is still undergoing content and wording changes makes little sense. Revising the content of an essay and proofreading it for errors are two very different tasks which as a general rule shouldn't be co-mingled. If you run across an occasional error as you write or revise a paper, you might correct it on the spot. However, the emphasis on error correction should be at the end, when your sole focus is on identifying and correcting errors.

Each lesson presents a different type of error problem that is common among writers, and within the twelve lessons you will learn how to eliminate the vast majority of errors that can plague writers. Some types of errors may not be a problem for you, and you needn't dwell on them. You will focus primarily on the types of errors that you are most prone to make and work on eliminating them in your writing.

Run-on and Comma-Splice Sentences

Aside from spelling errors, running sentences together is the most common error that writers make. Fortunately, it is also one of the most easily correctable errors once a writer focuses on it.

To eliminate run-on and comma-spice sentences in your writing, follow these guidelines:

1. **Most run-on sentences contain two sentences not separated by a period that are closely related in meaning:**

   We're going to be late for the concert it begins in ten minutes, and we're still a half hour away from the arena.

   The traffic on Shaw Avenue is terrible there must be a faster way to get to the arena.

2. **A comma-splice contains two sentences with a comma between them.** A comma between sentences is an incorrect punctuation mark since it is not an end mark and does not separate sentences:

   Clarissa jogs through Central Park every morning, she is training to run in the New York Marathon.

A different Republican presidential candidate leads in the polls each week, there is no strong frontrunner.

3. **Most run-on and comma-splice sentences are relatively short, and the second sentence often begins with certain types of words.** Pronouns such as "he," "she," "they," and "it" and "introductory" words such as "a," "an," "there," "the," "that," and "these" often begin the second sentence within a run-on or comma-splice:

   The Kwan family hold its annual reunion in a park there are over a hundred relatives that usually attend.

   The latest Beijing high rise complex is fifty stories tall, it took only three months to build.

4. **To correct run-on and comma-splice sentences, do one of the following:**

   A. Insert a period after the first sentence and capitalize the first letter of the second sentence within the run-on or comma splice:

   The rain isn't expected to last beyond the first of the week, it should be clear and dry for the Obon Festival.

   Corrected:
   The rain isn't expected to last beyond the first of the week. It should be clear and dry for the Obon Festival.

   B. Insert a "joining word" between the two sentences to create one sentence:

   I'm not going to the football game Saturday there are just too many other things going on.

   Corrected:
   I'm not going to the football game Saturday *because* there are just too many other things going on.

   C. Insert a semi-colon (;) between sentences. A semi-colon can correctly separate sentences, and it is often used between shorter sentences closely related in meaning:

   You're one of the best speakers in the class you seem completely natural and relaxed when you give a speech.

   Corrected:
   You're one of the best speakers in the class; you seem completely natural and

relaxed when you give a speech.

5.   **In general, to correct run-on and comma-splice sentences, insert a joining word or a semi-colon (;) between shorter sentences and separate longer sentences with a period (.):**

Kenisha is inseparable from her twin sister they do everything together.

Corrected:
Kenisha is inseparable from her twin sister, *and* they do everything together.

The women's restroom is on the north side of the gym, the men's restroom is on the south side.

Corrected:
The women's restroom is on the north side of the gym; the men's restroom is on the south side.

That pungent odor seems to be emanating from the backyard of the house on the corner from the smell, I'll bet they are doing a deep-pit barbecue for a party.

Corrected:
That pungent odor seems to be emanating from the backyard of the house on the corner. From the smell, I'll bet they are doing a deep-pit barbecue for a party.

Writing Activity 1.12

For practice identifying and correcting run-on and comma splice sentences, read the following paragraph and correct any run-ons or comma splices. Combine shorter run-ons with a joining word or semi-colon, and separate longer run-ons with a period.

Example:

One winter, about fifty geese migrated to the Roeding Park Lake, most of them left by March. A few, however, didn't leave, and park visitors began feeding them popcorn and peanuts. Within a year, the geese had multiplied two-fold and clearly had no intention of leaving they had become park residents, and their numbers continue to grow each year.

Corrected:

One winter, about fifty geese migrated to the Roeding Park Lake, *and* most of them left by March. A few, however, didn't leave, and park visitors began feeding them popcorn and peanuts. Within a year the geese had multiplied two-fold and clearly had no intention of leaving. They had become park residents, and their numbers continue to grow each year.

Major flooding occurred in different parts of the world in 2011, it was rare for that much flooding to occur in one year. In different parts of Southeast Asia, Europe, and North America, thousands of people had to evacuate their homes, causing millions of dollars in property damage. Many people had no disaster insurance they lost most of their worldly possessions. Climatologists, alarmed by the unprecedented amount of flooding worldwide, pointed to global warming as the likely cause. They contended that higher levels of precipitation created by an ever-warming atmosphere triggered the flooding, all of the areas that were flooded had experienced a deluge of rainfall. The 2011 floods were unexpected climatologists warn us to prepare for more of the same in the future.

Writing Activity 1.13

Proofread your draft for any run-on or comma-splice sentences, and make the necessary corrections. Separate longer sentences with periods and combine shorter sentences with joining words and/or semi-colons. You may find that you have no problem with run-on or comma-splice sentences, which eliminates a major proofreading concern for future writing.

Writing Activity 1.14

Proofread your draft for errors and make the necessary corrections. The following are among most common types of errors that writers make: comma usage, apostrophe usage (in possessives and contractions), pronoun usage, subject-verb agreement, easily confused words (there/their/they're, it/it's, know/no, affect/effect, your/you're, then/than), irregular verbs, sentence fragments, and misspelled words. Make sure to run the spell-check on your word processing program to correct any spelling error.

Use your current knowledge and writing experience to proofread your draft for errors, and don't be concerned if you aren't familiar with some grammatical areas. In future lessons, you will receive instruction on how to detect and avoid each type of error. In addition, you may not have problems in a number of these areas, and in the future, you can concentrate primarily on the types of errors that you tend to make.

Proofreading Tips

Writers often overlook errors in their writing for two reasons. First, they try to find and correct all types of errors at one time. Second, they unintentionally ignore certain types of errors, such as apostrophes in possessive words.

To give yourself the best chance of identifying and correcting any errors in your writing, proofread your draft for one type of error at a time, such as comma usage. Then proofread it another time for a different type of error, such as pronoun usage.

Finally, have a list of the types of errors you are looking for, and make sure to proofread your draft for each type. As you gain a greater awareness of your personal error tendencies, you will know what areas in particular to focus on.

Writing Activity 1.15

After you have completed proofreading your draft and correcting errors, exchange drafts with a classmate or two and proofread each other's papers. A second pair of eyes never hurts in detecting errors, and you will learn both from proofreading and finding errors in other writer's drafts and in seeing the types of errors you overlooked in your own draft.
.

Communicating with Readers

Essays are written to be read. To make your writing for the course most meaningful, it should be read by the audience for which it was intended, in this case your classmates. When you spend significant time and effort on a paper, and no doubt create a work of considerable interest, it deserves to be read by others.

Sharing your essay with classmates by reproducing copies or passing the essays around class is a simple matter. Your instructor may also design ways for you to get feedback from your readers. In later lessons, when you are writing for audiences outside the classroom, you will find different ways, with your instructor's help, to get your essays into the hands of readers. Your essay writing for the course, then, is more than just completing assignments to develop your writing skills. Through your essays, you will present your ideas and opinions to different reading audiences on a variety of topics that readers may find interesting, informative, or thought-provoking.

Lesson Two: Providing Examples

Objective: To write a biographical essay with an emphasis on providing examples to highlight a person's characteristics and qualities.

Purpose: To provide a clear depiction of a person for readers, including your relationship with him or her.

Audience: Classmates

Providing examples in your writing is one of the most effective ways to help readers understand your ideas. Writers use examples for a variety of purposes: to help readers understand a particular concept, to provide evidence that something exists or occurs, to support a particular point the writer is making, to "show" readers what a particular statement means, or to clarify an idea.

For example, a writer used the following example to help readers understand a theory and to provide evidence to support it.

> Evolution is still occurring today. For example, in the past few years, scientists have noted a significant increase in wing span among certain species of migratory birds. In other words, some birds are growing longer, larger wings than their predecessors. The reason for the evolving wing span, scientists speculate, is that these birds are having to fly longer distances in search of food, often against heavier winds brought about by climate change. Their wings have grown larger and longer through extended, vigorous use, adapting to survive in a changing environment.

The writer provides an example that helps readers understand how a specie evolves and provides evidence that such evolution is occurring today.

Another writer used the following example to show readers what she meant by "hands-on learning."

> Seventh grade science instructor Michael Renteria regularly provides students with "hands-on" learning. For example, rather than explain to students how carbon dioxide from auto and industrial emissions traps heat in the atmosphere and raises temperatures, he lets them discover the effect on their own. In the classroom, they create an artificial, enclosed environment, pump carbon dioxide into its atmosphere, and note any change in atmospheric temperature. As the temperature rises with the increased levels of $CO2$, they see first-hand the warming effect of $CO2$.

The writer provided an example of "hands-on learning" that helps readers understand how Mr. Renteria's students learn by doing rather than being told.

Incorporating Examples

Throughout your writing you will find opportunities to provide examples that will create interest and help readers understand your thoughts. An example such as the one about the evolving wing span of migratory birds creates interest for readers and helps them understand a concept in a way that textbook theory may not.

   To provide examples effectively in your writing, consider the following suggestions:

1. **When you present a general statement, provide an example to make it particular to the person or situation you are writing about.** For example, if you write, "Nathan can make anyone laugh," you are providing a general statement that could apply to many people. A good example, however, can make the statement particular to Nathan:

   > Nathan can make anyone laugh. He can imitate how anyone walks or talks, and he does hilarious imitations of some of our teachers. If you turn your back on him and hear people laughing, you can guess who he's imitating. He does it in a good-natured way, however, and no one is offended.

   The example reveals Nathan's own special brand of humor and personalizes the general statement, "Nathan can make anyone laugh."

2. **When you present a thought that readers may not fully understand, provide an example to clarify the thought.** For example, a writer presented the following example to clarify the statement, "Failure is often a self-fulfilling prophesy."

   > Failure is a self-fulfilling prophesy. If you think you are going to fail, there is a greater likelihood that you will. In a research study, one group of students were told that the task they faced was very difficult and that successful outcomes were rare. Another group of students were told that the same task was relatively easy and they could expect good results. The students who expected to do poorly were significantly less successful than those who expected to do well.

   The example helps readers understand what the writer meant by "self-fulfilling prophesy" and provides some evidence of its validity.

3. **Provide the best example possible to clarify a thought and create reader interest.** When you decide to use an example in your writing, ask yourself, "What is the best possible example I can provide that will both interest and accurately inform readers?" For example, compare the impact of the following two examples:

The effects of the hurricane on parts of the Southern coast were devastating. Seaside homes and businesses were inundated with water, and roads were flooded. Windows were broken, trees were blown over, and electricity was knocked out. The cost of property damage was incalculable, and insurance companies were working overtime to sort out the claims.

The effects of the hurricane on parts of the Southern coast were devastating. People were forced to evacuate their seaside homes, businesses were overrun by water, and cars were stranded in the flooded streets. People were injured by broken windows and blown-down trees, and electricity was knocked out for days, leaving hundreds of thousands of residents without heat or light. The cost of property damage was incalculable, and many residents lost everything they had. While insurance companies worked overtime to sort out the claims, the thousands of uninsured poor struggled to survive the disaster.

While both paragraphs present stark examples of the devastating effects of the hurricane, the second paragraph includes the human element that readers can relate to. The destruction of property is terrible, but its effect on human lives is even more gripping for most readers.

Writing Activity 2.1

For practice providing examples, write an example for each of the following statements. To personalize each statement, fill in each blank with your own word or words.

Student Examples:

Freda is an excellent cook. She can make anything from spaghetti to enchiladas to stuffed peppers. Growing up, she liked helping her mom in the kitchen, and she learned a lot of from her. Freda is always expanding her cooking repertoire, and recently she learned to make sushi. She also likes to experiment with different seasonings and sauces. I know all of this because she is my apartment roommate, along with two other girls, and she does most of the cooking for us. We always look forward to dinner and are more than happy to clean up the kitchen afterwards.

I hate being cold. In the winter, dad won't turn the heater beyond 67 degrees, so I have to wear sweaters and sweats to stay warm. In the summer, when I go to the movies or a restaurant, I always take a sweater because the air conditioning freezes me out. When I swim in cold water, my body turns blue and I shake uncontrollably. I am very skinny, so I have no insulation. My friends make fun of me for wearing a sweater when they are in short sleeves. I wish I lived in Hawaii.

My dog is very loyal. One cold, rainy day she followed me to the corner where I caught the school bus in high school. When I got on the bus, I told her to go home. When I came back on the bus seven hours later, she was still at the bus stop waiting for me, soaking wet. She ran up to me with her big doggy grin and I gave her a hug.

1. _____ is a _____ person.

2. I spend a lot of time _____.

3. _____ is very hard for me.

4. _____ is not very _____

    when it comes to _____.

Writing Activity 2.2

Read the following paragraph. With a partner, identify places within the paragraph where an example would help clarify a particular point, and discuss what the writer might include in the example that would interest readers.

American Influence

Anywhere you travel in the world, you can see the impact of American culture. In practically any country, if you long for a good old hamburger and fries, you'll find a McDonald's or Burger King to satisfy your craving. American food chains permeate the globe, and the Big Mac is an international fast-food staple. American music has also infiltrated foreign countries in interesting ways. In addition, if you're in Europe, Asia, or South America, you don't have to wait to get home to see the current American blockbuster movie. It's showing in theaters throughout the world. American capitalism has also changed the way that countries function economically, with rising powers such as China and India embracing the free-market economy, private business ownership, and entrepreneurial investment. Finally, American democratic ideals offer hope for all suppressed people longing for freedom, and many are risking their lives to change their governments.

Writing Assignment

For this lesson, you will write a biographical essay about a person that you know well. It may be someone who is special to you, who has made an impact on your life, for better or worse, whom you find particularly interesting, or whom you greatly admire. The purpose of the essay is to characterize this person in ways that allow readers to know him or her as you do.

Think of different people in your life that stand out for whatever reason. Then decide whom you would most like to write about, and why. The "why" provides you with the main point that you want to convey to readers. For example, if your mother is the most important person in your life, your essay should clearly reveal that. If a friend of yours is the biggest character you know, that is what you want to show readers. If a childhood bully made your life miserable, you want readers to know that person as you did.

Topic Selection Tips

What to write about? Every writer faces that same challenge, whether essayist, novelist, editorialist, or student writer. The right topic can spark your enthusiasm for writing and pique your readers' interest.

To help decide on topics for your essays, consider five "what" questions: What am I really interested in writing about? What do I feel strongly about? What do I know something about? What will interest some group of readers? What can I cover in an essay-length paper?

If you ask yourself these five questions when considering possible writing topics, you will most likely select a topic that you will enjoy writing about and will interest readers.

Preparation

Once you have decided on a person to write about, you can begin thinking about what you want to include in your essay. To help you prepare, consider the following questions:

1. **Why do you want to write about this person?** The reason you are writing about the person influences everything that you include in your essay: the qualities you present, the examples you use, the relationship you reveal between this person and yourself, and the way in which you want readers to see this person.

2. **What qualities and traits best characterize this person?** Since you want readers to know this person as you do, include those qualities, whether good or bad, that present the most accurate picture.

3. **What are the best examples to "show" readers the qualities and characteristics of this person?** Strong examples are the best way to bring the person to life for readers.

4. **What do you want readers to know about your relationship with the person?** Since you are writing about someone who has had some impact on your life, decide how you want to show that relationship and the examples that best capture that relationship and your feelings towards this person.

Prewriting Suggestions

To help you prepare to write the first draft of your essay, consider the following prewriting activities:

1. Either think through or write down responses to the four questions just presented.

2. Free write about the person for ten minutes or so, writing down anything that comes to mind about him or her.

3. Make a list of the person's qualities that you may include in your essay, and come up with at least one "real life" example for each quality.

4. Do a "clustering" diagram on the person, beginning with the main qualities you want to include and branching out to more detailed information under each quality. (See the following clustering diagram to get the idea.) A clustering diagram helps you generate material for your paper, including both main points and supporting examples and detail, and helps you organize your material.

Writing Activity 2.3

To help prepare to write your first draft, do one or more of the prewriting activities presented that you think would be most beneficial. If you find that the activities don't generate many ideas or much material regarding your subject, you may want to consider writing about another person.

Sample Prewriting Activity

Clustering Diagram

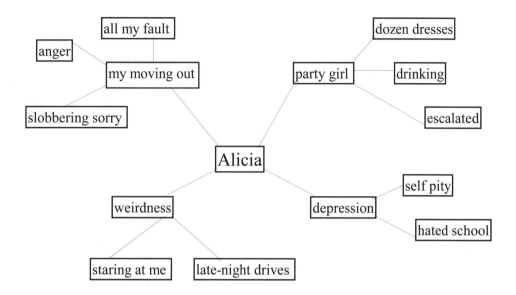

Notice how through the clustering diagram the writer generated four main ideas - "party girl," "depression," "weirdness," and "my moving out" - and some specific examples to clarify and help readers understand each idea.

Drafting

Now that you have selected a topic and done some prewriting preparation, you are ready to write your first draft. To help you get started, consider these drafting suggestions:

1. **Introduce your subject in a way that will interest readers and give some insight into the person.** Include why you are writing about the person and your relationship with him or her before you get into the main points of your essay. (Read the two-paragraph opening of the "College Roommate" draft in Activity 2.4 to see how one writer opened her paper.)

2. **Present the qualities that best characterize the person and the examples that bring those qualities to life for readers.** If your relationship with the person is an important part of the essay, provide examples that help reveal that relationship. (Read the fourth paragraph of the "College Roommate" draft to see how the writer both presented a quality and revealed the relationship between her and her roommate.)

3. **Include any descriptive detail that will help bring the person to life, show your relationship to him or her, or help readers visualize the examples you provide.** What you learned in Lesson One about using verbs, adjectives, and adverbs to describe sights, sounds, thoughts, and feelings can apply to most of the writing that you do. (Read a few paragraphs of "College Roommate" to see how the writer incorporated descriptive detail.)

4. **Write your draft in paragraphs, changing paragraphs as you introduce new qualities and examples.** Notice how each paragraph in the "College Roommate" draft deals with a different subject related to the topic.

5. **Feel free to add new ideas that come to you as you write: a new quality, a different example, a fresh insight.** The writing process itself often triggers new thoughts and connections that you will want to include. Don't be limited to what you generated during your prewriting preparation.

6. **Conclude your draft in a manner that brings closure to your topic: a final thought on the person you are writing about, an update on your relationship with him or her, the reason you find this person so memorable, a final quality that best typifies the person, or a final powerful example to leave readers with.** Read the two-paragraph conclusion to "College Roommate" to see how the writer ended her paper.

7. **Include dialogue in the draft if conversation is an important part of any example.** "Hearing" a person speak helps bring him or her to life and creates interest for readers. (See how the writer uses quotations in the "College Roommate" draft.)

8. **Don't be concerned with writing a "perfect" paper.** First drafts aren't intended to be finished products, so don't spend a lot of time agonizing over using just the right word, on rewriting sentences over and over, or on coming up with the "perfect" example. There will be plenty of time to revise your draft after you get your ideas on paper, and most writers do a better job of revising after they have completed a draft and set it aside for awhile.

9. **Keep your reading audience - your classmates - in mind as you write.** Keeping readers in mind helps you provide the best examples, details, and insights to hold the their interest and give them the clearest picture of your subject.

Paragraphing Tips

Paragraphing an essay is not that difficult if you follow a few basic principles:

1. In general, develop one main idea or thought in each paragraph.

2. Change paragraphs as you move to something new in your essay: a new idea, a different time or place, a different part of the essay (opening, middle, ending).

3. Avoid extremely short or overly long paragraphs. Combine short, related paragraphs and divide longer paragraphs.

By following these suggestions, you will paragraph your essays in ways that make your ideas most accessible to readers, the main purpose of paragraphing.

Writing Activity 2.4

Write the first draft of your biographical essay keeping the drafting suggestions in mind. You may first want to read the "College Roommate" essay to see how one writer developed her draft.

College Roommate - first draft

Audience: college students

My first-semester college roommate showed up with a dozen dresses to cram into her tiny closet space. "What are all those dresses for?" I asked. "For the dates and the parties I'm going to!" she bubbled. Alicia was short and a bit plump with dark, pretty eyes, and I wondered if her dating expectations were a bit high. I think I had brought one dress to school and had little anticipation of being in the date-and-party crowd. That was just one of the many differences between Alicia and myself.

Although her mother and mine were close friends, Alicia and I had grown up in different towns and didn't know each other very well. Our mothers had made the plans for us to room together in college, figuring we'd get along just as well as they did. Unfortunately, it didn't turn out as they had hoped.

I had come to school to get an education and Alicia had come to socialize. However, when her dating expectations fell flat, she began to get depressed. As her party dresses remained hanging in her closet, her mood turned darker and darker. "I hate this place," she'd say. "I went out in high school all the time. What's wrong with the guys here?" I tried to convince her that the first semester in college away from home wasn't easy for anyone, but that didn't seem to help. Then she'd fall into her self-pitying mode. "I'm just not pretty enough," she say. "I'll never get a date or get asked to a party. I'm just a loser." I'd try to get her out of her mood, but that got tiring pretty fast.

Alicia was very jealous and possessive. One weekend a couple friends from high school visited me, and we spent the weekend doing things together. I would invite Alicia to join us, but she always passed. When my friends left, she gave me the silent treatment for a long time. "What's the problem?" I finally asked her. "When your friends were around, you pretended like I didn't exist." "That's not true," I retorted. "I invited you to go everywhere with us." "Sure, I really wanted to be the third wheel," she said sullenly. My having other friends on our dormitory floor was another personal affront to her. "You like Megan and Grace better than me," she'd pout. "Of course not," I'd lie.

Alicia also had her rather strange side. Sometimes at night I'd wake up and she'd be lying in her bed staring at me. "What's the matter?" I'd ask, and she'd say nothing, like she was in a trance. Sometimes I'd wake up and she wouldn't be in the room. "Where were you last night?" I'd ask. "I took a long ride," she'd say. "I just needed to get out and clear my head." In the middle of the night?

Alicia began to drown her sorrow in booze. When there were Friday-night parties on campus to attend, she'd start drinking in the afternoon to get "fortified" for the party. Then she'd continue drinking at the party. She'd talk to any guy that was available, but she was usually so drunk that she'd turn people off. Then she'd wake up at noon the next day with a splitting headache and say, "Don't ever let me do that again," as if I had any control over her. The drinking didn't stop, and I began to worry about her.

I had my own life to lead, however, and dealing with Alicia was the last thing I needed. I began spending more and more time in some of my friends' rooms in the dorm, and I studied in the library instead of my room. I only saw Alicia when I had to, and she had basically stopped speaking to me by then. The one thing I knew for certain was that I couldn't spend another semester living with her, and I finally told her. "Good," she said. "I hate living with you. You're a judgmental bitch." A few days later, she came into the room slobbering drunk, wanting to hug and apologize for what she'd said and begging me to be her roommate. "I just can't tell my mom that you won't live with me anymore," she moaned. "Then just tell her that you don't want to live with me," I said dispassionately. "I already have new roommates for next semester." She broke into her self-pitying sobs, and I left the room.

Second semester I moved into an inexpensive apartment near campus with three friends from the dorm. I couldn't have been happier with my roommates; they helped change my college experience completely. Fortunately, the college campus was large, so I seldom ran into Alicia. When our paths did cross we were civilized enough to say, "Hi" and move on. I feel sorry for Alicia because when her fantasy vision of what college would be like didn't materialize, she couldn't handle it. All of her worst qualities came out, and I experienced them first-hand.

I think a school psychologist might be someone who could help Alicia, and during one of her fits of depression, I suggested she see one. I hope she has. Her first semester had been a nightmare, one that I unfortunately had to live in. I really wished things had worked out for us as roommates because of our moms, but I realized that my own happiness and well-being at college was more important than trying to please other people.

Revision

Once you get your first draft on paper, you can evaluate how well you have developed your topic and how the parts of your essay fit together. On rereading their drafts, writers sometimes discover that they left something important out, veered off the topic at times, put an example in the wrong place, created an "imbalance" by devoting too much time to one aspect of the topic, or wrote an overly long paragraph that needed dividing. Such problems are common in first drafts and often easily rectified. That is why for most writers, including professionals, revision is an essential part of the writing process.

Improving Examples

Since the lesson's emphasis is on developing your essay with examples, take a good look at the examples that you used and how effectively they develop and clarify the qualities of the person you are writing about. To evaluate your use of examples, consider the following questions:

1. **Have I provided one or more examples for each quality or personality trait that I presented?** Read your draft, look at each quality or characteristic that you have included, and see whether you have followed it with a "real life" example. If you haven't, add examples where they would help.

2. **Have I provided the best possible examples to "show" readers the person's qualities?** Read each example to see whether it most accurately shows the person's quality and creates interest for readers. If you think of a better example on rereading, include it. If you think a current example could be improved, revise it.

3. **Are my examples "balanced" enough in length to develop each quality effectively?** If you find that you have devoted a great deal of space to one or two examples and very little to others, consider balancing their length. Writers tend to begin with lengthier examples and end with shorter ones as time, space, and enthusiasm dwindle. If, however, there is a special quality that you are highlighting, a lengthier example(s) may be appropriate.

4. **Are there examples to add that I hadn't thought of before?**   On rereading a draft, sometimes new ideas will pop up, including examples you hadn't previously considered. Feel free to add any new example that will improve your essay.

Writing Activity 2.5

Applying the four revision suggestions presented, read your draft and make any changes in examples that will improve your essay.

Example

Added example from "College Roommate" draft (added words in "bold."):

    Alicia also had her rather strange side. Sometimes at night I'd wake up and she'd be lying in her bed staring at me. "What's the matter?" I'd ask, and she'd say nothing, like she was in a trance. Sometimes I'd wake up and she wouldn't be in the room. "Where were you last night?" I'd ask. "I took a long ride," she'd say. "I just needed to get out and clear my head." In the middle of the night? **Beyond that, I never knew which Alicia would come into our dorm room. Would it be the bubbly, happy Alicia, the mournful, depressed Alicia, or the cold, silent Alicia? It was like living with three different people. I quit reacting to her every mood, realizing that was exactly what she wanted.**

Sentence Wording Improvement

When you write a first draft, you are putting your ideas on paper for the first time. It is not surprising, then, that you don't always word those ideas perfectly. You may have used more words than necessary or settled for some words that didn't precisely convey your meaning. Writers frequently improve the wording of first-draft sentences, which can lead to a more smoothly worded, enjoyable essay to read.
    To improve your first-draft sentences, consider the following suggestions:

1. **Look for overly long sentences that are "wordier" than necessary to express the thought.** When writers first express an idea, they often produce a lengthier version than needed: unnecessary words, repeated words or phrases, wordy sentence constructions. Revise wordy sentences to make them more concise and effective.

   First-draft sentence:

   Last night's wind storm, which was the strongest of the year, blew off the remaining autumn leaves on our trees and covered the lawn with a brown and orange carpet of leaves.

   Revised:

   Last night's wind storm~~, which was~~ the strongest of the year, blew off ~~the~~ **our trees'** remaining autumn leaves ~~on our trees~~, ~~and~~ cover**ing** the lawn with a brown and orange carpet ~~of leaves.~~

   First-draft sentence:

   Unaccustomed as I was to public speaking, I had no choice but to speak before the college board of trustees if I was to have the courage of my convictions and speak against the outrageous tuition increase.

Revised:

Unaccustomed ~~as I was~~ to public speaking, I ~~had no choice but~~ **felt obliged** to ~~speak before~~ **address** the college board of trustees ~~if I was to have the courage of my convictions and speak against~~ **about** the outrageous tuition increase.

2. **Replace questionable word choices with more appropriate words.** Finding the best word to express a thought or action or describe a situation most vividly is a challenge. Those more questionable words often stand out when you reread a draft, and you now have the opportunity to replace them.

First-draft sentence:

The troubled congressman gave up his senate seat rather than expose himself to the rigors of a bribery investigation by the Ethics Committee.

Revised:

The ~~troubled~~ **beleaguered** congressman ~~gave up~~ **resigned** his senate seat rather than ~~expose~~ **subject** himself to a bribery investigation by the Ethics Committee.

3. **Revise awkward sentences to improve their smoothness and readability.** Sometimes a first draft sentence just doesn't read well, often the result of an awkward sentence structure. To revise an awkward-looking sentence, you may have to move words or phrases around, delete words, or completely restructure the sentence.

First-draft sentence:

Not only are there too many stop signs on Shaw Avenue, but also there are some that are difficult to see due to overhanging tree limbs that partially obscure them.

Revised:

There are too many stop signs on Shaw Avenue, some of which are partially obscured by overhanging tree branches.

4. **Revise vague sentences whose meaning may be unclear to readers.** Sometimes although a writer knows what she wants to say, the thought doesn't come out clearly. If you run across a first-draft sentence whose meaning may not be clear to readers or that could be interpreted more than one way, revise it to clarify the thought.

First-draft sentence:

Clarence's attitude was a factor in the way he was treated by his colleagues.

Revised:

Because of Clarence's upbeat attitude, his colleagues enjoyed being around him.

Writing Activity 2.6

Read the following paragraph. Revise sentences to eliminate the types of problems you may encounter in your own drafts: wordiness, faulty word choice, awkward phrasing, vague meaning. The resulting sentences should be clearer, smoother, more concise, and easier and more enjoyable to read.

Example:

New electric cars such as the Nissan Leaf and Chevy Volt, which are two of the most popular electric cars, sound better than they may be in reality. For example, while the Nissan Leaf advertises a hearty 100-mile driving range between battery charges, if you go on their website and read the details, you find that the 100-mile range can't really be reached. In fact, if you drive a slow-like 55 m.p.h. on the freeway with no air conditioning or heater turned on in the car, your driving range drops to around 65 miles, a humongous drop-off from the 100 miles that caught-off-guard motorists might expect to achieve.

Revised:

New electric cars, such as the **popular** Nissan Leaf and Chevy Volt, ~~which are two of the most popular electric cars~~, **may** sound better than they **actually are** ~~may be in reality.~~ For example, ~~while~~ the Nissan Leaf ~~advertises a hearty~~ **claims a** 100-mile driving range between ~~battery~~ charges, **but the Nissan website admits that the range is only 65 miles when driving 55 m.p.h. without air conditioner or heater on, which may shock unsuspecting motorists.** ~~if you go on their website and read the details, you find that the 100-mile range can't really be reached. In fact, if you drive a slow-like 55 m.p.h. on the freeway with no air conditioning or heater turned on in the car, your driving range drops to around 65 miles, a humongous drop-off from the 100 miles that caught-off-guard motorists might expect to achieve.~~

Music Programs

While music programs in many elementary schools across the country have vanished as more and more class time is spent on preparing students for standardized test taking, the Slater Unified School District has kept its choir, band, and orchestra programs intact in all elementary schools. Slater stresses test performance on the state's STAR testing, and its students' test scores are good, but many students also choose to take part in the choir, band, or orchestra, and some participate in two of the programs.

Music programs are put on for parents, friends, and relatives at each elementary school in the fall and spring semesters, and district-wide choral and band competitions are also sponsored by the District, where thousands of elementary level students participate in the competition. Slater relishes itself on its students' academic achievements, but it takes no less pride in its students' musical achievements, and its commitment to the arts remains unremittingly the same at a time when some districts have stopped the sounds of elementary children singing and playing instruments in their schools.

Writing Activity 2.7

Reread each sentence of your draft, looking for sentences whose wording could be improved. Revise sentences by eliminating unnecessary words and phrases, smoothing out awkward sentences, replacing questionable word choices, and clarifying any vaguely worded sentences. The resulting revised sentences should be clearer, smoother, more concise, and more effective.

Writing Activity 2.8

Now that you have revised your paper to improve examples and sentence wording, make any further revisions in the following areas, which will apply to most writing that you do:

1. **Check your opening and conclusion**. Are you satisfied with how well you introduce your topic and how effectively you conclude your essay?

2. **Check your paragraphing.** Have you changed paragraphs as you move from one thought to the next? Do you need to divide any overly long paragraphs or combine any short, related paragraphs?

3. **Check you paper's "balance."** Do you give relatively equal space to each quality and example you present? (An exception would be if there is a particularly important quality or characteristic that you want to highlight.) Do your opening and conclusion seem in proper "balance" with the overall essay?

4. **Check your use of descriptive detail.** Do you provide details that help readers see, hear, and feel what you want them to? Check your use of verbs, adjectives, and adverbs to provide effective description.

5. **Check your use of dialogue.** Do you use dialogue to create interest and capture the

most dramatic or insightful comments or conversations?

Reader Feedback

As mentioned in Lesson One, getting feedback on a draft from readers is a valued part of the writing process for many writers. Professional writers have editors and agents to read their drafts, and student writers have a ready-made audience in their classmates and instructor. No matter how experienced the writer, having his draft viewed through someone else's eyes provides a different perspective, and, quite frequently, some useful revision suggestions.

Getting feedback from classmates comes after you have done your own revising for one reason: you are in control of your writing. After you have made your own revision decisions and shaped the paper the way that you want, you can see what readers think about it. They may make some excellent suggestions which will not only improve your current draft but future writing. What suggestions you decide to incorporate or ignore is up to your judgment. Ultimately, every writer is responsible for what he writes, and every decision that you make adds to your growth as a writer.

Reader Feedback Tips

Students sometimes ask, "How can I help someone revise a paper when I'm still learning myself?" These thoughts may allay your concerns:

1. *Most people's reading skills are more advanced than their writing skills. You are using those reading skills to evaluate the draft.*

2. *You aren't expected to be an expert revisionist. If the writer get one or two helpful suggestions from you, that's great.*

3. *Keep a couple questions in mind as you read someone's draft: Are there some things that I would like to know more about? Are there some things that I don't completely understand? Let the reader know what those things are.*

> ### 4.   *Every draft you read will have some things that you like. Let the writer know what she's done well as well as what might be improved.*
>
> ### 5.   *Your evaluative skills will grow as you continue providing feedback throughout the lessons. In turn, evaluating other people's writing will help improve your own revision skills.*

Writing Activity 2.9

Exchange drafts with a classmate or two and read each other's drafts. Provide any suggestions that you feel will help the writer improve his paper.

Writing Activity 2.10

Based on feedback from your classmate, make any further revisions in your draft that you feel will improve it. Then set your draft aside for awhile before giving it a final reading (or two) to see if there are any other changes you might want to make.

Editing

For most writers, the final step in the writing process is to proofread their revised drafts for errors and make the necessary corrections. Producing error-free writing is often the result of careful, meticulous proofreading, and your readers - whether instructors, fellow students, the general public, or a future employer - will appreciate the results of your effort.

The editing emphasis in this lesson is on correct comma usage, which is important in helping readers navigate your sentences most successfully. You will also proofread your draft for other types of common errors, focusing in particular on the types of errors you are most prone to make.

Comma Usage

The purpose of inserting commas in your sentences is to show readers where to pause to read each sentence with the greatest understanding. When you read an essay aloud, you can hear the natural pauses that create a reading rhythm for listeners. That same rhythm helps readers read your sentences most effectively.

Fortunately, there are some basic comma usage rules that will help you insert commas correctly. These rules are based on how people read sentences, identifying the places where readers naturally pause. The rules, then, provide a practical guide for comma usage rather than a prescription for how readers *should* read a sentence.

To use commas effectively in your writing, keep the following general rules in mind:

1. **Insert a comma between each entry in a series of three or more words or groups of words, most frequently joined by "and:"**

   Juanita might apply for the nursing, dental hygiene, or medical technician program at her local community college.
   Working and going to school, caring for her young daughter, and keeping her apartment clean take up most of Freda's time.
   Our cat sits motionless for minutes, slowly stalks her prey, and then pounces with lightening speed on her rubber mouse.

2. **Insert a comma after the *coordinate conjunction* (and, or, but, so, for, yet) in a *compound sentence* - two complete sentences joined by a coordinate conjunction:**

   There are eight Republican candidates in the presidential race, *but* only two candidates appear to have a chance of receiving the nomination.
   Interstate I-5 over the mountains is impassable due to snow, *so* the only way to get south of the mountains is to take an eighty-mile detour around them.

3. **Insert a comma after an introductory word or group of words which include the following:**

Prepositional phrases:	*Within* a few minutes, *After* the football ball game, *From* the looks of the outside of the house,
Participial phrases:	*Listening* to the new Train album, *Ignoring* the will of the voters, *Delighted* by the drop in interest rates,
Subordinate clauses:	*Because* you have been so kind to me, *Unless* we do something about the leak in the roof, *Until* Joshua has the money to buy his books, *While* you were changing the tire,
Transitional wording:	*First, Next, Meanwhile, In conclusion,*

After the football game, let's get something to eat at the grill across campus.
Ignoring the will of voters, the governor proposed an increase in the sales' tax.
Until Joshua has the money to buy his books, I'm going to share mine with him.
First, try to find the best route to get from your house to the college.

4. **Insert a comma before and after *interrupters* - a word or group of words that stops the flow of the sentence:**

I ran into your uncle, *by the way*, at the supermarket last evening.
The price of tomatoes, *incidentally*, went up the same amount as the price on yams.
The water level of the lake, *as you can see*, is lower than it's been in years.
Fortunately, there is something we all can do to reduce air pollution.

5. **Insert a comma after an ly-ending adverb such as *especially* or *particularly* that is preceded by a natural reading pause:**

I like walking in the early morning, *especially* when the air is crisp and clear.
Reynaldo loves to eat sushi, *particularly* the calamari rolls at Sendai Sushi.

6. **Insert commas before and after a *relative clause* beginning with *who, which,* or *whose*:**

Olin Brown, *who owns the dry cleaners on "R" Street,* is eighty-three years old.
Gold, *which went up thirty dollars an ounce,* is still a risky investment.
The city's philharmonic orchestra, *whose string section is terrific,* is putting on a Christmas concert next weekend.

Note: Commas are *not* used with *restrictive* relative clauses, which are needed in a sentence to identify clearly the person or thing they modify: The woman *who runs the outdoor flower concession* is always friendly. (The relative clause is needed to identify the woman.)   The pavement company *which sends in the lowest bid* will receive the contract for repaving the college parking lot. (The relative clause is needed to identify which company receives the contract.)

7. **Insert a comma before an ending clause beginning with *which, where,* or a *participial phrase* at the end of a sentence:**

The three top swimming teams in the conference all lost duel meets on Saturday, *which puts the conference championship up for grabs.*
A high-rise condominium complex has been proposed by the city renovation committee, *which would dramatically change the downtown skyline.*
The stock market dropped 400 points Friday, *causing widespread fear among investors.*
Ms. Kwan requested a parent-teacher conference with the parents of Anthony Glick, *troubled by his dramatic change in behavior.*

8. **Sentences will often have multiple commas that fall under different rules:**

Before we buy a new rug, let's replace our old swaybacked sofa, which is ugly and uncomfortable. (Comma after an introductory subordinate clause and before an ending "which" clause.)
After the big wind last night, leaves covered the dormitory lawn, so we raked them into a huge pile and, needless to say, jumped into them. (Comma after an introductory prepositional phrase, before a conjunction in a compound sentence, and before and after an "interrupting" phrase.)

9. **Avoid inserting commas where they aren't needed, such as before a subordinate clause that *ends* rather than begins the sentence or before an "and" or "or" that connects groups of words, not sentences.**

I'm not going into work today *because* I can work from my home computer.
There is no need to shop for food today *unless* you don't want to eat leftovers.
Gretchen waited an hour for the bus *and* finally gave up and walked downtown.
You can have my old magazines *but* not my old albums.

Writing Activity 2.11

Insert commas in the sentences in the following paragraphs following the rules provided. Some sentences may not require any commas.

Example:

There was an early-evening shooting outside a restaurant on Shaw Avenue near Armstrong. The shooting which surprised residents of the area was allegedly drug-related. Up until recent times the Shaw-Armstrong area was crime free but drug trafficking has spread throughout the city causing alarm in once-safe neighborhoods.

Revised:

There was an early-evening shooting outside a restaurant on Shaw Avenue near Armstrong. The shooting, which surprised residents of the area, was allegedly drug-related. Up until recent times, the Shaw-Armstrong area was crime free, but drug trafficking has spread throughout the city, causing alarm in once-safe neighborhoods.

Weight Gain

There may be some truth to the "freshman ten" weight gain prophesy which refers to the ten pounds on average that college freshmen tend to put on. When you think about it it is not surprising that freshmen often add a few pounds.

First college freshmen often aren't as active as they were in high school where they often participated in a sport or other physical activity. Second college freshmen tend to eat more high-calorie junk food particularly when they live away from home. It is not uncommon for example for a college student to eat at McDonald's for breakfast Carl Jrs. for lunch and back to McDonald's for an inexpensive dinner.

In addition college freshmen tend to have more time on their hands than in high school and they often fill that time with snacking. Of course they don't usually go for the healthier snacks like fruit or trail mix opting more often for the chips pretzels and soda. This snacking can also pick up late at night when students study into the a.m. hours especially if they have no classes the next morning.

As you can see the changing lifestyle of students from high school to college lends itself to their packing on a few pounds which isn't that difficult for anyone. The solution to the "problem" is equally obvious. College freshmen like all people need to be more active eat healthier food and keep the snacking to a minimum. For some reason most college students don't continue to gain extra weight after their first year perhaps because their metabolism adjusts to their changing lifestyle because they get smarter about what they eat and how much they exercise or because their "freshman ten" weight gain is a wake-up call. Of course many students avoid the dreaded "freshman ten" and they are often the ones that continue to do the right things to control their weight throughout their lifetime.

Writing Activity 2.12

Check your use of commas in each sentence of your draft, adding or deleting commas according to the rules for comma usage.

Comma Usage Tips

    When making decisions on inserting commas in your sentences, the best advice is to follow the basic rules. However, when you are uncertain whether to insert a comma in a particular place, keep in mind the old adage, "When in doubt, leave it out."

    Sometimes when writers focus their attention on comma usage, they litter their sentences with too many commas, creating unnecessary reading pauses and hindering the sentences' natural flow. For example, they begin putting commas before every "and" or "but" rather than reserving them for "ands or "buts" in compound sentence or words in a series.

    On the flip side, if you find a place in a sentence where you naturally pause but can't recall a rule for inserting a comma, you are probably safe to insert it. If you find such a natural reading pause in a sentence, no doubt readers will read it the same way.

    Reread the previous three paragraphs, identifying a rule for the placement of each comma. Note how the commas indicate the natural reading pauses without restricting the flow of each sentence.

Writing Activity 2.13

Proofread your draft for other common errors -*run-on sentences and comma splice sentences, fragments, pronoun usage, subject-verb agreement, easily confused words* (there/their/they're, it/it's, know/no, affect/effect, your/you're, then/than), *irregular verbs, and misspelled words* - and pay particular attention to the types of errors you are most prone to make. For the most thorough proofreading job, read your draft a number of times, looking for a different type of error each time.

Writing Activity 2.14

Exchange drafts with a classmate and proofread each other's drafts for errors. Correct any errors that your classmate finds in your draft, and make a note of the kinds of errors that you overlooked, if any.

Communicating With Readers

As with your essay in Lesson One, your reading audience for your biographical essay is your classmates. Reproduce copies of the essay for classmates, and enjoy reading one another's papers.

Lesson Three: Providing Illustrations

Objective: To write an essay using an illustration to support the main point.

Purpose: Writer's choice

Audience: Writer's choice

In the first lesson, you wrote about a personal experience and its impact on your life, providing descriptive details to bring the experience to life. In the second lesson, you wrote about a particular person and provided examples to reveal particular qualities or characteristics. In this lesson, you take something from both lessons to develop an essay that makes a point by using an *illustration*: an extended example that brings the point home to readers.

In Lesson One, you narrated your personal experience and used descriptive details to recreate that experience for readers. In this lesson, you narrate a real-life experience that serves as an example for the main point that you are making in your essay. In Lesson Two, you provided a number of examples to "show" readers the qualities that typified your subject. In this lesson, you provide one extended example to help readers understand a particular point. What you have learned about vividly narrating a story, using descriptive detail, and providing compelling examples will help you in writing your upcoming essay.

For example, on reflection, a student felt that joining a gang is one of the worst things that a young person can do, the main point that he wanted to make in an essay. To illustrate his point, he decided to relate the experience of his younger brother, whose entire life changed when he joined a gang in junior high school: his attitude towards his mom, his attitude towards school, his getting into trouble, his getting into drugs, and eventually, his being stabbed to death one night outside a mini-mart. The downward spiral of his brother's life would vividly illustrate his point that joining a gang can lead to disaster.

As another example, a student wanted to make the point that a person should never give up on her education. To illustrate the point, she told the story of a friend who got pregnant in high school but stayed with her education. She went to continuation school and got her GED. Although she had to work days and attend night classes at the community college, she made the sacrifices, and after four years, she got her associate degree in secretarial science. Today, she works at the financial aid office at the college, has great benefits, and provides a life for her son that wouldn't have been possible without her education.

Illustrating a Point

There are different ways to make a particular point in your writing, including providing factual and comparative evidence, which will be covered in future lessons. The benefits of using an illustration to make a point are that an illustration creates interest for readers, provides a "real life" example involving people, and gives readers something that they may relate to.

For example, a writer wanted to make the point that the armored vests that the military provided its combat soldiers in the Middle East were inadequate. He could write of the tests that were done on the vests that showed that they could be penetrated by high-powered rifle bullets, or he could tell the story of a friend serving in Afghanistan whose armor was pierced by a sniper's bullet, critically wounding him and almost costing his life. For most readers, the illustration of his friend's harrowing experience would be the most compelling way to make his point.

To provide an effective illustration for your upcoming essay, consider the following suggestions:

1. **Provide the best illustration to make your point.** What illustration would have the biggest impact on readers? What illustration would make your point in the most convincing way? What illustration would provide the most accurate, relevant example of your point? For example, the writer who told her friend's educational success story to illustrate the importance of an education used a persuasive example. Without that education, the young woman and her son would no doubt be living in poverty.

2. **Provide an illustration you are most familiar with.** To illustrate a point with the most effective detail and clearest insight, you need to know the experience well. Ask yourself, "What illustration can I provide that I have the most intimate knowledge of?" For example, the writer who used his brother as a cautionary example against joining gangs could tell the story as if it were his own.

3. **Provide an illustration that is substantial enough to fill an essay.** For your upcoming essay, the illustration you provide is the central focus of the paper. Use an illustration that has the significance and weight to justify that focus. (See the essay "A Lesson in Courage" in Activity 3.3 as an example of such an illustration.)

Writing Activity 3.1

For practice writing an illustration to make a point, select one of the following statements and provide a supporting illustration: a "real life" example that validates the statement. You may illustrate an experience from your own life or from someone's that you know well.

Example:

Statement: A lot of young people don't know what hard work really is.

Illustration:

The summer after my senior year in high school, I was looking for work and saw an add in the newspaper about job openings in a commercial laundry. That sounded like a pretty good job to me. Maybe I'd get to drive a truck to deliver laundry or something. I talked to a friend, and we decided to apply together.

   I was surprised by the size of the laundry building: a huge warehouse full of noisy machinery. There were large washing machines, round, spinning dryers, big hot-air dryers, and rectangular-shaped steam irons. Pounding, whirring, sloshing, hissing, and buzzing sounds filled the hot, steamy air. Mounds of towels and sheets were piled high in canvas bins, which were being wheeled in every direction. Over two-hundred workers were silently manning the machines, working robotically at their stations.

   In a small front office we met the foreman: a large, no-nonsense guy who said, "Can you get started tonight?" "Sure," we said, and he took us to the area with the large spinning dryers. He explained our job, which was to load the wet towels and sheets from the bin into the dryer, run the dryer, unload the towels and sheets into another bin, wheel the bin to the area with the hot-air dryers, and help load the towels and sheets into the hot-air dryers. "You've got to keep moving," he said, " so the bins from the washing machines don't get backed up."

   We began loading the wet towels and sheets into the dryer, and they were heavier than we expected. Then we started the dryer on its five-minute cycle. Half way through the cycle, the dryer started kicking and making an awful racket. The foreman came over and turned it off and said, "That's what happens when the load isn't balanced. Rebalance the load better and start it again." We moved the towels and sheets around and started it up. In the meantime, two more loads of wet towels and sheets had appeared.

   Once the cycle finished, we loaded the laundry into another bin and I wheeled it quickly to the hot-air dryers while Marvin started loading the next batch into our dryer. I helped load the laundry into the hot-air dryers and ran back to help Marvin. We took turns wheeling the laundry and helping to load the hot-air dryer while the other began loading our dryer. It was a non-stop process, and within an hour, my arms felt like they would fall off. Only seven hours to go.

   When I got home from that night shift, I'd never been so tired in my life. My arms were aching and my legs were tired from standing for eight hours. At the end of the shift, all the foreman said was, "See you guys tomorrow night." I wondered if I would make it.

   I did make it back, but Marvin and I only lasted two weeks . You hear of the "backbreaking" manual labor that some people do. I experienced it first hand. I hated every minute working in the laundry, and I couldn't believe that some people had worked their for ten or fifteen years. The heavy loads of laundry, the non-stop assembly line speed, the hot, stifling air, and the ever-present foreman seemed more than anyone could endure for long. When we quit, the foreman said, "You college guys never last." He was right.

I realized that I, like a lot of young people, had no idea what hard work really was and how millions of people spend their lives doing work that I could only handle for two weeks. I gained a lot of respect for people who do the really hard work. I also felt lucky that I was going to college and wouldn't have to spend my adult life working in a commercial laundry.

1. Younger brothers (or sisters) can be a real _____.

2. Working full-time and going to college is _____.

3. Many high school students often aren't that well prepared for college.

4. Mothers (or fathers, grandmothers, etc.) often sacrifice a lot for their children.

5. _____ can really mess up your life.

6. Dropping out of high school can be a bad decision.

7. Finding a job today is harder than some people think.

8. Being bullied in school can be a terrible experience.

Writing Assignment

For this lesson, you will write an essay using an illustration to make a particular point: something of significance that you believe to be true. The illustration will provide an extended example from life that supports your point and helps readers understand why you believe as you do. The illustration might come from your personal experience, from a friend or relative's, or from another person whose experience you are familiar with.

You might approach your topic selection in two ways:

1. Think about different experiences that you or other people have had and consider whether an experience might reveal a particular "truth" that you could share with readers. For example, one writer reflected on her older sister's experience of marrying a guy she didn't love because she was pregnant. They spent three miserable years together, he wasn't a good father, she regretted marrying him, and they finally got a divorce. The writer used this example to illustrate her point: "No pregnant woman should get married because she feels she *has* to."

2. Think of some of the things that you believe in - particular "truths" that you feel certain about - and then think of a good illustration that could support each belief.

For example, a writer hadn't decided on a major and felt that it was best to wait until she had taken more classes and had a better idea of what interested her. To illustrate the point that students shouldn't rush into choosing a major, she used her friend's experience as an example. Jessica had changed majors twice, taken many more classes than she would have needed to, and spent more time and money on her first years of college because she had felt pressured to choose a major early.

Using the two approaches to topic selection, decide on a topic for your essay - the main point that you want to convey to readers - and the illustration that you want to use to develop your essay. Select the topic for which you feel you have the strongest, most compelling illustration.

Example:

Main point: Courage can mean doing what is right when your friends are doing wrong.

Illustration: How Leticia showed courage by befriending a girl that her friends had shut out and ridiculed.

Preparation

Having decided on a topic for your essay and the illustration you are going to use, you have already done considerable preparation for your first draft. You know what the point of your essay is and how you are going to develop it. Further preparation may include fleshing out your illustration in a way that provides the strongest support for the main point of your essay.

   For example, let's say that a writer wants to make the point that childhood obesity is a solvable problem. To illustrate the point, she uses her nephew's experience. Since the purpose of the illustration is to show that childhood obesity can be overcome, she emphasizes exactly what her nephew did, with the help of his parents and physician, to lose considerable weight and keep it off. She wants her illustration to convince readers that if her nephew could go from obesity to normal weight, other children can do the same. In addition, she wants to show how overcoming obesity changed her nephew's life for the better.

   To use your illustration most effectively to support your main point, consider the following suggestions:

1. **What exactly is my purpose in providing the illustration?** What do you want to accomplish by providing it?

2. **What aspects of the illustration most strongly support my main idea?** Make

sure to include those aspects in your draft. For example, the writer who illustrated how joining a gang can ruin your life included the following aspects of his brother's experience: not respecting his mother, getting in trouble in school, his failing grades, his drug use, his staying out late at night, and, finally, his being stabbed to death.

3. **What should I *describe* in the illustration to have the greatest impact on readers?** For example, the writer illustrating the weight-loss experience of her nephew felt it was important to describe what her nephew looked like before and after his weight loss. She also wanted to describe his feelings about himself and his life when he was obese and when he was a normal weight. She also wanted to describe how he was treated differently by children before and after his weight loss. Finally, she wanted to describe in some detail how he went about losing the weight and keeping it off: a successful diet-and-exercise program that other children and families could follow.

Writing Activity 3.2

In preparation for writing your first draft, answer the three questions provided to help use your illustration to greatest effect.

Example:

(From upcoming draft "A Lesson in Courage")

1. My purpose in providing the illustration is to show readers that it takes real courage to stand up to peer pressure, and I hope that the example I use makes that point clearly and in an interesting way.

2. In the illustration, I think an important aspect to emphasize is the contrast between how the "gang" treated Araceli and how Leticia treated her. I also want to emphasize what Leticia gave up by befriending Araceli. Finally, I want to emphasize the impact that Leticia's courage eventually had on me, and perhaps my illustration could have some impact on readers.

3. I need to describe in detail the "gang's" treatment of Araceli, including the snubbing and the taunting. Next, I want to describe Araceli's reaction to being ostracized. I also want to describe my conflicting feelings throughout the experience, especially since it involved my good friend Leticia and I being on opposite sides. I want to include a considerable amount of dialogue since most of what took place was verbal, and what different girls actually said most dramatically relates the experience.

Audience and Purpose

A writer's reading audience is usually determined by his writing topic and purpose for writing. Some writings are intended for general reading audiences, such as anyone who reads the newspaper or uses the Internet. Other writings are intended for more specific audiences, such as hockey fans, women over fifty, liberal Democrats, or college students.

A writer's audience and purpose go hand in hand. For example, the writer who wrote on the problem of childhood obesity had a clear purpose in mind: to convince readers that childhood obesity was a solvable problem. She may decide that she wants to reach a very general audience, since childhood obesity and its effects should be of concern to everyone, or she may want to focus her message on those who can most make a difference: the parents of young children and the children themselves. Whom she decides to write for will influence how she writes her essay and what she includes. To help you decide on the best audience and purpose for your upcoming essay, ask yourself these questions:

1. **Whom do I most *want* to read my essay?** What readers would be most interested in your topic? What readers would be most affected by its message? What readers might take something from it that could influence their lives? Your primary audience might be college students, the college board of trustees, newspaper readers, high school seniors, foreign students, or pregnant teens.

2. **What would my primary purpose be in writing to this audience?** Do you want to change people's minds? Reveal to them a particular "truth?" Provide some useful information? Get readers to act? Give them hope?

3. **How can I best accomplish my purpose given my chosen reading audience?** What do you need to emphasize? What may make the greatest impact on readers? What should you definitely include?

Writing Activity 3.3

To decide on a reading audience and purpose for your essay, answer the three previous questions on audience and purpose.

Example:

from the writer of "A Lesson in Courage"

1. I think I'd most like young girls - elementary and junior high school - to read the essay. They are the ones I am writing about in the essay, and they may have had similar experiences to the one I will illustrate. It may make them think about what

goes on in their lives, be more aware of how they treat others, and at best, help them make courageous choices when they are faced with them.

2. My purpose would be for girls to see that what they may be going through, whether on one side of the experience or the other, is not uncommon. My further purpose would be to show that there is a right and wrong way to act towards other girls, and that they have the courage within them to make the best choices.

3. I need to present the illustration so that it feels "real" to readers and they can relate to it. I want them to see how I felt the same conflicting feelings that they may feel some times, and that I didn't have the courage at the time to do what I should have. I don't want to write in a way that dismisses the difficulty in going against peer pressure and doing the right thing. I want them to know that I understand how hard it is, but at the same time, not impossible. I also want to give them the upside: how good it can feel to do the right thing and, ultimately, how it can change your life for the better.

Drafting

Your prewriting preparation has provided you with some direction for writing your first draft and, no doubt, the confidence that comes from knowing what you want to say. Exactly how you put those thoughts on paper - what you include in your illustration, what you emphasize, what you describe, how you tie your illustration to your main point, how you word you thoughts and develop each paragraph - is something that you work out sentence by sentence, paragraph by paragraph as you write the draft.

Writing is often a process of "discovery" where the act of writing itself helps you figure out what you want to say. Each sentence is related to the previous sentence as well as the other sentences in the paragraph. What you write in one sentence influences what you write in the next, and writers often go back and reread previous sentences in a paragraph to help decide how best to continue. Thus, writing is a *rescursive* activity, where writers continually return to what they have already written to help them continue moving forward.

As you write your first draft, if you frequently reread sentences, grapple with what you want to write next, have trouble wording a thought the way you want, or struggle to bring an emerging idea into clear focus, you are experiencing what all writers do. That is why writing can be challenging, frustrating, and exciting by equal turns. Writing is a continuous decision-making process which can test the skill and tenacity of the most experienced writers.

Writing Openings

How do you open your paper? That is the first consideration for writers as they begin their draft. As readers read your opening, they are poking their heads into your paper to see what's going on. If the opening gets their attention, they will want to read further. If it doesn't, they may set it aside or read on with little enthusiasm.

To write an opening that leads effectively into the main body of your essay, consider the following:

1. **In general, an opening introduces your topic and creates reader interest.** Two questions on readers' minds as they begin an essay are, "What is this essay about?" and "Why would I want to read it?" An effective opening can answer those questions.

2. **There are different ways to open an essay.** There is no "formula" for writing an effective opening, and writers have different options for introducing their topic: an interesting or relevant fact, a brief anecdote, some relevant statistics, a fabricated incident or situation, a vivid description, a significant quote, or some combination of options. Ask yourself, "For my particular a topic, what would be the most interesting or effective way of opening the draft?"

3. **An opening should be relatively brief.** Most essay openings are a paragraph or two in length. You don't want to take too long or expend too much space on introducing your topic since the main part of your paper lies ahead.

4. **An opening often expresses the writer's viewpoint on the topic.** For example, in the draft "Lessons in Courage," the writer expressed this viewpoint in her opening: Courage is more than just braving danger; it can mean doing the right thing despite peer pressure to do the opposite. Your viewpoint - the main idea you are developing in your essay - is called an essay's *thesis*, which will be emphasized in future lessons.

To understand better the options available for opening an essay, read the following openings, which may give you some ideas about how to begin your draft. Each opening concludes with the writer's main point that she will illustrate in her draft.

Factual opening

In the last two years, three financial magnates have gone to prison for phony investment schemes that have bilked thousands of people of their life savings. Glossy investment portfolios induced people into investing millions of dollars in building projects, international corporations, and land deals, none of which ever existed. Unfortunately, the unsuspecting victims will never get their money back. With all of the investment opportunities available today, people need to be extremely cautious when it comes to investing and heed the advice, "If an investment looks to good to be true, it probably is." (Essay followed with an illustration of the writer's grandmother's investment disaster.)

Statistical opening

Over seven million children in America have no health insurance. Another three million children have inadequate coverage, preventing them from getting the best treatment. These ten million children are more likely to contract diseases, less likely to be diagnosed at early onset, and less likely to take badly needed medication than children who are fully insured.

In comparison, all children in Canada, England, France, Italy, and Japan are covered by their country's universal health care program, and the childhood mortality rate in those countries is 20% lower on average than in the U.S. There is something terribly wrong with America's health care system, and our children are among the victims. (Essay followed with an illustration of the health problems of an uninsured child who was related to the writer.)

Anecdotal opening

Dominique became alarmed when she noticed some blisters in her genital area and fever blisters on her lips. She went to the doctor, who diagnosed her as having genital herpes. Rather than being alarmed, her first reaction was one of relief. "Thank goodness I don't have AIDS," she said. "I can deal with herpes."

As more and more sexually active young adults contract STD's (sexually transmitted diseases), there is a certain sense of fatalistic acceptance. They know they aren't going to die from herpes, syphilis, or gonorrhea, and they don't have AIDS. What they don't realize is that they may be living with a terrible lifetime disease that affects not only them but also their partners and in some cases, their unborn children. Contracting any kind of STD is horrible, and every high school student should be educated about these terrible diseases and how to prevent them.
(Essay followed with an illustration of the terrible impact of herpes on the life of one young woman whom the writer knew.)

Fabricated scenario

What if every child were required to do some kind of community service work as part of their education? They could participate in food and clothing drives, help younger children with reading problems, bring cheer to the elderly in rest homes, or put on performances at children's hospitals. This would not be a one-time experience but a regular part of their K-12 education. Helping others would become a part of their lives, and its importance a part of their value system. To help create service-minded children, every school district should implement a service program required for every student.
(Essay followed with an illustration from the writer's own life, whose parents instilled such a belief and commitment in her, and how it affected her life.)

Description

The lawn in front of the house is dead, and waist-high weeds grow everywhere. The fence on the north side of the property is leaning badly. Windows are broken, shutters are hanging loosely, the paint on the house is chipped and cracking, and someone has graffitied the side of the house with black spray paint.

Sitting vacant for months, this house is one of thousands of foreclosures in the city, a neighborhood eyesore and target for vandals and thieves. Of all the problems associated with America's foreclosure epidemic, one that is often overlooked is the negative effects that foreclosures have on the neighborhood's residents.
(Essay followed illustrating the impact of foreclosures in the writer's neighborhood.)

Writing Activity 3.4

For practice and to develop some material for your draft, write an opening for your essay, or try writing a couple different openings and decide which you feel is most effective. Include the main point on your topic that you are going to illustrate. Then exchange openings with classmates to see how other writers introduced their topics.

Example

Trinity College has over 8,000 students that attend during the day, many of whom drive to campus. For those 8,000 students, Trinity has only three parking lots which can hold a maximum of 3,000 cars. There is also parking available on the street on two sides of the campus and in a large vacant dirt lot across from one street. However, that additional parking space is woefully inadequate for the number of cars that need parking. Trinity College has a severe student parking problem that affects thousands of students, and it needs to invest in more parking space.
(Essay continues by illustrating the writer's own parking experiences at the college.)

Optional opening:

At 8:45 in the morning, an army of cars whiz around the north parking lot aisles, competing for those rare available spaces. Brakes screech and tires squeal as one car dives into a parking space in front of another. Eventually a lot of the cars leave the lot in hopes of finding parking in more remote areas. Many students who parked in the lot arrived for class over an hour early just to get parking. That hectic scene is duplicated every school day in the three inadequate parking lots that Trinity College has for its 8,000 day students. The college has a severe student parking problem that affects thousands of students, and it needs to invest in more parking space.

Drafting Suggestions

As you begin writing your first draft, consider the following suggestions:

1. **Begin your draft using one of the openings that you generated in the previous activity.** If you aren't satisfied with your opening, try something different. Be sure to express the main point of your essay in the opening so that readers will know the purpose of your forthcoming illustration.

2. **Illustrate your main point in a way that provides the best support.** Emphasize those things that most clearly show readers why you believe as you do.

3. **Include descriptive details so that readers see, hear, and feel what you want them to.** In this regard, writing your illustration is no different from relating your personal experience in Lesson One.

4. **Paragraph your draft, and change paragraphs as you move to a new thought or to a different part of your paper: opening to middle to conclusion.** Avoid overly long paragraphs that readers can get bogged down in or extremely short paragraphs that may need combining or further development.

5. **If dialogue is an important part of your illustration, provide quotations for the most important or dramatic comments to spark reader interest.** Put quotation marks (" ") around the spoken words and identify the speaker: "You can not use the car until your grades improve," mom said resolutely.

6. **With a first draft, don't worry about perfection.** The purpose of the first draft is to get your thoughts on paper. You will have time to sharpen and polish your draft during the revision process.

7. **Conclude your paper in a manner that reinforces your main thought in some manner.** You might conclude with an important illustrative point, a restatement of your main point and its effect on people, some thoughts on what the future may hold for your topic, or some suggestions on what should be done regarding the topic. Since your ending is the last thing that readers read, think about how you could make the greatest impact on them.

8. **Keep your reading audience in mind: the people that you would most like to reach with your essay.** Write in a way that you feel would be most effective for this particular audience.

Drafting Tip: Getting Stuck

At one time or another, all writers get "stuck" in their writing, uncertain what they want to say next. These "writer's block" moments can have different causes: writing exhaustion, momentary boredom, jumbled thoughts, or paralyzing indecision. Whatever the reason, if you get "stuck" in a paper, try some of these ideas:

1.   Get away from your paper for awhile. When you return, your direction might appear much clearer.

2.   Reread a couple times what you have written to that point. That may help you decide how to proceed.

3.   Get some sleep. You may be low on energy, and need a recharge.

> **4.** *Concentrate on connective thoughts. If there is a memory that needs unlocking for you to proceed, think of things associated with that memory: people, places, times, incidents, feelings.*
>
> **5.** *Do some exercise. Get the blood flowing, which increases oxygen to the brain. Physical and mental energy go together.*
>
> **6.** *Write something. It may not be what you want, but it may help get you there. Sometimes the act of writing helps you discover what you want to say next.*

Writing Activity 3.5

Read the following first draft, noting its opening, which includes its main point, the illustration it uses to support that point, its use of descriptive detail and dialogue, its paragraphing, and its conclusion. Then write your first draft keeping in mind the drafting suggestions provided.

A Lesson in Courage - First Draft

Reading audience: school-age girls

When I was in seventh grade, I learned that courage comes in different types of acts and behavior and is not restricted to confronting the dangerous. You don't have to jump into a burning building or take on the school yard bully to show courage. Courage can be doing what is right when your friends are doing wrong. My friend Leticia showed me the best example of that.

As a seventh grade girl, it was hard for me to admit I was wrong about anything, especially when I was behaving like the popular majority. I always stayed on the popular side, but my former friend Leticia took the unpopular side and paid a big price. But the courage that she showed stayed with me and eventually caused me to rethink the kind of person I wanted to be.

A girl named Araceli was always on the fringe of the popular girl group, and she always tried too hard to get on the inside, kissing up to the leaders and basically doing anything they asked of her. The leaders started making fun of Araceli behind her back, and the rest of us joined in, happy with our status as "insiders." One day one of the leaders said, "You know, Araceli really makes me sick the way she acts. I hate her hanging around us." "Yeah," the rest of us chimed in, only too happy to kick Araceli to the curb. And from that moment on, she became an outcast.

When Araceli came around at recess the next day, Ramona, one of the most vocal leaders, said, "Get away from us. We don't want you around." As Araceli looked around the group for some sympathetic faces, all she got were "mean girl" scowls and silence. "What did I do wrong?" she asked plaintively. "Nothing," said Ramona. "You're just not one of us. Now get lost." With tears running down her face, Araceli turned and ran away, obviously crushed by the group's sudden rejection. "Good riddance to bad rubbish," said Callie, who would never cross Ramona. "Yeah," the rest of us said, laughing at Araceli's fate and happy that it wasn't us.

The big snub was officially on. If Araceli tried to sit at our table in the cafeteria, we'd close ranks so she had no where to sit. If anyone was caught talking to Araceli, someone would say, "Why were you talking to that bitch?" No one ever made the same mistake twice. Not content to shut Araceli out, the taunting on the school grounds began, with comments like, "Hey Araceli, you should 'moo' instead of talk. You look like a cow," as we all made mooing sounds, or "Hey Araceli, Halloween isn't until next month. Why are you dressed like a witch?" The taunts were followed by hoots and laughter, and I hooted and laughed like everyone else. It seemed like the more miserable we could make Araceli, the better we felt.

One day at the cafeteria, one of our gang said, "Look across the room. Leticia is sitting with Araceli!" No one could believe it. Leticia was one of us. Why on earth was she sitting with the outcast? Some of us walked across the cafeteria to see what was going on. "Leticia," I asked, "why on earth are you sitting with *her*?" Leticia looked at me calmly and said, "Araceli is my friend. She never did anything wrong." Shocked by this outrageous break with popular-girl protocol, we just stood there dumbfounded. Finally, someone said, "Well, you're dumber than you look, Leticia. You just made a really bad choice." And we walked away.

Troubled by this defection of one of our own, Ramona needed to put this into perspective for us. "I never really liked Leticia anyway," she said. "She was always too quiet. She wasn't really one of us." "Yeah," we agreed. "Leticia and Araceli deserve each other," said Callie. "They're both losers." That settled that. Leticia was out, and everything was right in the popular-girl world. But I was still troubled by what Leticia had done because she was really my friend. I was mad at her for doing something so stupid.

Leticia knew that what she had done would alienate her from the gang, and apparently she was prepared for it. She didn't try to hang around us or talk to us. She truly befriended Araceli and spent time with her. When we passed in the corridor, she'd smile and say "hi" and I'd do the same, but I wouldn't talk to her at school. No one ever made fun of Leticia the way we did Araceli, and I think some of us grudgingly admired what she had done even though we thought it was crazy.

I couldn't be seen talking to Leticia at school, so I went to her house one Saturday morning. "Why did you do that Leticia?" I asked. "Araceli just got what she deserved." "No she didn't," said Leticia. "She just wanted so badly to be a part of our group that she tried too hard. It was wrong the way that we treated her, and I just couldn't keep doing it." "But you chose her over us!" I retorted. "That's crazy." "I wish it wasn't that way," she said. "But it was you guys who did the choosing. I never shut anyone out." "You're still my friend Leticia," I said, "but you really screwed up." "I don't regret what I did," said Leticia. "Araceli is a nice person."

When I look back in hindsight, I envision myself having the courage to side with Leticia against the gang, spurring on other girls to do the same and ending the cruel treatment of Araceli we had all been a part of. But that's not what happened. I continued to go along with the gang, Leticia remained an outcast along with Araceli throughout our eighth grade year, and then Leticia moved to a town up north and I didn't see her anymore. But I have thought about her often, admiring the courage that it took to side with Araceli against the popular girls, knowing that it would shut her off from her friends and make her an outcast. I certainly didn't have that courage, and I went along with the gang knowing deep inside that what we were doing was wrong.

Leticia's example wasn't lost on me, however. As I got older, when peer pressure was on the side of doing something I felt was wrong or of treating someone unfairly, I did my best not to go along. I tried to do the right thing in spite of the consequences. Admittedly, I never had to make a choice as drastic as Leticia's, where she lost all her friends, but I made some hard decisions I never would have made in junior high. I also chose my friends more wisely, not just gravitating to the lower orbit of the most popular girls in school, who weren't always the nicest.

Today, I like myself more as a person than I did when I was younger, and there is no question that Leticia played a role in that. Courage takes all kinds of forms, and anyone who has been a seventh grade girl knows the courage it takes to resist the tremendous peer pressure of the group. Leticia showed me what courage looks like, and it was the best lesson I learned in junior high.

Revision

Completing your first draft is the biggest step towards your ultimate writing goal: producing a final, polished essay to share with readers. You have done the "heavy lifting," getting your ideas on paper in a relatively organized manner. Now you can take a look at what you have written, see what you have done well and what you might do better. Your revisions might include improving some sentence wording, adding some detail in certain places, combining a couple short, related paragraphs, or strengthening your opening. You now have a completed draft to work with, and through revision, you can develop and shape it exactly the way you want.

To revise your current draft, consider the following suggestions:

1. **Take a good look at your opening.** Do you clearly introduce your topic in a way that may interest readers? Do you present the main idea that you are illustrating in your essay? Is the length of your opening in "balance" with the rest of the draft? Make any changes that will strengthen your opening.

2. **Evaluate your illustration, the main focus of your draft.** You are using your illustration to show readers why you believe as you do. Make sure that they understand clearly the connection between the illustration and the main point that it is supporting. Are there details you might add to help readers see and hear what is happening and understand what you or others are thinking and feeling? Have you used dialogue, if appropriate, to create reader interest and bring people to life? On rereading, do you recall new things about the experience that you want to add?

3. **Check your sentence wording.** Usually you will find some first-draft sentences that can be improved by eliminating unnecessary words, rewording an awkward-sounding sentence, clarifying a vaguely worded sentence, or improving your word choices. Make any changes that will make your sentences smoother, clearer, more concise, and more vivid.

4. **Check your paragraphing.** Make sure that you have changed paragraphs as you move from one idea to the next or to different parts of the draft: opening to middle to conclusion. Divide any overly long paragraphs and combine or develop extremely short paragraphs.

5. **Check your organization.** The organization of your draft is pretty straightforward. Check to make sure you presented your illustration in the chronological order in which the experience unfolded. If a particular paragraph or a sentence within a paragraph appears out of place, move it to a more logical location.

6. **Evaluate your conclusion.** Does your ending reinforce the main point of your essay in some manner? Does it leave readers with a sense of closure? Is its length in "balance" with the rest of the essay? What final impression does it leave with readers? Make any changes that will strengthen your conclusion and its impact on readers.

7. **Read your draft from your readers' perspective.** Since you are writing the essay for a particular audience with a purpose in mind, read the draft from your readers' perspective. Make any changes that you feel will help them understand the illustration, engage their interest, or help you accomplish your writing purpose.

Revision Tips

What is the best way to revise a paper when there are a number of different elements to consider? Try the following approach to revise your draft most effectively:

1. First, revise for content. Make any changes - adding descriptive detail, inserting a new example, emphasizing a particular point, or replacing a weak introduction - to improve the essay's content.

2. Second, revise for wording. Once you are satisfied with content, make all of the sentence wording improvements that will present your content most effectively.

3. Third, revise for paragraphing and organization. Make any changes that will improve your paragraphing and strengthen your organization.

4. Fourth, revise for overall effect. Give your draft a final once-over and make any revisions that you feel will heighten its impact.

While some writers prefer tackling all revision elements at once, revising one element at a time gives you a systematic, focused approach which leaves nothing out.

Writing Activity 3.6

Since sentence-wording improvement is a common focus for most writers, it receives some extra attention in different lessons. For practice, revise sentences in the following paragraph to eliminate wordiness, awkward phrasing, or weak word choice. The revised sentences should be smoother, clearer, and more concise.

Example:

The food that they have in the cafeteria is so good that I seldom go off campus to eat lunch.   The cafeteria is actually divided up into several small "restaurants," each of which is run by a different vendor that the cafeteria leases space to. For example, the restaurants include ethnic choices such as Mexican, Chinese, and Italian, so as you can see, you have a great choice of what to eat, and it is all good.

Revised:

The **cafeteria** food ~~that they have in the cafeteria~~ is so good that I seldom go off campus ~~to eat~~ **for** lunch.   The cafeteria is ~~actually~~ divided ~~up~~ into several small "restaurants," each ~~of which is~~ run **and leased** by a different vendor. ~~that the cafeteria leases space to.~~ ~~For example,~~ **T**he restaurants include ~~ethnic choices such as~~ Mexican, Chinese, and Italian **cuisine**, so ~~as you can see,~~ you have a great choice of ~~what to eat, and it is all~~ good **food.**

School Library

The college library is not located in a very good place for students to use it. It is located far off in the north end of the campus, far away from the campus center whose buildings include most of the classes that students take. It is a good ten-minute walk from my classes to the library, and it is not a walk that I frequently take. When you do go out to the library, few students can be seen within it, which tells the story of its bad location. Most students, instead of going to the library to study, study instead in the centrally located student union, leaving most of the large study space in the library without students. There is no real solution to the problem of the library's crummy location. Unless you badly need a book or periodical to find information to help you do a research paper for some class, there is no real reason to have to go to the library, and therefore, few students do.

Writing Activity 3.7

Revise your first draft by applying the revision suggestions provided, making any changes that you feel will improve it.

Example:

Revisions from "Lessons in Courage" (Deleted words crossed out; added words in bold)

Fifth paragraph:

The big snub was ~~officially~~ on. If Araceli tried to sit at our table in the cafeteria, we'd close ranks so she had no where to sit. If anyone was caught talking to Araceli, someone would ~~say~~ **ask**, "Why were you talking to that bitch?" No one ever made the same mistake twice. Not content to shut Araceli out, the taunting on the school grounds began, with comments like, "Hey Araceli, ~~you should "moo" instead of talk.~~ **why aren't you mooing?** You look like a cow," ~~as~~ **and** we all made mooing sounds, or "Hey Araceli, **today isn't** Halloween. ~~isn't until next month.~~ Why are you dressed like a witch?" The taunts were followed by hoots and laughter, **including my own.** ~~and I hooted and laughed like everyone else.~~ It seemed like the more miserable we could make Araceli, ~~feel,~~ the better we felt. **But deep down, I was also feeling guilt.**

Last paragraph:

Today, I like myself more ~~as a person~~ than I did when I was younger, and there is no question that Leticia ~~played a role in that~~ **helped make that happen.** Courage takes all kinds of forms, and anyone who has been a seventh grade girl knows the courage it takes to resist the tremendous peer pressure ~~of the group~~. Leticia showed me what courage looks like, and it was the best lesson I learned in junior high. **What I still wonder about is how our treatment of Araceli affected her. Did we help to ruin her young life or leave her with emotional scars? You never know the damage that your words and deeds can do to someone, a lesson that I try to carry with me.**

Writing Activity 3.8

When you finish revising your draft, exchange drafts with a classmate or two. Read each other's drafts, ask questions, and make suggestions that will give the writer some revision ideas. Make any additional changes that you feel will improve your paper.

Editing

Once you have revised the draft to your satisfaction, you are one short, critical step from completing your essay: correcting any errors you may find. Now is the best time to run the spell check on your word-processing program since you have made all of your wording revisions. Now is also the time to proofread your draft systematically for errors, particularly those that you are most prone to make.

In the first two lessons, you learned to identify and correct run-on and comma-splice sentences and to insert commas correctly in your sentences. In this lesson, you are introduced to *subject pronouns* and *pronoun-antecedent agreement,* two potential problem areas for writers. Since you probably used pronouns in your illustration, now is a good time to focus on them.

Subject Pronouns

Using the correct subject pronouns - *I, he, she, we, you, they* - is not a problem for writers when there is one subject in a sentence. For example, no one would write, "*Her* went to the singing audition," or "*Them* are really interested in sub-leasing our apartment." However, when the subject is *compound* - two or more subjects - the incorrect pronoun form doesn't sound as bad to some writers, and mistakes can occur:

> Amanda, Noppakan, Gracelia, and *her* went to the singing audition.
> The Singh family and *them* are interested in sub-leasing our apartment.

To use the correct subject pronoun forms in your sentence, follow these basic rules.

1. **The *subject* of a sentence is who or what the sentence is about, and it usually comes at or near the beginning of the sentence:**

   He is no longer a member of the chess club.
   We enjoy taking long walks on cool autumn mornings.
   During the summer, *they* often sit on their porch to enjoy the afternoon breeze.

2. **The correct subject-pronoun forms are *I, he, she, we, they, it*, and *you*.** Always use these pronouns as the subjects of your sentences. The *object* pronoun forms - *me, him, her, us, them* - should never be used as subjects.

3. **Subject-pronoun problems occur with *compound subjects*: two or more subjects.** Always use the correct subject-pronoun forms in compound subjects:

   Jonas and *I* ride the city bus to school in the morning.
   Matilda and *she* have been best friends since grade school.

He and *I* are taking the same classes this semester.

4. **To choose the correct pronoun form in a compound subject, listen to how the pronoun sounds if it were the *only* subject.** For example, in the sentence (Him, He) and (Me, I) are good friends, ask yourself, Would I say "*Him* is a good friend" or "*He* is a good friend?" Would I say "*Me* is a good friend" or *I* am a good friend?" The correct forms - *he* and *I* - are obvious. With a compound subject, if you isolate the pronoun and see how it sounds as the only subject, you will always use the correct pronoun.

Writing Activity 3.9

Correct any subject-pronoun errors in the following paragraph.

Example:

My cousin Samantha and me are very close. Since we were babies, her and I were together every day at our grandma's house. We grew up together like sisters. Although our other cousins and us are all good friends, Samantha and me have a special relationship.

Corrected:

My cousin Samantha and *I* are very close. Since we were babies, *she* and I were together every day at our grandma's house. We grew up together like sisters. Although our other cousins and *we* are all good friends, Samantha and *I* have a special relationship.

Our family and the Iwamoto family have done things together for over thirty years. Them and us were neighbors for twenty years, and we spent New Year's Eve together every year. Their daughter August and me were on the same basketball and volleyball teams for years, and her and I got along great. The Iwamotos and us went on a lot of vacations together, and us kids played at each other's houses all the time. It was great having the Iwamotos as our neighbors, and them and us will always be friends.

Pronoun-Antecedent Agreement

As with subject pronoun usage, pronoun-antecedent agreement is not a problem for writers in most situations. For example, we know that when you refer by pronoun to the word "boy" in a sentence, you would use *he, him, his,* or *himself,* depending on the situation. If you refer to the word "girl," you would use *she, her, hers, or herself.* You always use the pronoun that agrees in *number* and *gender* with its *antecedent:* the word in the sentence that it replaces.

Pronoun-antecedent agreement problems occur most frequently when the *antecedent* of a pronoun is an *indefinite pronoun* like *someone, somebody, no one, everyone,* or *everybody*. For example, would you write, "Everyone at the soccer game took out *their* umbrella when it began to rain," or "Everyone at the soccer game took out *his or her* umbrella when it began to rain?" Some writers would puzzle over the correct usage.

To use the correct pronouns with their antecedents, and in particular when the antecedent is an *indefinite pronoun*, follow these basic rules:

1. **A pronoun agrees with its *antecedent*, the word in the sentence that it replaces, in *number (*singular or plural) and *gender* (male, female, or neutral):**

    (antecedent underlined, pronouns replacing antecedent in italics)

    Frances brought *her* daughter to work because the day care center was closed.
    Herman never takes *himself* too seriously.
    I don't believe that the debate team members performed *their* best at the contest because *they* had so little time to prepare.
    My cell phone loses *its* reception in the mountains.
    No matter how far our team got behind, *we* always believed in *ourselves*.

2. **When an *indefinite pronoun - one, someone, somebody, no one, everyone, everybody, anything, anybody, neither, none, each, either -* is the antecedent, the pronoun(s) replacing it is always *singular*.**

    Everyone in the women's choir should bring *her* choir robe to practice Monday.
    Neither of the male singing contestants had a chance against *his* female opponents.
    Everybody hopes to reach *his* or *her* goals in life.

3. **When a *collective noun* - a word referring to a group of people - is an antecedent, the pronoun replacing it may be singular or plural, depending on the situation.** Collective nouns include words like *team, committee, family, legislature, club* or *group*. In a sentence, when the collective noun is referring to a single unit acting together, use singular pronouns to replace it:

    The football team played *its* best game of the season last night.
    The state legislature gave *itself* two days to complete budget negotiations.

    When the collective noun is referring to people acting individually within the group, use plural pronouns to replace it:

    All of our family do *their* own Christmas shopping separately.
    The sequestered jury were finally allowed to return to *their* homes.

4. **When a singular antecedent can include both males and females, use the pronoun tandem** *he or she*, *him or her*, **or** *himself or herself* **to replace it:**

A <u>student</u> should do *his or her* best to find a quiet place to study on campus. <u>No one</u> wants *his or her* reputation tarnished by unfounded accusations. After completing an essay, a <u>writer</u> should treat *himself or herself* to some relaxation.

Pronoun-Antecedent Tips

Referring repeatedly to singular antecedents with "him or her," "he or she," or "himself or herself" can become monotonous and create a distraction for readers. This problem can be solved in two ways:

1. *Make the singular antecedent plural. For example, instead of writing, "A writer usually finds one place where he or she can write most productively," try, "Writers usually find one place where they can write most productively." Instead of writing, "A person needs to call upon his or her inner strength to finish a marathon," try, "People need to call upon their inner strength to finish a marathon."*

2. *Alternate between using the masculine and feminine pronoun forms. For example, in this book, with so many potential "his or her," "he or she," and "himself or herself" references, the masculine and feminine references are used alternately to replace antecedents that include males and females: "A writer often does his most productive writing under the pressure of a deadline. No one likes such pressure, but it sometimes motivates a writer to complete her task."*

In general, change singular antecedents to plural when possible, use "his or her" and "he or she" references if they come up infrequently in an essay, and alternate between the masculine and feminine pronoun forms when writing longer papers with numerous pronoun references.

Writing Activity 3.10

Correct any pronoun-antecedent agreement problems in the following paragraph. Change some singular antecedents to plural to avoid awkward "his or her" references.

Example:

Every teaching retiree vested in the state pension system got a shock when their most recent check was 10% smaller than usual. The state legislature had exercised their right to reduce the pension payout amount if the pension deficit exceeded $2 billion, which occurred last month. Everyone in the system had believed that their monthly pension payout was a fixed, unchangeable benefit.

Corrected:

~~Every~~ *All* teaching *retirees* vested in the state pension system got a shock when their most recent check was 10% smaller than usual. The state legislature had exercised ~~their~~ *its* right to reduce the pension payout amount if the pension deficit exceeded $2 billion, which occurred last month. Everyone in the system had believed that ~~their~~ *his or her* monthly pension payout was a fixed, unchangeable benefit.

Higher Ticket Prices

Student ticket prices for home basketball games increased $5.00 per game this year. No one was aware that their tickets would cost more until after the ticket lottery had been held. Since the basketball team was predicted to have their best season, nobody really wanted to give up their tickets. However, with the price increases totaling over $70 for the season, some students felt that he or she had no choice but to give it up. Every student agreed that the college shouldn't have held the lottery before warning them and that they didn't need to raise the price that much.

Writing Activity 3.11

Proofread your draft for any subject pronoun or pronoun-antecedent agreement problems, and make corrections if needed. Then proofread your paper for other common errors, including run-on or comma splice sentences, comma usage, subject-verb agreement, quotation marks usage, or frequently confused words such as there/their/they're, know/no, affect/effect, its/it's, your/you're, to/too/two, or were/we're.

Writing Activity 3.12

Exchange drafts with a classmate and proofread each other's papers. Make any necessary corrections, noting the types of errors, if any, that you overlooked in your draft.

Communicating with Readers

When you finish your essay, you are ready to share it with readers. Given the readers that you wrote the essay for, what might be the best way to get the essay to them? For example, the writer who wrote the essay "Lessons in Courage" for young girls to read disseminated copies to girls in local 6th and 7th grade classes with the approval of their instructors. Your instructor may have some ideas on how you might best reach your reading audience and get perhaps get some feedback.

Lesson Four: Thesis Support

Objective: To write a thesis-based essay with the emphasis on providing effective supporting points.

Purpose: To reveal something of yourself by sharing with readers an activity, pastime, or event that you find particularly enjoyable or fulfilling.

Audience: Classmates

Most essays that you read - editorials, letters to the editor, periodical articles, readings in anthologies - have a *thesis*: a main point that the writer introduces and supports in the essay. The thesis reveals the writer's *viewpoint* on the topic - what she thinks, feels, or believes about it. The essay goes on to explain *why* the writer holds that particular viewpoint.

In this lesson, as well as in subsequent lessons, you will write a thesis-based essay. The emphasis in this lesson is on providing the best possible *support* for your thesis: the reasons you believe as you do. The writing topic - an activity, pastime, or event that you find enjoyable or fulfilling - is suitable for a thesis-based essay and something that you can write on knowledgeably. The purpose of the lesson is to give you some experience generating and supporting a thesis, which will be useful for your upcoming essays.

Thesis Generation

While the term "thesis" may sound rather formal and academic, it applies to any type of writing where the writer takes a position on a topic and explains or defends that position. A thesis-based writing might be a political science essay with the thesis, "The Southern states' political shift from the Democratic to the Republican Party can be traced to the far-left politics of Democrats in the 1960's," or it might be a mother-to-son e-mail with the thesis, "I think you are making a mistake trying to work full-time during school."

Thesis-based essays have been around for centuries because they provide an effective format for a writer to present his ideas and for readers to follow them. Simply put, the writer introduces his topic, tells what he believes or how he feels about it, and explains why he believes or feels as he does. For readers, there is a clear topic, a viewpoint to consider, and the writer's supportive reasoning to evaluate.

For example, let's say that a writer's topic is the new proposed amphitheater at the college. Her viewpoint, the thesis of the essay, is that the amphitheater would be a great addition to the campus. In the essay, she explains her reasoning:

1. The amphitheater will hold more students than any venue on campus.
2. It will provide very comfortable seating.
3. Students will enjoy the relaxed atmosphere that an outside venue provides.
4. With the greater seating capacity, the college can attract more big-name entertainers.
5. The weather during the fall and spring is great for outdoor concerts.

Readers can evaluate the writer's reasoning and decide whether it makes sense to them.
  To generate a thesis for an essay, consider the following:

1. **Your thesis is the *main point* of your essay: the idea that you are developing in your paper.** If an essay lacks a thesis, readers may ask themselves, "What is the point of the essay?"

2. **Your thesis provides your *viewpoint* on the topic: what you think, feel, or believe about it.** For any writing topic, decide on a thesis that best expresses your viewpoint.

3. **Generate a thesis that you can *support* in an essay.** The success of any thesis lies in how well it is supported. The more convincingly you can support your viewpoint, the greater likelihood readers will agree with it or at the least, understand why you hold it.

4. **An essay's thesis is usually expressed in a *thesis statement*: a sentence expressing the writer's viewpoint on the topic.** For example, with the topic "America's Shrinking Middle Class," the writer's viewpoint may be that the "American Dream" has become unattainable for many people His *thesis statement* in his essay may read, "With America's middle class shrinking dramatically, the American Dream of home ownership and a secure financial future is dying for millions of Americans." A writer who evaluated the options of leasing or buying a car generated the following thesis statement for her essay: "For many people, the only realistic way to get a new car is to lease it."

Writing Activity 4.1

Generate a thesis statement for at least half of the following topics that expresses your viewpoint on the topic and that you could support in an essay.

Examples:

Topic: Eiffel Tower

Thesis: The Eiffel Tower is the most incredible landmark in the world.

Topic: Snorkeling

Thesis: The only time I want to be near fish is at a restaurant.

Topic: Reggae music

Thesis: The Reggae beat sets it apart from all other music.

1. Topic: Playing video games

    Thesis:

2. Topic: The price of college textbooks

    Thesis:

3. Topic: Rock concerts

    Thesis:

4. Topic: Mexican food

    Thesis:

5. Topic: Facebook

    Thesis:

6. Topic: Rap music

    Thesis:

7. Topic: You Tube

    Thesis:

8. Topic: Electric cars

    Thesis:

Thesis Support

In a thesis-based essay, the main task of the writer is to explain to readers *why* she thinks or believes as she does. The more convincingly a writer can support her thesis, the more likely that readers will understand and accept her reasoning.

For example, a writer felt that burning wood in fireplaces should be banned in the valley where she lived because of the pollution it generated. However, she also knew that thousands of families heated their homes in winter with their fireplaces or wood-burning stoves. She knew that she would have to provide strong support for her viewpoint to influence people.

To that end, she provided the following reasons why wood burning should be banned: the high level of pollution in the valley; the degree to which wood burning contributed to that pollution; the ugly brown haze that hung over the valley in winter; children's asthmatic and respiratory illnesses caused by pollution; the ever-increasing "bad air" days where children can't play outside at school; and the many positive effects of improved air quality if fireplace burning was banned. The writer felt that those points made the best case in support of her thesis.

To provide the best support for your thesis, consider these suggestions:

1. **Generate as many reasons as you can think of to support your thesis.** You may not use them all, but you can decide on those that you think are the strongest.

2. **Generate support that you strongly believe to be true.** The more convinced you are that your supportive reasons are valid, the better you can convince readers.

3. **Consider your readers as you evaluate your support.** What reasons would make the greatest impact on readers, particular those who may not be particularly knowledgeable on your topic?

4. **If you can't think of some compelling support for your thesis, consider changing topics.** Sometimes we may have a strong feeling or opinion about something, but upon analysis, little reasoning to support it. For example, a writer didn't like a particular movie, but could only conclude that it was "boring." She decided not to write about the movie.

Writing Activity 4.2

For practice generating support for a thesis, pick two of your thesis statements from Writing Activity 4.1 and make a list of reasons in support of each thesis.

Examples:

Topic: Eiffel Tower

Thesis: I'd love to climb to the top of the Eiffel Tower

Reasons: 1. The view from the top of the tower would be fantastic.
2. I love heights.
3. The climb to the top of the tower would be exciting.
4. It would be very romantic at the top of the tower with my girlfriend.
5. It would be a once-in-a-lifetime experience.
6. I could take some amazing pictures of the "City of Lights."

Topic: Snorkeling

Thesis: The only time I want to be near fish is at a restaurant.

Reasons: 1. Fish swimming around me would freak me out.
2. I'd be terrified of being attacked by sharks or sting rays.
3. When snorkeling, my friend got sea urchin spikes in his foot and suffered indescribable pain and swelling
4. I'm not that comfortable swimming in the ocean, let alone snorkeling.

Writing Assignment

For this lesson, you will write a thesis-based essay about something that you enjoy doing with an emphasis on providing the best support for your thesis. For your topic, consider different activities that you enjoy, hobbies you might have, events you like attending, volunteer work you might do, or any clubs or organizations you are involved in.

Select a topic that interests you, that you are knowledgeable about, that you could develop in an essay, and that may be different from your classmates' topics. Take your time selecting a topic, settling on one that you would like to share your enthusiasm or passion for with readers.

Examples:

Samples of student topics:

Attending the annual state fair
Working as a candy striper volunteer at Valley Children's Hospital
Playing in my garage band
Following my favorite team, the Chicago Bulls

Fixing up old cars
Singing in the school pop choir
Playing my favorite video game, Madden 10
Shopping, shopping, shopping!
Working at the college day-care center

Preparation

Once you have decided on a topic, you can do a number of things to help prepare to
write your first draft. Each "Preparation" section provides you with some optional
prewriting activities to get you thinking about your topic and to generate some potential
material for your draft.

Deciding on a Thesis

The thesis for your upcoming essay, which expresses your viewpoint on the topic,
should be relatively easy to generate. Since you are writing about something that you
enjoy doing, your thesis is obviously going to be a positive statement. Your main task
is to come up with the wording for your thesis statement that best expresses your
attitude towards the topic.

As examples, take a look at some of the thesis statements that students generated for
the sample topics at the end of the "Writing Assignment" section:

Topic: Attending the county fair
Thesis: I always look forward to September when the big state
            fair comes to Akron.

Topic: Working as a candy striper volunteer
Thesis: Nothing gives me more pleasure than my volunteer work at
            Valley Children's Hospital.

Topic: Playing in my garage band
Thesis: Playing in a garage band is my creative outlet.

Topic: Fixing up old cars
Thesis: I'm never happier than when I'm under the hood of a '57 Chevy.

Topic: Shopping, shopping, shopping!
Thesis: When I have the money and the time, the only place you'll find me is at the
            Fashion Fair Mall.

Writing Activity 4.3

Generate a thesis statement for your upcoming essay. Of course, you might revise the wording as you write your draft, but you will have something to start with.

Example:

Topic: raking leaves
Thesis: Some people make think I'm crazy, but I love raking leaves in the fall.

Thesis Support

You will develop your upcoming draft primarily by providing supporting points for your thesis: the reasons that you feel the way you do about the topic. Your thesis support will answer the readers' question, "*Why* do you enjoy this particular activity?" The answer will both fill the paragraphs of your essay and reveal to readers something about yourself.

To help prepare for your upcoming draft, consider the following prewriting options:

1. **Make a list of reasons for enjoying this particular activity.** Write down any reason that comes to your mind, and later you can evaluate their relative importance and decide what to include in the draft.

2. **Free write for ten minutes or so on your topic.** Write down anything that comes to mind about your topic, which may create some potential material for your draft, explore your feelings towards the topic, and perhaps unlock some ideas you hadn't thought of.

3. **Do a clustering diagram, beginning with the reasons that you enjoy your topic and then connecting details to each reason.** A clustering diagram helps you identify both supporting points and some developmental details for your paragraphs.

4. **Visualize yourself doing the particular activity, and the enjoyment that you get from each aspect of it.** For example, a writer who loved playing golf "visualized" playing a round on the course, including her feelings at different times, and came away with these reflections: the beauty of the course, the feel of hitting an iron flush, seeing how far a really good drive traveled, the camaraderie with golfing friends, the thrill of holing a tough putt, the mounting excitement of playing a low-scoring round. Putting yourself into the activity may put you in touch with those positive feelings.

Writing Activity 4.4

Select one or two of the prewriting options to generate some ideas for your draft.

Example:

Topic: the state fair
Thesis: I always look forward to September when the big state
          fair comes to Akron.

Clustering Diagram (Main supporting points in bold)

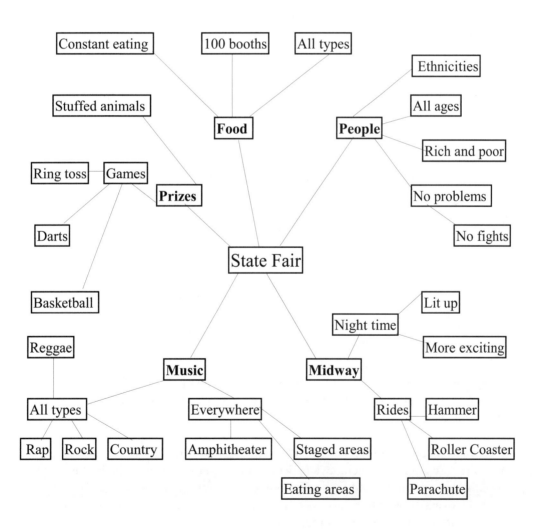

Drafting

Now that you have done some prewriting preparation, you are ready to write the first draft of your essay. Many of your drafting considerations from earlier lessons - creating an interesting opening, providing descriptive detail and examples, paragraphing your draft, including your thoughts and feelings - are also applicable to this draft.

A new drafting emphasis in this lesson is on providing a strong ending that leaves readers with a lasting final impression. Sometimes in the drafting process, writers are somewhat fatigued by the time they get to the ending and consequently dash off something short and fast to finish the paper. Before writing an ending, it helps some writers to take a break, mentally recharge, and then give the ending the time and thought that it deserves.

Writing An Ending

To write an effective ending for an essay, consider the following suggestions:

1. **An essay can be concluded effectively in a number of different ways**. You might reinforce the thesis in some manner, provide a critical supporting point for the thesis, summarize the support presented in the middle paragraphs, indicate what the future may hold regarding the topic, reveal the effects of the topic on the writer or on readers, or emphasize the purpose of the essay. How you conclude a particular draft depends on your topic, on what has come before it in the essay, and on what you want to accomplish with your ending.

2. **Bring something new to your ending.** Your conclusion should be more than a rehash of previously presented material or a reworded thesis. Give readers a reason for reading your conclusion by providing something new for them to consider or understand.

3. **Keep your ending "balanced" with the rest of your draft.** An abruptly short ending or one that goes on interminably may seem out of kilter with the rest of the draft and leave readers underwhelmed.

4. **Reread your draft before writing your ending.** Writers seldom know exactly how they are going to conclude a paper until they get to the end. The best ending usually flows naturally and logically from the previous paragraphs and is in keeping with the overall content of the essay. Before writing the conclusion, reread the entire draft to help give some direction to the ending.

5. **Keep your readers in mind when you write your conclusion.** What would be an interesting way to end the draft from a reader's perspective? How might you end the draft to give readers something to think about or remember?

A writer might end the same draft in a variety of ways. The following endings provide examples of how the writer of the "The Big Fair" draft may have concluded her essay. Read the essay "The Big Fair" in Writing Activity 4.7, including the original ending paragraph in the draft, and then read the following optional endings.

Optional Ending #1

Perhaps the greatest thing about the fair is that there is something for all ages. As a child, I loved the kiddie rides and games. As a young adult, I love the midway and the music. As a parent, which I hope to be someday, I'll love taking my own children to the fair and sharing in their enjoyment. As an older person, I'll enjoy all of the exhibits, the music, the horse races, and, of course, the food. I can't think of too many events that a person can enjoy from childhood until older age, and the fair is definitely one of them.

Optional Ending #2

The fair provides an example of how I wish life could be like every day. At the fair, everyone comes together - young and old, rich and poor, every ethnicity and race - to have a good time. No one hassles anyone else, and everyone is respectful of others. That's the way the world should be outside the fair, and it is one reason that I enjoy going so much. If we could just treat people every day the way that we do at the fair, a lot of the problems in our society would disappear. The fair provides a model for how to treat people every day.

Optional Ending #3

I think one of the reasons I enjoy the fair so much is that it only comes once a year. I'm sure I'd get tired of it if there was a fair every month, and of course I couldn't afford it anyway. That the fair only comes once a year, giving me twelve months to save up money and build my anticipation, makes it very special. In addition, the things I do at the fair, riding the big rides and playing the games, are things I can't do in the city the rest of the year. I'm sure that getting to ride the hammer or giant parachute just once a year makes those rides more thrilling. How many things are there that you really enjoy doing that you have to wait a year for? For me, the fair is always worth the wait.

Optional Ending #4

It's twelve o'clock on the last night of the fair as we slowly make our way to the tunnel leading to the south parking lot. I see the lights going out in the midway, and a feeling of sadness comes over me. I won't see those lights again for another year. I always feel a little sad when I leave the fair for the last time, knowing I won't be back for a year and that tomorrow the wonderland of rides, music, and food will be a huge vacant lot again. Like magic, it appears, then vanishes. I think that "magical" best describes how I feel about the fair. I hope I never lose that feeling.

Optional Ending #5

For me, one of the things I'll always treasure about the fair are the memories. I can still remember what it was like going to the fair with my parents when I was little. Then I remember being dropped off at the fair with my friends in junior high, and riding rides with boys for the first time. When I get older, I'm sure I'll have great memories of the times I'm having now with my college friends. And there will always be the fair pictures to revisit my experiences. My mom was a camera bug, and I inherited that from her, so there are plenty of fair pictures around. Reliving those great memories is a part of my enjoyment, including the good times with family and friends.

Writing Activity 4.5

With a classmate or small group, evaluate the different optional endings (including the one in the draft), and based on the entire essay, decide which ending or endings you preferred as a reader. What was there about certain endings that you liked, and what made other endings less effective?

Drafting Suggestions

As you write your first draft, consider these suggestions:

1. **Apply what you learned in Lesson Three to help you write an effective opening.** Introduce your topic, create reader interest, and include your *thesis statement* at or near the end of the opening.

2. **If your topic may be unfamiliar to some readers, provide some explanation following your opening.** For example, the writer who worked as a candy striper volunteer at a hospital explained what a candy striper was and her duties at the hospital before getting into the reasons she liked the work. The writer whose hobby was working on old cars explained the things he did to fix up the cars before giving the reasons that he enjoyed doing it so much.

3. **Present your supportive reasons for your thesis in separate paragraphs.** Develop each paragraph by providing examples, descriptive detail, and explanations

to help readers understand each reason. For example, the writer who worked as a candy striper developed one reason in the following way:

Being around the children at the hospital inspires me. While many of the children have serious illnesses such as cancer or heart problems, they remain cheerful and upbeat and are happy to see me. My heart goes out to them, but the last thing they want is anyone's pity. Their courage inspires me to be more fearless in facing my own problems, although they don't compare to what the children are going through. These children are my heroes, and I love being around them.

4. **Use some *topic sentences* to present your supportive reasons in the middle paragraphs.** A *topic sentence* introduces the main idea of a paragraph, which is developed in the subsequent sentences. For example, in the sample paragraph in 3., the topic sentence is "Being around children at the hospital inspires me," and the rest of the sentences explain what the writer means and provide details and examples. Note the topic sentences beginning paragraphs 2, 3, 4, 5, and 6 in the upcoming draft "The Big Fair," and how each paragraph is developed.

5. **Finish your draft with a strong conclusion, applying what you have learned about effective endings.** Write a conclusion in keeping with your thesis and supportive reasons, and provide something new to leave with readers.

6. **Keep your reading audience - your classmates - in mind and your writing purpose: to reveal something about yourself by sharing with them something that you enjoy doing.** As you write, consider what your classmates may find most interesting about your topic.

Topic Sentence Tips

Writers frequently begin paragraphs with a topic sentence, which introduces the topic of the paragraph. The following tips will help you use topic sentences in your writing.

1.   A topic sentence provides an effective way to introduce a paragraph's topic, and it helps readers follow your ideas clearly. No doubt you are already using some topic sentences in your writing.

2.   Use topic sentences to begin paragraphs that develop a single point or idea. For example, if one reason that a writer enjoys

---

jogging is the challenge, his topic sentence for a paragraph might read, "I enjoy the challenge of extending my jogging distance every week." The rest of the paragraph would tell "why."

3.   *Before beginning a particular paragraph, consider an appropriate topic sentence for introducing the main idea of the paragraph. For example, if one reason that a writer enjoys working on old cars is spending time with his dad, a topic sentence for a paragraph might be, "Spending time with my dad is a big reason I like working on cars."*

3.   *All paragraphs won't begin with a topic sentence. Opening and concluding paragraphs or paragraphs that tell a story or provide an example or explanation often don't have a topic sentence. Don't try to "force" topic sentences onto paragraphs; use them when they provide the most effective opening for single-topic paragraphs.*

Writing Activity 4.6

Select one of the following topics and generate a thesis statement and some supportive reasons. Then write a paragraph beginning with a *topic sentence* to develop *one* of the supportive points.

Example:

Topic: Christmas break

Thesis: I always look forward to Christmas break

Reasons: Get to go home
           See my friends
           Christmas with family
           Relax

(Topic sentence in italics)

When I'm home on break, I can relax and take it easy. After a semester of studying, taking tests, and working part-time, I have two weeks with no responsibilities. I can stay up late, watch T.V., sleep in, and not worry about a term paper that is due or passing a calculus mid-term. After sixteen busy, stressful weeks of school and work, I'm ready to do nothing productive for a while and recharge my battery. After a relaxing two-week break, it's back to the school-and-work routine. For me, Christmas break is a time to forget about school and do as little as I want.

Topics (select one): A favorite television program
A favorite movie
A favorite time of year
A favorite type of weather
A favorite sport's team

Writing Activity 4.7

Read the first draft of "The Big Fair," noting the writer's opening, thesis statement, reasons supporting the thesis, *use of topic sentences* (in paragraphs 2-6), paragraph development (details, explanations, examples), and conclusion. Then write the first draft of your essay, keeping in mind the drafting suggestions presented.

The Big Fair (First draft)

Reading audience: classmates

Driving down Kings Canyon Boulevard, the first thing I see are the blue, green, and red lights of the giant ferris wheel spinning in the warm night air. We're almost there, and my adrenaline starts pumping. Every September I look forward to the State Fair coming to the city fairgrounds. I have been going since I was a little kid, and I've never missed a year. The fair runs for two weeks, and I go at least twice and always have a terrific time.

People watching is a fun part of the fair for me. It is the one time all of the city gathers in one place: young and old, rich and poor, and every ethnicity that makes up our diverse city. Everyone is there to have a good time and not hassle anyone. Even the rival gang members cool it during the fair. It is just fun to see thousands of people walking around enjoying themselves, and sometimes my friends and I will just sit on a bench for a half hour and watch the human parade pass by.

Of course, you can't go to the fair without eating. There are probably a hundred booths offering any kind of food you could imagine: Mexican, Italian, Chinese, Indian, corn dogs, barbecue, hamburgers, corn-on-the-cob, and a lot more. My friends and I like to eat throughout the day: a corn dog here, a taco there, some kettle corn later, all washed down with a continuous flow of soda. I come home from the fair stuffed every time and with my wallet a lot lighter.

Music is everywhere at the fair, and I like to catch my share of it. There are different bands playing at every eating area, and there is a large stage with benches around it and grassy knolls to sit on where different performers sing and dance throughout the day and evening. You can hear any kind of music you want including rock, rap, country, hip hop, alternative, reggae, you name it. I always go to at least one evening concert in the 5,000 seat outdoor amphitheater, and this year I went to two. One night I saw Sick Puppies with my friends and another night I went to Anthony and the Imperials with my mom. The music is always loud, which I like, and the crowds really get into it and have a good time.

I love going to the midway part of the fair at night when all of the rides are lit up. The rides seem more exciting at night, and my friends and I always hit our favorites: the giant ferris wheel, the roller coaster, the hammer, the parachute drop, and the giant swings. We'll ride anything with speed, and for a total rush, the parachute drop is hard to beat. I haven't gotten up enough nerve to try the bungee jump yet, but next year I'm determined to try. We usually spend about an hour at the midway because with rides costing four and five dollars a pop, our money goes fast.

Finally, you can't come home from the fair empty-handed, so I always budget some money to play some games. I've tried everything: ring tosses, balloon bursting, electronic horse racing, coin tosses, fishing for prizes, basketball shooting, knocking down milk cans with a baseball. I lose a lot more than I win, but I'll always win something, whether a small stuffed animal or a gold fish. Occasionally I've gotten lucky and won a stuffed dog or tiger so big that I could barely carry it to the car. That's when everyone you walk by smiles and gives you that envious look.

I always spend more money at the fair than I should, but it's the one time of the year when I really splurge on entertainment, and I'd rather spend it at the fair than anywhere else. If you go to the fair worried about every dollar you spend, or complain about how everything is overpriced, you're going to spoil your fun. When I go to the fair, I just go with the flow, have a good time, and later, start putting away money for the next year. I'll probably still be going to the fair when I'm an old lady on a walker, like some of the senior citizens I see every year. In fact, there was an article and picture in the paper today about a ninety-year old woman who did the bungee jump. Hey, if she can do it, I'd better try!

Revision

After completing their first draft, writers usually have a sense of how well the drafting went. There may be some areas they know they want to work on: a less-than-satisfactory opening, a minimal number of supportive points, or the inadequate development of a couple paragraphs. Some dissatisfaction with a first draft is not uncommon since you are both exploring and expressing your thoughts simultaneously. Writers who feel they have nothing to improve in a first draft usually need to take a closer look.

The good news is that there is no problem that the revision process can't fix. You can rewrite an unsatisfactory opening or conclusion, reword any sentence you don't like, move sentences or paragraphs to more appropriate locations, and add or delete anything you want. Nothing is sacred in a first draft, and sometimes improving a draft may require some bold strokes rather than just tinkering around the edges.

For example, a writer who wrote about her love of shopping got halfway through her draft and decided she didn't like anything about it. As she analyzed the draft, she realized it wasn't the writing but the topic that was the problem. Writing about shopping seemed boring to her, and she figured readers would feel the same. She abandoned her topic and selected a new one. Another writer, on rereading the reasons he had presented for enjoying working on cars, knew he had left out a major reason: he began fixing up older cars because he couldn't afford newer ones. He added a new paragraph developing that practical reason for his hobby.

Revision Suggestions

As you read the suggestions for revision in different lessons, you will find some obvious repetition. There may be some special revision considerations in different types of essays, such as effective descriptive detail in narratives, quality of support in thesis-based essays, or feasibility of a solution in a problem/solution essay, but there are also many revision constants that apply to all essays.

With any essay, most writers strive for clear organization, effective paragraphing, well-constructed sentences, strong openings and conclusions, relevant examples, and a clear writing purpose. While the particular revisions that you make are specific to a given draft, many of the *types* of revisions that you consider are applicable to any essay that you write. Your familiarity with these considerations grows with each draft that you evaluate, leading to increasingly effective revision.

To revise your current draft, consider these suggestions:

1. **Read through your draft once to get an overall sense of its effectiveness.** Some things may jump out at you as you read: an overly long paragraph, some sentences that seem out of place, the need for an example to clarify a point, a rather short, abrupt ending. Keep such concerns in mind as you begin revising your draft

sentence by sentence, paragraph by paragraph.

2. **Read your opening, and consider what improvements you might make.** Have you clearly introduced your topic for the essay? Have you created interest for readers? Have you included your thesis statement? Is your opening in "balance" with the rest of your essay?

3. **If readers may not be that familiar with your topic, have you provided some explanatory information to help them?** The best place to provide such information is right after your opening. Don't assume that readers are as knowledgeable about your topic as you are.

4. **Read your middle paragraphs to see how well you have presented and developed your reasons in support of your thesis.** Do you provide examples and description to help readers understand each reason? Do you use some topic sentences to begin paragraphs? Have you presented your reasons in the most effective order for readers? On rereading, do other reasons come to mind that you might add? Revise your middle paragraphs in ways that will help readers better understand *why* you feel or believe as you do about the topic.

5. **Revise your sentences to make them clearer, smoother, and more concisely worded.** Eliminate any unnecessary words, reword awkward sentences, and replace questionable word choices.

6. **Check the effectiveness of your paragraphing.** Do you change paragraphs as you move to each reason in support of your thesis? Do you change paragraphs to begin different parts of your draft: opening, middle, and conclusion? Divide any overly long paragraphs and combine or develop any overly short paragraphs.

7. **Read your conclusion and consider what improvements you might make.** Have you reinforced your thesis in some manner? Have you added something new for readers to consider rather than merely summarizing what came before? Does your conclusion follow logically and naturally from your middle paragraphs?

8. **Read your draft through your readers' eyes.** What might you add, change, or delete to help readers best understand why you wrote about this particular topic?

Reader-Consideration Tips

Since most essays are written for readers, when revising, it is useful to consider how your readers might respond to what you write. To help you view your draft through your "readers' eyes," ask yourself these questions:

1. *What do readers need to know to understand my topic? Do they need to know exactly what "needle point" is? Do they need examples of the kind of things I do as a day-care worker? Do they need to understand why every bowling lane is different to bowl on?*

2. *How can readers best understand a particular point that I am making? Do they need some descriptive detail, a clear example, or a comparison to help clarify the point?*

3. *How will readers react to what I am writing? Will they find it interesting? Will they find it boring? Will they have trouble understanding why I feel or think the way I do? What can I do to get the response from readers that I would like?*

4. *Will readers understand my writing purpose? How can I best make it clear to them why I am writing about this topic and what it means to me?*

By asking such questions, you will become increasingly adept at considering your readers' perspective and revising accordingly.

Writing Activity 4.8

Revise your draft keeping the revision suggestions in mind. Read your draft several times, focusing each time on one or two particular areas of revision.

Example:

Sample revisions from paragraphs in "The Big Fair" draft

(Deletions crossed out, additions in bold print)

I love going to the midway ~~part of the fair~~ at night when all of the rides are lit up **in bright blues, greens, and reds.** The rides ~~seem~~ **are** more exciting at night, and my friends and I always hit our favorites: the giant ferris wheel, the roller coaster, the hammer, the parachute drop, and the giant swings. We'll ride anything with speed, and for a total rush, the parachute drop is hard to beat. **You go up 60 feet into the air in an enclosed basket and then drop at breakneck speed to the ground. I scream the entire time without even realizing it.** I haven't gotten up enough nerve to try the bungee jump, **where you leap off of a high tower with a long elastic cord attached to a harness on your chest,** but next year I'm determined to try. We usually spend about an hour at the midway because with rides costing four and five dollars ~~a pop~~ **each**, our money goes fast.

Finally, ~~you can't~~ **I don't like to** come home from the fair empty-handed, so I always budget ~~some~~ money to play some games. I've tried everything: ring tosses, ~~balloon bursting~~ **throwing darts at balloons,** electronic horse racing, coin toss, fishing for prizes, basketball shooting, **and** knocking down milk cans with a baseball. I lose a lot more than I win, but I'll always ~~win~~ **come away with** something, whether a small stuffed animal or a gold fish **that survives for a few months**. Occasionally I've gotten lucky and won a stuffed ~~dog or tiger~~ **animal** so big that I could barely carry it to the car. That's when ~~everyone~~ **most people** you walk by smile and give you that envious look. **I still have a huge bulldog sitting in one corner of my bedroom that I won a few years ago.**

Writing Activity 4.9

After you make your revisions, exchange drafts with a classmate(s) to give and receive some reader feedback. Ask questions if there is anything you don't understand or would like to know more about, and make any suggestions that you feel would help your classmate improve her draft. Take from your classmate's feedback any revisions suggestions that you feel will improve your paper.

Editing

By now, you probably have a good idea of the types of errors that tend to crop up in your writing. A good way to begin your proofreading is to focus on those areas first, which may eliminate most of the errors in your draft.

Each lesson focuses on one type of common writing error. To this point, you have covered run-on and comma-splice sentences, comma usage, subject pronouns, and pronoun-antecedent agreement. The focus for this lesson is on *subject-verb agreement*: choosing the correct verb form to agree with its subject. Since you probably wrote your thesis-based draft in the *present tense*, the verb tense to which subject-verb agreement applies, now is a good time to focus on that grammatical area.

Subject-Verb Agreement

Most writers have little problem with subject-verb agreement when the verb follows directly after the subject (subject underlined, verb in italics):

The prevailing wind *blows* from the northwest every afternoon.
Most word processing programs *contain* an automatic back-up system to retain working files in case a program *shuts* down unexpectedly.

Subject-verb agreement problems usually occur when the subject and verb are separated in the sentence so that the correct verb form isn't as easily distinguishable:

The sound coming from rocks at the top of the hill (indicate, indicates) that rattle snakes make be lurking.

Due to the separation of subject and verb, the incorrect form - *indicate* - does not look as obviously wrong as it would if it followed the subject "sound" directly. Fortunately, there are some basic rules that take the guesswork out of selecting the correct verb form that agrees with the subject:

1. **The *subject* of a sentence is what the sentence is about, or who or what performs the action of the sentence** (subject underlined):

   The apples nearest the top of the tree are the biggest.
   In the evening, hummingbirds flit from flower to flower in our front garden.

2. **The *verb* of a sentence shows action or a state of being.** It tells what the subject is doing or the subject's "state of being:"

   The running back *jumped* to his feet after being tackled hard. (Action)

I *am* very tired after working a ten-hour shift. (State of being)
A layer of fog *covered* the valley floor. (Action)
No one *was* happy about the negotiated salary settlement. (State of being)

Verbs that express a *state of being* are the "to be" verbs *am, is, are, was, were, be, been, being.*

3. **Subject-verb agreement involves *present tense verbs*: verbs that show something occurring or existing in the present.** *Past tense* and *future tense* verb forms remain the same with any subject.

    (Exception: The past tense verbs "was" and "were" must agree with their subject: The <u>boy</u> *was* tired of hoeing weeds. The <u>boys</u> *were* tired of hoeing weeds.)

4. **If the subject of a sentence is *singular* - *one* of anything - the verb ends in "s;" if the subject is *plural* - *more than one* - the verb does *not* end in "s:"**

    The <u>cat</u> *stalks* its prey with the stealthiest of moves.
    The <u>cats</u> *stalk* their prey with the stealthiest of moves.

    (Exception: The only verbs that end in "s" with a plural subject end in a double-"s": *miss, kiss, dress,* and *press*: The <u>twins</u> *miss* their old apartment.)

5. **When a group of words separates a subject and verb, *ignore* those words when deciding on the correct verb form:**

    The <u>aroma</u> of barbecuing steaks from the backyard *fills* the air. (The verb "fills" agrees with the singular subject "aroma.")

    (Exception: When the subject is an "amount" word - *all, some, a lot, none* - followed by a *prepositional phrase - all of the cake, none of the boys, some of the noise, a lot of the reasons* - the verb must agree with the last word in the prepositional phrase, called the *object of the preposition*: All of the <u>cake</u> *looks* moldy. None of the <u>boys</u> *like* ice skating. Some of the <u>noise</u> *bothers* me.)

6. **In sentences beginning with "There," the subject and verb are often *inverted* with the verb coming first. In such sentences locate the subject found *after* the verb to determine the correct verb form:**

    There *are* many <u>ways</u> to season chicken.
    There *appears* to be a large purple <u>stain</u> on the dining room curtain.
    There *is* <u>no one</u> in the travel group who has visited Taiwan before.

7. **In sentences that have more than one present tense verb that goes with the**

same subject (*compound verbs*), all verbs must agree with the subject:

The <u>smell</u> from the garbage bin in back of the apartments *is* very strong by the end of the week, *gets* even worse when the wind blows, and *becomes* intolerable when the dirty diapers pile up.

Subject-Verb Agreement Tips

Most writers have an occasional problem with subject-verb agreement, particularly in sentences when the incorrect verb form doesn't "sound" too bad. To eliminate any subject-verb problems in your writing, consider these suggestions:

1. *Make subject-verb agreement the sole focus of one proofreading scan of your draft.*

2. *Look for sentences where the subject and verb are separated by other words. Mentally cross out the "separating" words and consider the subject and verb side-by-side, which will make the correct verb form more obvious.*

3. *Look for longer, more complex sentences where subject-verb agreement problems often lurk.*

4. *In sentences where the subject and verb are separated, errors can occur when a word close to the verb is singular and the subject is plural, or vice-versa: "Our dogs in the backyard seldom bark at night," or, "One of the men looks guilty." Look in particular for those types of situations, ignoring the word close to the verb.*

Writing Activity 4.10

To proofread your drafts for subject-verb agreement problems, you need to be able to identify subjects and verbs in your sentences. Underline the subject(s) and circle the verb(s) in each sentence in the following paragraph. Some sentences have more than one subject and verb, and some sentences may contain both helping and main verbs: *has run, is going, have been sleeping, are trying.*

Example:

The Christmas <u>decorations</u> on Fremont's Christmas Tree Lane are spectacular. Every house's front <u>yard</u> is decorated beautifully, and <u>it</u> seems that each <u>house</u> tries to outdo its neighbors. Colored <u>lights</u>, nativity <u>scenes, snowmen, angels</u>, and <u>candy canes</u> adorn the yards, and <u>Santas, reindeer</u> and <u>sleighs</u> sit atop the rooftops. The <u>houses</u> glisten with light, and a steady <u>stream</u> of cars crawls along the street. <u>People</u> from all over the area visit Christmas Tree Lane, <u>which</u> has dazzled visitors for over fifty years.

The elementary girls' "C" basketball games are wild. The "C" team is composed of the leftover girls who didn't make the "A" or "B" squads, and the girls receive very little coaching. Their coaches are volunteers from the schools, and they often know very little about basketball. The "C" games are filled with fouls, double dribbling, mad scrambles for the ball, and wild shots. There are no referees, so anything goes. Unfortunately, the girls are learning nothing about how to play basketball, and it is sad that they get such indifferent treatment. Amazingly, most of the girls seem to have a good time, and they look forward to playing each game. At least they benefit from the exercise, but with the lack of supervision, surely someone is going to get hurt in a game, and the schools are completely to blame.

Writing Activity 4.11

Some sentences in the following paragraph have subject-verb agreement problems. Locate the subject and verb in each sentence, determine whether they are in agreement, and correct any incorrect verb forms.

Example:

One of the problems on many country roads in the county are the lack of stop signs. A lot of intersections has no stop signs, and sometimes cars zip through the intersections without looking for cross traffic. There has been a few accidents at such intersections, some of which involved fatalities, and then the county puts in stop signs. However, no one on the board of supervisors, which oversee the county roads, seem to anticipate the problems before they occur.

Corrected:

One of the problems on many country roads in the county ~~are~~ *is* the lack of stop signs. A lot of intersections ~~has~~ *have* no stop signs, and sometimes cars zip through the intersections without looking for cross traffic. There ~~has~~ *have* been a few accidents at such intersections, some of which involved fatalities, and then the county puts in stop signs. However, no one on the board of supervisors, which ~~oversee~~ *oversees* the county roads, ~~seem~~ *seems* to anticipate the problems before they occur.

Many of the businesses on main street in downtown Exeter is hurting. Since a WalMart and Kmart have opened in the northern end of town, regular downtown shoppers who used to do their shopping on main street now goes to the big discount stores. Many of the downtown businesses specializing in clothing, shoes, or jewelry has seen a dramatic drop in sales in the last year. One of the shoe stores have closed, and other stores are losing money. Local businessmen lobbied the city council for months to keep WalMart and Kmart out of town, knowing the impact they would have on downtown businesses. However, the council succumbed to the desire to increase their tax base and bring more employment to the city, and the downtown, much to the chagrin of many residents, who suffer as a result. The long-term impact on downtown businesses remain unclear, but business owners and residents are fearful that Exeter's downtown will never be the same.

Writing Activity 4.12

Proofread your draft for any subject-verb agreement problems and make corrections if necessary. Then proofread your draft several times to correct any errors involving run-on or comma-splice sentences, comma usage, subject pronouns, pronoun-antecedent agreement, apostrophes in contractions or possessive words, quotations, spelling, or frequently confused words (their/there/they're, its/it's, affect/effect, no/know, your/you're, etc.). Concentrate in particular on the types of errors that you have a tendency to make.

Writing Activity 4.13

Exchange drafts with a classmate and proofread each other's drafts for errors. Correct any errors that your classmate may uncover in your draft, noting the kinds of errors that you had overlooked.

Communicating with Readers

Since your reading audience for this essay is your classmates, your instructor may have you reproduce copies for them, pass a copy or two around class for a "read-around," or have essays read aloud. Your instructor may devise some way for you to get feedback from classmates, whether through written or verbal responses.

Lesson Five: Explanatory Writing

Objective: To write an essay explaining how to do something or how something works or occurs.

Purpose: To heighten the readers' understanding of a particular process for their own use or edification.

Audience: Writer's choice

Many of the books and articles that find large reading audiences are *instructional* in nature: how to add software to your computer, how to stay physically fit, how to make money selling real estate, how to study for tests most efficiently, how atoms store and release energy, how animal species evolve to survive in changing environments. People have a natural curiosity about how things work and a strong self-interest in finding ways to improve their lives.

The best instructional writings explaining how to do something or how something works share similar qualities: a topic of interest, a clear, understandable explanation of the process, a step-by-step delineation of the process, and accurate, valid information that readers can rely on. These qualities will be the focus for your upcoming essay, where you will explain to readers a process for doing something or for how something works. You will find the ability to provide clear, accurate explanations useful for much of the writing you do.

Explicating a Process

The primary goal in explaining a process for doing something or for how something works is to make the process most understandable to readers. By following the process, readers should be able to replicate the results that the process leads to - a successfully installed PDF conversion program on their computer, a functioning bluetooth telephone system in their car, a more efficient and effective golf swing - or understand clearly how something works or occurs - global warming, volcanic eruptions, or an electric-powered car.

To explain a process in a way that readers will clearly understand, consider the following questions.

1. **What is the specific process that I am explaining?** Readers need to know the exact process you are presenting before you begin explaining it. For example, if you are explaining how to transfer pictures from a camera to a computer, it may be

important to specify that the process is intended for digital cameras and PC's.

2. **Why should readers be interested in the process?** How might readers benefit from understanding the process? How might it help them do something worthwhile or understand something of importance?

3. **What terminology may need defining?** For example, you may need to explain what a "timing belt" is in a car, what "sensor reheat" means on a microwave oven, what "greenhouse gases" are in regards to global warming, or what "in vitro fertilization" means regarding pregnancy. It is important to define any term that readers may be unfamiliar with.

4. **What is needed to complete the process or for the process to occur?** For example, what tools are needed to change the lock on a door, what ingredients are needed to make a pineapple upside-down cake, what atmospheric conditions are needed to produce fog, or what thinking skills are invaluable to playing chess?

5. **In what order do the steps in the process occur?** In many processes, the order in which the steps occur is critical to the outcome. For example, with most word-processing programs, you must highlight the word, sentence, or paragraph that you want to cut and move *before* you click on "Copy" under the "Edit" tool bar heading.

6. **How accurate is the information I am presenting?** Most readers assume that the process information you are providing is accurate and will produce the correct results. If you have any doubts, check to ensure the accuracy of any information that you provide. If you are explaining a process that doesn't have a guaranteed result - how to make money in the stock market, how to win a student body election, how to negotiate the best deal -, make sure that readers understand that you are providing a process to "improve their chances" rather than guarantee their success.

7. **What useful tips might be included to help readers duplicate the process?** From your experience, you may have discovered some things that make the process easier that you can pass on to readers: labeling each section of the artificial Christmas tree for easiest assemblage; troweling a new walkway in the cooler morning hours when the concrete doesn't set up as fast; closing all programs on your computer before installing the latest Microsoft program.

8. **What can I assume that readers know?** Gear your process explanation to the particular audience you are writing for. Are your readers experienced computer users or neophytes? Are they students just learning to cook or who know their way around a kitchen? Explain the process in a way that you feel is most effective for your specific readers, and when in doubt, err on the side of explaining more than may be necessary.

Writing Activity 5.1

Keeping the previous questions in mind, read and evaluate the following process essay. How well do you understand the process based on the essay? What, if any, terms need to be defined? What could be added or revised to help your understanding? What does the writer do well in explaining the process?

Playing the Piano by Ear

Audience: College students who don't play the piano

I took two years of piano lessons when I was nine and ten and hated every lesson. I didn't like playing the endless warm-up runs, I hated practicing, and I wasn't interested in the songs I was having to learn. My mom knew my heart wasn't in it, and she let me quit.

However, one song that I had learned, "Country Gardens," stayed with me. It was in the key of "C" and contained four left-handed chords which went with different notes in the right-handed melody. After I quit lessons, I tried applying those same chords to some popular songs, and they sounded pretty good. Through trial and error, I learned how to play a number of songs, and today I can play just about anything that I hear. I am going to teach anyone how to play the piano by ear who has an interest, and it's a lot of fun and a great hobby, even for anyone who hated piano lessons.

First, you need to learn the four basic left-handed chords, two beginning with the "C" note, one beginning with "B," and one with "A." Each chord contains three notes. The "C" chord includes every-other note - "C," "E," and "G - and the "F" chord includes "C," "F," and "A." The "G" chord includes "B," "D," and "G," and the "A" chord includes "A," "C," and "E." Play the three notes in each chord simultaneously with your left hand, creating one sound, and then alternate between the four chords. Practice playing them in different orders as you will in different songs.

Once you know the chords well, you can learn which chords go with which right-handed melody notes. In most cases, the chords go with the same right-handed notes that are in the chord. For example, the "C" chord is played with the "C," "E," and "G" melody notes and the "F" chord is played with the "F," "A," and "C" melody notes. Practice playing the right-handed melody notes and their corresponding left-handed chords together, one melody note at a time. You will notice that there is some overlap of chords with certain notes; the "C" melody note, for example, can be played with the "C" chord, the "F" chord, and the "A" chord. In playing a song, the trail and error comes about by listening to which chord sounds the best with a particular melody note for a particular song.

After you have practiced playing the four left-handed chords with their corresponding right-handed melody notes, you are ready to try a simple melody.

Start with something simple like "Twinkle, Twinkle, Little Star." Play the right-handed melody first: C, C, G, G, A, A, G, F, F, E, E, D, D, C, G, G, F, F, E, E, D, G, G, F, F, E, E, D, C, C, G, G, A, A, G, F, F, E, E, D, D, C. Play this simple melody a few times until you can play it easily. Then you are ready to play the left-hand chords with the melody.

Play a left-handed chord together with the first melody note, and then play a chord *each time you change notes on the right hand.* In most cases, you will be playing a chord with every-other right-hand melody note. Beginning with the first melody note, play the chords in this order: C, C, F, C, F, C, G, C, C, F, C, G, C, F, C, G, C, C, F, C, F, C, G, C. Play the song very slowly to begin with until you are comfortable playing the right-handed melody notes and the left-hand chords together. Then gradually increase the tempo.

You have now learned how to play a song which includes playing three of the four chords you have learned. The fourth chord - the "A" chord - has a more "minor" sound and is used in many songs. Now the fun part begins: figuring out the right-hand notes for a particular melody, which you learn through trial and error, and then adding the best-sounding left-hand chord for each melody note, *which is often the same right-hand/left-hand combination you used in "Twinkle, Twinkle, Little Star."* Start with some other simple songs like "Row, Row, Row Your Boat," "Mary Had A Little Lamb," and "Silent Night" (a bit more challenging). Begin "Row, Row, Row Your Boat" and "Mary Had a Little Lamb" with the "C" note and "Silent Night" with "G."

Finally, move on to some popular songs that you like. You will find that many of them are surprisingly easy to play. Others are more challenging and will take more time to learn. Learning to play by ear is a lifetime learning process. You will learn more chords as you progress to apply to different songs, including some that use the black keys. You will also learn to play "broken" chords - one chord note at a time in succession - when it sounds best for a particular song. You will discover all of these things on your own, just as I have done over the years, and you now have the basics to get started.

Writing Activity 5.2

For each of the following process topics, decide on the following:

1. Who would be an appropriate reading audience?
2. What terms, if any, may need defining?
3. How might you order the steps?

Example:

Topic: How to play the card game "Frustration"

Steps: Evaluate the strength of your hand: the number of "high" cards you have.
            Bid the number of tricks you think you can take.
            Deal out ten cards the first hand, nine the second, and so on down to one.
            Play a trick at a time, following suit, the high card taking the trick.
            The winner has the highest point total from making his bid the most.
            After dealing, turn over one card in the deck, which is the "trump" suit.
            You can play a trump card when you can't follow suit, which wins the trick.
            You must get the exact number of tricks you bid to "make" your bid.

Audience: Anyone age 12 or over who likes to play cards

Define: hand, trump, bid, trick, suit

Ordered steps:

            Deal out ten cards the first hand, nine the second, and so on down to one.
            After dealing, turn over one card in the deck, which is the "trump" suit.
            Evaluate the strength of your hand: your high cards and trumps.
            Bid the number of tricks you think you can take.
            Play a trick at a time, following suit, the high card taking the trick.
            You can play a trump card when you can't follow suit, which wins the trick.
            You must get the exact number of tricks you bid to "make" your bid.
            The winner has the highest point total from making his bid the most.

1. Topic: How to interview for a job

    Steps: Look the interviewer in the eye.
              Answer questions honestly.
              Thank the interviewer for her time.
              Research the job and company to show some knowledge and initiative.
              Be enthusiastic and express a willingness to work hard.
              Make interviewer aware of the qualities, skills, and experience you have.
              Be pleasant and polite.

2. Topic: How rain forms

    Steps: Water condenses in the air as tiny droplets that form clouds.
              Water droplets collect around solid particles suspended in the air
              and grow larger and larger.
              The vapor rises and reaches a cooler level in the atmosphere where it
              condenses.
              When the droplets become too heavy, they fall back to earth as rain.
              Heat from the sun causes ocean water to evaporate.
              Rain water comes mainly from the oceans.

Writing Assignment

For this lesson, you will write an essay explaining how to do something or how something works or occurs. Since this is not a "research" assignment, think about processes that you are knowledgeable about and that may be of interest to a particular reading audience. Your purpose will be to explain how to do something so that readers may replicate the process or to show how something works or occurs to enhance your readers' understanding.

Consider your topic and reading audience simultaneously since your topic may be appropriate for some readers and not for others. For example, explaining how rain forms and falls to earth may be a great topic for 6th grade students but too elementary for your college classmates. As you consider different process topics, ask yourself, "Is there a reading audience that would be interested in or could benefit from reading about this topic?" You also want to steer away from processes that are too simple or commonly understood to benefit readers, such as changing a tire, boiling water, or registering for classes.

Think about different processes that you are familiar with and that may be of interest to readers, and select a process topic for your upcoming essay and an audience that may benefit from reading about it. While this is not a research assignment, you may need to check with some "expert" source to make sure that all of the process information you provide is accurate.

Sample Topic: Putting a video on You Tube

Audience: College students who aren't familiar with the process

Preparation

Preparing to write the first draft of your process essay should not be that difficult. Since you are writing about a process that you are familiar with, you already have the basic content of the essay in your mind. The greatest challenge will be to explain the process to readers in the most understandable way.

To help prepare for writing your draft, consider the following questions:

1. What is needed (materials, tools, ingredients, conditions) for the process to work?

2. What are the steps in the process that need to be followed or that need to occur?

3. What, if anything, do you need to check on to provide the most accurate information? While this is not a research essay, feel free to double-check any aspect of the process that you aren't one-hundred percent certain of. You might

find confirmation through someone you know or from an Internet search.

4. What are the most important aspects of the process for readers to focus on? What are the absolutely essential components of the process that you need to emphasize to readers?

Writing Activity 5.3

Answer the previous four questions to help you prepare to write your first draft. You can either write down your responses or think them through. Some writers like having something tangible on paper to work from while others prefer working from a mental roadmap.

Sample responses:

Topic:	How to Put a Video on You Tube
What is needed:	a computer with Internet access a camcorder or other video-recording device Windows Movie Maker (optional) firewire cable (USB adapter may be needed.) MP4 video format
Steps:	Video record something to put on You Tube Load video onto computer Convert video to MP4 format Upload video in MP4 format on You Tube
Check on:	See whether Macs have same firewire port as PC's
Emphasize:	Importance of using camcorder for best video results Exact procedure for uploading video at You Tube

Drafting

Writing the first draft of your process essay should be relatively straightforward. You know the process well, you know the steps that it takes to produce the result, and you know what is needed to complete the process. Your greatest challenge is to explain the process in the best way for readers to understand it clearly.

As in writing any draft, you have a number of ongoing decisions to make: What are the best words to use to explain each step in the process? What terms do I need to explain to readers? How can I make it easiest for readers to complete each step in the process? Since no process is foolproof, what precautionary advice might I provide at one step or another? When there is more than one way to complete a particular step successfully, should I present different options or just my preferred way? You continually make such decisions as you work through your draft, deciding what to include, what to omit, what to emphasize, what to define, and what to describe to explain your process in the most understandable way for readers.

As you write your first draft, consider the following suggestions.

1. **Introduce your topic in the opening and create reader interest.** Why should readers be interested in this particular topic? How might it benefit them? Create an opening that will encourage readers to keep reading. (See the opening for the draft "Put Your Video on You Tube" in Writing Activity 5.4.)

2. **Write the draft as if you were talking readers through the process.** If you are explaining a process that readers can duplicate, you might use the pronoun "you" (meaning your readers) so that readers feel that they are going through the process themselves.

3. **Present each step in the process in the order it occurs, and change paragraphs as you move to different steps.** Provide as much detail as necessary for readers to understand each step, explaining clearly how to complete it (or how it occurs) and defining any terms that readers may be unfamiliar with.

4. **Provide your expertise on the topic in the way of caveats, suggestions, and reminders.** Knowing the process well, you can interject that expert knowledge that will help readers avoid common problems that can come up during the process, the best way(s) to complete a particular step successfully, or crucial reminders of critical things that people may tend to forget.

5. **Conclude your draft in a manner that keeps readers interested in the process.** Since you have explained a process that readers may want to duplicate, your conclusion may provide the motivation that will get readers to try it. (See the conclusion of the"Putting Your Video on You Tube" draft, Writing Activity 5.4.)

Process Writing Tips

In explicating a process, writers often make the mistake of explaining it in a way that knowledgeable readers would understand. In other words, they are explaining it for people like themselves. Thus, they make assumptions about how much readers know that are often wrong.

To avoid this common pitfall, make this more valid assumption about your readers: they may know little or nothing about my topic. Write about each step in the process in a way that the least knowledgeable reader can understand.

Of course, if you have purposely selected a more knowledgeable audience for your essay, say readers with experience playing online fantasy football, you can delineate the process for achieving fantasy football success with their experience in mind. In most cases, however, you are explaining a process that is new to most of your readers, so make sure to explain the process in clear detail.

Writing Activity 5.4

Read the first draft "Putting Your Video on You Tube" and note the opening, the explanation of each step in the middle paragraphs, the "how to" details that are included, the terms that are defined, the way in which the writer "talks" to her readers, and the conclusion. Then write the first draft of your essay, keeping your reading audience in mind.

Putting Your Video on You Tube   (First Draft)

Audience: Any college students unfamiliar with the process who have computer knowledge.

Have you ever thought about creating a video to put on You Tube? It might be a humorous video, a music video of your band, a short skit or movie, a cartoon you created, a "how to" video, or whatever strikes your fancy. No one ever knows what You Tube video may go viral, and yours might be the next one. The good news is that the process for putting a video on You Tube is not that difficult, and once you've done it, you probably won't want to stop at one.

The first step, of course, is deciding what to put in your video, and that is entirely up to you. You might want to go onto You Tube and sample the wide range of videos to get some ideas. You might also consider collaborating with a friend or two if you have similar interests. The most important thing is to make a video that you'd have fun doing and that could be entertaining, interesting, or instructive to a broader audience than your immediate family or friends.

Filming your video with a camcorder is your best option. While you can also do video filming with some digital cameras and I-Phones, the visual and audio quality of the video is a prime consideration when putting it online, and the camcorder will produce the best quality. If you don't have your own camcorder, no doubt you can borrow one from a friend or even rent one from a camera shop.

Since you are now in the "movie making" business, you will probably want to film your video several times to get the best possible result, unless you have unexpectedly captured some hilarious, shocking, or outrageous event with your camcorder such as we might see on "America's Funniest Videos." If you are interested in a more polished final product, Windows XP has a program called Windows Movie Maker which allows you to edit your video and create special effects, and you can download it free on the Internet.

Once you have shot your video, the next step is to load it onto your computer. For that, you'll need a Firewire cable, which you can buy at any number of stores such as Radio Shack, Target, or Best Buy for under $10.00. The firewire cable will have a smaller and larger plug at its ends. The smaller end plugs into the camcorder port, and the larger end plugs into the computer port in the back of the computer. While most computers have a firewire port, some do not. If you find that there is no compatible port in your computer to plug the firewire into, you need to get a USB adaptor for the computer-end of the firewire cable, which will allow you to plug into the USB port. Once your camcorder is connected to the computer, your computer will import the video to whatever file you choose.

Once you have the video on your computer, the next step is to convert it to the best format for You Tube. While You Tube takes different video formats, MPEG4 (MP4) is the recommended format for the best quality video. To convert your video file to MP4, go to the Any Video Converter website to download its video-conversion software for free. Once the download is completed, click on the video conversion button and your computer files will come up so that you can select the video file you want to convert. The conversion process takes less than a minute, and your video is MP4 formatted and ready to upload at You Tube.

Now you are ready to put your video on You Tube, which is a simple process. Go to the You Tube site and click on "Create Account" if you aren't already signed in, which is required to upload your video. Once you have created your free account, hit the "upload" icon and your computer document files will come up. Click on the Any Video Converter file and when it comes up at You Tube, type in the name of the file, which will be a number. Your video will now be uploaded to You Tube. Next, you will provide a brief description of your video, check the category it belongs in, and check whether you want it viewed by the public or only privately by friends and family. You can locate your video by entering your description in the "Search" window.

Once you have gone through the process once, you will see how easy it is to upload your next video on You Tube. Once you have a video made to upload, you can complete the entire process in about fifteen minutes.   Putting your videos on You Tube can be a lot of fun for you and your friends, and it might become to your next big hobby.   And you never know when you might have a hit. Annoying Orange started as a You Tube video, and now Annoying Orange products are in toy stores nationwide and a cable cartoon show is in the works.   You may create the next Annoying Orange.

Revision

Now that you have completed your first draft, you can evaluate how well you have explained the process and determine what changes you might make. No matter how satisfactorily the drafting process went, most writers always find things to improve: an overly wordy or awkward sentence, an underdeveloped paragraph, a term that readers may not understand, a process step out of sequence. Such problems are not unexpected in first drafts, and that is why the revision process is so invaluable to most writers.

A new revision consideration in this lesson is the incorporation of *transitional wording* in your writing: words and phrases that help move readers from one step to the next in a paper and that show relationships between ideas. No doubt you already use some transitions in your writing, and a greater awareness will help you incorporate them even more effectively.

Transitional wording is introduced in this lesson because of its common usage in process-oriented writing. The different steps in a process are often introduced with transitions such as *first, second, next, now,* and *finally.* In this lesson, you will analyze your use of transitions in your draft and determine whether additional or different transitions may be useful.

Transitional Wording

To give you an idea of the purpose of transitional wording, read the following two versions of the same paragraph. The first paragraph contains no transitional wording; the second paragraph contains transitional wording in italics.

Many newer cars do not require an ignition key to start them. Make sure that you have the key to the car in your pocket or purse. You won't need to take it out because the car "knows" the key is present. Put your foot on the break pedal and push in the large ignition button on the dash. The car's engine will start up automatically. The push-button starting mechanism is much easier than having to insert and turn a key, and it's also faster. If you aren't used to the push-button starter, it is easy to forget to push the button to turn the car off, leaving the car running. I taped a reminder message on the dash after I left the car idling overnight one time.

Many newer cars do not require an ignition key to start them. *First,* make sure that you have the key to the car in your pocket or purse. You won't need to take it out because the car "knows" the key is present. *Next,* put your foot on the break pedal and push in the large ignition button on the dash. The car's engine will start up automatically. *As you can see*, the push-button starting mechanism is much easier than having to insert and turn a key, and it's also faster. *However,* if you aren't used to the push-button starter, it is easy to forget to push the button to turn the car off, leaving the car running. *Consequently*, I taped a reminder message on the dash after I left the car idling overnight one time.

As you can see, the transitional wording in the second paragraph introduces the steps in the process (*first, next*) and shows relationships among the writer's thoughts (*as you can see, however, consequently*). Transitional wording helps readers navigate the paragraph with greater understanding.

   The following information will help you use transitions most effectively in your writing.

1. **Transitional words and phrases introduce a writer's thoughts in ways that help readers best understand them.** For example, when the steps in a process are introduced with transitions such as *first*, *second*, *then*, and *last*, readers can distinguish between the different steps and see the sequential relationship between them. (Notice that the previous sentence begins with the transition "for example," which indicates to readers what is coming in the sentence.)

2. **Different types of transitions are used for different purposes.** The following are among the most commonly used transitions, grouped according to their function:

    To introduce different points, steps in a process, or the events in a sequence: *first, second, next, then, now, once, finally*.

    To add one idea to another: *furthermore, in addition, also, moreover, additionally, on top of that, beyond that, besides that*.

    To introduce an example: *for instance, for example, such as*.

    To indicate a conclusion: *finally, lastly, as you can see, in conclusion, in summary*.

    To show a contrast: *however, on the other hand, nevertheless, nonetheless, on the contrary, despite, in spite of, whereas*.

    To show a cause-effect relationship - one thing occurring as the result of another: *therefore, consequently, thus, as a result, to that end, because of that*.

    To emphasize a particular point or idea: *in fact, actually, of course, in reality, needless to say*.

    To show a time relationship: *in the meantime, until then, prior to, before, after, while, meanwhile, during*.

3. **Use a transition in your writing wherever you feel it will introduce an idea most effectively and help readers understand what you are trying to convey.**

For example, transitions such as *of course, as you can see, consequently,* and *moreover* (meaning "more importantly" or "beyond that") not only introduce a thought but express your *viewpoint* towards that thought.

4. **Don't overuse transitions.** When some writers become aware of using transitional wording in their writing, they try to work a transition into every sentence. While a few well-placed, appropriate transitions can be very effective, piling on the transitions can be distracting for readers.

5. **Provide some variation in the transitions you use**. As you can see from the previous lists of transitions, there are a number of words and phrases that accomplish similar purposes. Work on incorporating different transitions to create reader interest and add to your transitional repertoire.

Transitional Wording Tips

While paragraphs are discrete, separate units, they are also related parts of the whole essay. Transitional wording can tie paragraphs together and help readers navigate your essays most smoothly.

When you begin a new paragraph, consider its relationship to the previous paragraph. If it introduces the next step in a process, you might begin the paragraph with "Next," "Then," or "Second." If it introduces the next supporting point for a thesis, you might begin with "Another," "In addition," or include an "also" within the sentence.

If the main idea of the paragraph contrasts with the previous paragraph, you might begin with "However" or "On the other hand." If the new paragraph presents an "effect" resulting from a "cause" presented in the previous paragraph, you might begin with "Therefore" or "Consequently." If a paragraph sums up what has been presented in the previous paragraphs, you might begin with "As you can see."

Of course, the first sentence of every paragraph won't contain a transitional tie-in to the previous paragraph. However, as you begin a new paragraph, consider its relationship to the previous paragraph and whether some transitional wording in the first sentence will help readers see that relationship. (See the transitional wording in the first sentences of paragraphs in the "Putting Your Video on You Tube" draft.)

Writing Activity 5.5

Fill in the blanks in the following sentences with appropriate transitions, using a number of different transitions from the lists provided.

Example:

The landscape crew weeded the large lot in front of the dormitory. <u>Then</u> they rotor tilled the ground to loosen the soil. <u>Next</u>, they took large weighted rollers and smoothed out the area. <u>Finally</u>, they seeded the soil with bermuda grass and fenced off the area with stakes and tape so no one would walk on it. By April the dormitory had a nice carpet of green grass in front of it. <u>Needless to say</u>, the students preferred it over the previous weed-strewn lot.

The Columnar Manor apartment complex on "R" Street is in bad shape. _____, the roof is sagging in several places, an indication of rotting roof beams. _____ , the white paint on the building is chipping off, exposing patches of pink paint beneath it. The garbage bins at the back of the complex are often overflowing with garbage, with trash blown onto the driveway and sidewalks and a foul smell hanging over the apartments. _____, the tenants complain regularly to the apartment manager about the conditions. _____, their complaints usually go unheeded, and since many of them are undocumented workers, they don't cause too much of a ruckus.
_____ there is the problem of the apartments' location. The complex lies just outside the city limits. _____, it isn't subject to city inspections and ordinances, which would force the owners to bring the apartments up to code. The apartments are under the purview of the county, which appears to have no interest in improving the safety or health conditions of apartments such as Columnar Manor. The city has been trying to annex the property south of town, which includes Columnar Manor. If that happens, changes will definitely occur. _____, the apartment complex will continue to deteriorate, and unfortunately, most of the residents can't afford to live anyplace better.

Writing Activity 5.6

Insert transitions in the following paragraphs where you feel they would benefit readers and tie the writer's thoughts and paragraphs together most effectively.

Example:

I applied for a part-time job at the college's financial aid office. I had to fill out an application. I had an interview with one of the financial aid officers. She explained to me what the job entailed. She asked if it sounded like something I would like to do. I said that it certainly was, and that I had the time to do it. A day later I received the news that I had gotten the job. I was very happy to get a job on campus.

I applied for a part-time job at the college's financial aid office. *First,* I had to fill out an application. *Next,* I had an interview with one of the financial aid officers. She explained to me what the job entailed. *Then* she asked if it sounded like something I would like to do. I said that it certainly was, and that I had the time to do it. A day later I received the news that I had gotten the job. *Needless to say*, I was very happy to get a job on campus.

My old car is in pretty bad shape. The tires have over forty thousand miles of wear, and they have lost most of their tread. I don't have four hundred dollars for a new set, so I can't replace them for awhile. The front window has a good-sized crack in it. A rock hit the window when I was driving on a freeway about a year ago, and the crack has continued to grow across the width of the window. The seats are torn in the front. The car is over twenty years old, so the seats have gotten a lot of wear. I put on cloth seat covers to cover the tears. They look very tacky.

The car is leaking and burning oil. It leaves oil spots on the ground wherever I park it, and I have to put in at least a quart of oil every thousand miles or so. My car has a lot of problems, and they all require money to fix. When I get enough money, I'll replace the tires first because they are the biggest safety hazard. I'll just keep driving as safely as possible and hope I don't get a blowout.

Writing Activity 5.7

Read your draft to see if you have used some transitional wording to help move readers from step to step in the process and to tie your thoughts together most effectively. Add any transitions that you feel will improve your essay, including adding a transition to the beginning sentence of a paragraph to tie it to the previous paragraph.

Revision Suggestions

By now, you have revised a number of drafts in previous lessons and no doubt are developing a revision process that works well for you. Some writers like to revise their drafts in one area at a time: sentence wording, paragraphing, adding information and details, improving the opening or conclusion. Other writers prefer covering all areas at a time, handling whatever problems they come across as they read their drafts, whether it be adding an explanation, revising an awkward sentence, separating an overly long paragraph, or strengthening a weak ending.

However you choose to revise your draft, the most important thing is to cover all revision considerations. It is a good idea to maintain a revision checklist to make sure that you cover every area that may need some attention. In time, this checklist will become an indelible part of your revision process, a set of mental guidelines that you will apply effectively to every draft.

To revise your current draft, consider the following suggestions.

1. **Read through your entire draft once or twice to get an overall sense of how well you have explained the process.** Note any concerns that you have - a flat opening, a process step out of order, an explanation that isn't clear, a pair of noticeably short paragraphs - and keep them in mind as you begin revising your draft a sentence and paragraph at a time.

2. **Reread your opening to evaluate how well you have introduced your topic and drawn your readers into the paper.** What changes might you make to ensure that after reading the opening, readers will want to continue?

3. **Evaluate how well you explain each step of the process.** Is there anything you could add or change that would make each step easier or clearer for readers to follow? Have you provided any expert tips or cautionary notes that would help readers perform each step of the process most successfully?

4. **Check the order in which you presented the steps in the process.**   Are they in the proper sequence to produce the result or outcome that the process leads to?

5. **Check the terms that you use and determine whether some may need defining.** If there is any word associated with the process that some readers may not understand or be familiar with, explain what that word means.

6. **Read each sentence to see how it may be improved.** Delete unnecessary words or phrases, smooth out awkward sentences, replace questionable word choices, and reword vague or ambiguous sentences.

7. **Check your paragraphing, making sure that you change paragraphs as you move to different steps in the process or different parts of the draft - opening to middle to conclusion.** Divide any overly long paragraphs and combine or develop short, related paragraphs.

8. **Evaluate your conclusion and its impact on readers.** Have you added anything new in the conclusion to interest or edify readers? Make any changes in your conclusion to make it more substantial, interesting, or memorable.

9. **Read your draft a final time from your readers' perspective.** Make any changes that would help readers understand the process better or carry it out most successfully.

Writing Activity 5.8

Keeping the revision suggestions in mind, revise your current draft and make any changes that you feel will improve it and make the process more understandable for readers.

Sample revisions from three paragraphs of "Putting Your Video on You Tube" draft

(Deleted material crossed out; added material in bold print)

The first step~~, of course,~~ is deciding what to put in your video, ~~and that~~ **which, of course,** is entirely up to you. You might want to go onto You Tube and sample the wide range of videos to get some ideas. You might also consider collaborating with a friend or two if you have similar interests. ~~The most important thing is to~~ **Most importantly,** make a video that you'd have fun doing and that could be entertaining, interesting, or instructive to ~~a broader audience than your immediate family.~~ **whatever audience you want to see it, whether just family and friends or anyone who goes on You Tube.**

For the best results, filming your video with a camcorder is your best option. While you can also ~~do video filming~~ **film videos** with some digital cameras and I-Phones, **the camcorder will produce the best quality, and** the visual and audio quality of ~~the~~ **a** video is a prime consideration when putting it ~~online, and the camcorder will produce the best quality~~ **on You Tube**. If you don't have your own camcorder, ~~no doubt~~ you ~~can~~ **might** borrow one from a friend or ~~even~~ rent one from a camera shop.

Since you are now in the "movie making" business, you will probably want to film your video several times to get the best possible result, unless you have ~~unexpectedly~~ captured some hilarious, shocking, or outrageous event with your camcorder ~~such as we might~~ **like you** see on "America's Funniest Videos." If you are interested in a more polished final product, Windows XP has a program called Windows Movie Maker, which allows you to edit your video and create special effects, and you can download it free on the Internet. **It is worth going online to Windows Movie Maker to see the kinds of editing and special effects that are available.**

Writing Activity 5.9

Exchange drafts with a classmate or two and provide feedback from a reader's perspective. Ask questions when you aren't sure what the writer means or when you'd like more information or a clarifying example. Make any revision suggestions to the writer that you feel would improve the draft. Then based on your classmate's feedback, make further revisions to your own paper that you feel would benefit readers.

Editing

In each lesson, proofreading your draft should become increasingly easy as the number of errors diminish with each new writing assignment. If you have focused on the types of errors that you most frequently made in earlier essays, you have undoubtedly made some progress towards eliminating them.

In addition, what you have learned about avoiding the more common problems - run-on sentences, comma usage, subject pronouns, pronoun-antecedent agreement, subject-verb agreement - has probably helped you eliminate such errors in your drafts. Increasingly, most errors that appear are probably the result of inadvertent slips rather than chronic problems, the types of slips that all writers occasionally make.

In this lesson, you learn about sentence fragments and how to avoid them before proofreading your draft to correct other types of errors. Sentence fragments are not as common a writing problem as run-on or comma-splice sentences, and you may have little or no problem with them. As with the grammatical and punctuation concerns introduced in each lesson, focus on those areas where you have some difficulties and spend little time on those that you don't.

Sentence Fragments

While run-sentences result from failing to end a sentence with a period, sentence fragments occur when a sentence is ended before it is completed. To avoid fragments, writers need to understand what a complete sentence is. The most typical correction for sentence fragments is quite simple: eliminating the period which incorrectly separates two parts of the same sentence.

To avoid sentence fragments in your writing, follow these guidelines.

1. **A sentence contains a subject and verb and expresses a complete thought:**

    (Subjects underlined, verbs in italics)

    I *am going* to night school this semester and *working* during the day.
    Migrating geese often *take* up permanent residence at the city's holding ponds.
    For 2011, the government *granted* a one-month extension for income tax returns.

2. **A sentence fragment is an incomplete sentence that does not express a complete thought and often leaves an unanswered question.**

    When we returned from our vacation. (What happened when you returned?)
    While you were babysitting your niece. (What happened during that time?)
    Walking along the railroad tracks at dawn. (Who was walking?)
    A gaping hole in the middle of the street. (What about it?)

3. **Sentence fragments usually result from incorrectly separating two parts of a sentence with a period (fragment underlined):**

<u>When we returned from our vacation.</u> Our apartment had been burglarized.
You received five text messages. <u>While you were babysitting your niece.</u>
<u>Walking along the railroad track at dawn.</u> I saw several rabbits and a coyote.
<u>A gaping hole in the middle of the street.</u> Was caused by the earthquake.

4. **Most fragments can be corrected by deleting the period and capital letter that incorrectly separate the two parts of a sentence:**

When we returned from our vacation, our apartment had been burglarized.
You received five text messages while you were babysitting your niece.
Walking along the railroad track at dawn, I saw several rabbits and a coyote.
A gaping hole in the middle of the street was caused by an earthquake.

5. **Sometimes a colon (:) can connect an ending fragment to the sentence it belongs with when the fragment contains a list of words:**

We will need a number of things for the science experiment. Copper wire, galvanized nails, a battery-operated timer, and five jumper leads.

Corrected:
We will need a number of things for the science experiment: copper wire, galvanized nails, a battery-operated timer, and five jumper leads.

Nopakan has several hobbies. Playing the violin, collecting ceramic frogs, and playing pool.

Corrected:
Nopakan has several hobbies: playing the violin, collecting ceramic frogs, and playing pool.
(Note: An alternative to using a colon to connect an ending fragment is to add the words "such as:" Nopakan has several hobbies *such as* playing the violin . . .)

Writing Activity 5.10

Identify and correct the fragment among each of the following sentences by connecting it to the sentence it belongs with.

Example:

We're not going to the Beyonce concert. Although it should be a great show. The tickets are just too expensive.

Corrected:
We're not going to the Beyonce concert although it should be a great show. The tickets are just too expensive.

1. Students on campus froze in their tracks. When a deer appeared in the quad area. It must have come down from the hills above campus.

2. While many sections of Business II are still open for students to register. The sections taught by Dr. Watamura are all closed. He is a very popular instructor.

3. I am interested in working as a dormitory hall monitor this semester. Apparently there are many shifts still available for monitors. 9:00 to 11:00 a.m., 1:00 to 3:00 p.m., 5:00 to 7:00 p.m., and the four-hour late-night shift.

4. If I have my preference, I'd like to work the late-night shift. Because I could make more money and it is the easiest shift. I'm sure other students will also want it.

5. It is going to be very difficult to get our car out of the downtown parking lot. Until most of the cars have exited. We'll be one of the last cars out of the lot.

6. Sarah Hughes seems like the best candidate for city mayor. A woman who is known for her honesty and good judgment. I think I'll vote in a city election for the first time.

7. Tickets for the George Lopez concert in December are selling very fast. We'd better go online to Ticketron. Before all of the good seats in the arena are taken.

8. We can work on our science project in the biology lab this afternoon. Unless you'd rather wait until tomorrow morning. I am free either time.

Writing Activity 5.11

The following paragraph contains some sentence fragments. Eliminate the fragments by connecting them to the sentences they belong with.

Example:

Anna enrolled her young daughter in the college's day care program. Which is run by students who are child development majors. She enrolled her daughter in the program from 8:00 to 12:00 on Monday, Wednesday, and Friday mornings. Because that is when Anna takes classes at the college.

Corrected:
Anna enrolled her young daughter in the college's day care program, *which* is run by students who are child development majors. She enrolled her daughter in the program from 8:00 to 12:00 on Monday, Wednesday, and Friday mornings *because* that is when Anna takes classes at the college.

Identical twin sisters who were separated soon after birth and raised by different parents in different parts of the country were reunited in their late twenties. They dressed similarly, wore their hair the same, and were both employed in the medical profession. None of which was surprising to biological scientists. They were both married and had two children each. The sister's interests were also very similar. Attending their children's sporting events, reading mystery books, and doing daily exercise. Neither of them particularly liked to cook, and they preferred bringing home take-out food from a restaurant to cooking a meal. These similarities between twins with identical genetic make-ups who were raised apart no longer surprise scientists. Who have seen similar results with other sets of twins. The findings confirm the power of "nature" over "nurture." The genetic bond between twins having a stronger effect than the environments in which they were raised.

Writing Activity 5.12

Proofread your draft for sentence fragments, and eliminate any fragments that you find by connecting them to the sentences that they belong with. If you aren't sure whether a particular group of words is a fragment, check with your instructor. If you have no problem with fragments, great. You needn't proofread for problems that don't exist.

Writing Activity 5.13

The following paragraph contains some of the types of errors that have been covered in previous lessons: run-on and comma-splice sentences, problems with subject pronouns, pronoun-antecedent agreement, comma usage, subject-verb agreement, and commonly confused words (e.g. their/there/their, know/no, effect/affect). Before proofreading your own draft, proofread the following paragraph for errors and make the necessary corrections.

The food in the college cafeteria isn't great, it is no different than the food they served twenty years ago. Basically, all you can get is American food and there is very little variety from day to day. There is a couple "main" dishes to choose from each day and you can always get a hamburger or hot dog along with a bag of fries. You can also heat up a pre-packaged burrito or pocket sandwich in the microwave. Then there is always the mashed potatoes, green beans, and corn. One of my friends fill their plate with the same food everyday I don't see how she can stand it. My friends and me do eat in the cafeteria on most days, because we have no time between classes to go off campus. When I think of the food that's available in the cafeteria at a nearby college I get very frustrated. While there students are eating pizza, tacos, enchiladas, chow mein, teriyaki chicken, and berrocks I am eating my fried cod, mashed potatoes, and green beans. Even my old high school serves a better variety of food then our college cafeteria.

Writing Activity 5.14

Proofread you draft for errors and make the necessary corrections. Read the draft several times, concentrating on one problem area at a time and focusing in particular on the types of errors you are most prone to make. Make sure to run the spell-check on your word processing program.

Writing Activity 5.15

Exchange drafts with a classmate and proofread each other's drafts.   Correct any errors that your classmate finds in your draft, noting the types of errors that you overlooked.

Communicating with Readers

When you have your essay in "publishable" form, you are ready to share it with readers. Decide the best way to get your essay into the hands of your reading audience or representatives. Your instructor may have some ideas on how to proceed. You also have a built-in audience of classmates, some of whom may be interested in the process you described.

Lesson Six: Comparative Writing

Objective: To write an essay comparing two or more subjects with an emphasis on providing relevant criteria and reasoned conclusions.

Purpose: Writer's choice

Audience: Writer's choice

Comparisons are among the most common and effective types of writing development. Writers use comparisons to analyze and evaluate similar subjects: the Iraqi and Afghanistan wars, the Great Depression and the Great Recession, Michelin and Goodyear tires, elementary school children who attended pre-school and those who didn't. Writers also use comparisons to help make their points. For example, a writer pointing out the difficulty of achieving the "American Dream" of home ownership made two comparisons: the prices of homes today and thirty years ago and the percentage of income that went towards mortgage payments. The comparison revealed that housing price inflation has far outstripped earning power, with Americans spending nearly three times as much of their income on mortgage payments today than thirty years ago.

   Writers also use comparisons to help explain and clarify particular concepts and ideas. In particular, writers often use *analogies* comparing two dissimilar things in a way that helps readers understand the writer's idea. For example, a writer who believed that patching a mud levee every time the valley's flooding river broke through it was a waste of time used the following analogy: "Patching the levee is as futile as Sisyphus rolling the bolder up a hill," a reference to the mythological king whose punishment was to roll a large bolder up a hill eternally, only to have it roll back down each time.

   Because of its effectiveness, common deployment, and varied uses, comparative writing will be covered in two consecutive lessons. In this first lesson, you will write an essay comparing two or more subjects, drawing conclusions for readers based on your evaluation of the subjects. In the next lesson, you will use comparisons to help support your thesis and convince readers of its validity. In the future, you will be able to apply what you learn about using effective comparisons to much of your writing.

Comparing Subjects

Writers compare similar subjects for a variety of purposes: to present their similarities and differences, to evaluate their relative quality, or to suggest to readers the best decision to make: which car to buy, mayoral candidate to support, or college to attend.

The most effective comparative essays usually cover the most critical points of comparison, provide details that reveal the differences between subjects, present accurate, objective information, and draw insightful conclusions for readers based on the comparative information presented.

An important aspect of comparative writing is deciding on the *criteria* on which to base the comparison: the set of standards, rules, qualities, or features used to compare and evaluate your subjects. For example, if you were comparing presidential candidates, your comparative criteria might include the candidates' political experience, positions on key issues, integrity, and leadership qualities. If you were comparing singers, your criteria might include their quality of sound, strength of voice, performance ability, and song choice. Deciding on a criteria for your comparison is an important first step in writing a comparative essay.

Comparative Criteria

When a friend recommends a particular restaurant, lauds a particular physician, or says that a particular quarterback is the "best" in college football, you would probably want to know *why* he believes as he does. His response would indicate his *criteria* for making each judgment: the things that he feels are most important in a restaurant, physician, or quarterback. For example, his "restaurant" criteria might include the quality of food, the range of choices, the atmosphere, and the quality of service. His "physician" criteria might include the doctor's friendly manner, her expertise, and the quality of treatment she provides. His "quarterback" criteria might include percentage of passes completed, touchdown-to-interception ratio, and the success of his team. How closely your friend's criteria corresponds to your own could influence the degree to which you agree with him.

To write the most convincing comparative essay, the criteria you decide on should include those elements that are most important in evaluating the subjects. To that end, consider the following suggestions:

1. **In deciding on a criteria to evaluate your subjects, ask yourself, "What are the most important considerations for comparing these subjects?** For example, if you are comparing two different driving routes to get to a particular destination, the most important considerations may be the length of time each takes, the quality of the roads, the relative amount of traffic, and the easiest route to navigate.

2. **More comparative points are better than fewer.** You never know what comparative point may interest some readers, so it is better to be more inclusive rather than leave out a point or two that some readers may be looking for. For example, in the "driving routes" criteria, some readers may only care about how long each route takes, others may prefer the easiest route, and still others may prefer the nice freeway route even if it takes longer. You never know what consideration may be most important to readers.

3. **When deciding on your criteria, look at your subjects from different perspectives.** For example, for some readers, the cost of a product may be most important. For others, the quality may be most important. For others, the durability may be most important: how long will it last? Depending on your subjects, there might also be a moral component to consider (Was the Iraqi or Afghanistan war more morally justified?), a "fairness" component (Should cheaper non-union carpenters be hired over more expensive union carpenters?), or a "right-and-wrong" component (Should college-bound illegal aliens pay the same in-state tuition as American students?) .

4. **Keep your readers in mind when considering your criteria.** In making the comparison, ask yourself, "What can I include to help readers make a decision on what to buy, whom to vote for, or what to believe?" Regarding your subjects, consider what you think your particular readers would think most important, which could vary among different reading audiences: high school students, young working adults, senior citizens, or people just scraping by financially.

Writing Assignment 6.1

For any three of the following comparative topics and reading audiences, decide on a criteria by which to evaluate the subjects. Include what you feel are the most important points of comparison, keeping in mind the four suggestions presented. Then share your criteria with a classmate or two, and explain why you chose each criteria. Note how your criteria are similar to or different from your classmates', and decide whether you might change (add to or delete) any criteria.

Example:

Topic: Comparing apartment and dormitory living

Audience: College students

Criteria: Cost (rent, food, transportation)
            Convenience
            Freedom
            Space
            Choice of roommates
            Privacy

Topic: Comparing local community colleges

Audience: High school seniors

Criteria: Size of campus
            Parking availability

Programs offered
Quality of instructors
Social life
Facilities
On-campus resources (library, computers, Internet access, tutors, etc.)

1. Topic: Comparing two teams (any sport, any level)

    Audience: College students

    Criteria:

2. Topic: Comparing two similar stores (e.g. Target and Kmart)

    Audience: College students

    Criteria:

3. Topic: Comparing two similar fast-food restaurants

    Audience: Families with young children

    Criteria:

4. Topic: Comparing two reality musical television shows

    Audience: College students

    Criteria:

5. Topic: Comparing two presidential candidates

    Audience: All voting-age readers

    Criteria:

6. Topic: Comparing two gaming stations (e.g. Wii, X Box, Play Station)

    Audience: High school students

    Criteria:

Writing Assignment

In your upcoming essay, you will compare two-to-four similar subjects and draw conclusions based on the criteria you use for evaluating your subjects. To help you decide on what to compare, consider these suggestions:

1. **Compare subjects that your reading audience wouldn't already be knowledgeable about.** For example, comparing fast-food restaurants like McDonald's, Burger King, and Wendy's would be of little value since most people are familiar with fast-food restaurants. Compare subjects that would provide your readers with some new and useful information.

2. **Compare subjects that interest you and that you are knowledgeable about or want to learn more about.** Think of subjects that you are familiar with and have perhaps compared for yourself. If you are interested in knowing more about some subjects - e.g. different LED television brands, colleges you may transfer to, or similar jobs, such as licensed practical nurse, registered nurse, and nurse practitioner - you might research and compare those subjects.

3. **Compare subjects that are substantial enough to warrant a comparison.** For example, comparing different brands of bottled water wouldn't produce much of an essay. However, comparing three or four different sport's drinks that have have different ingredients, flavors, prices, and results might be of interest to people who work out a lot.

4. **Make sure to compare similar subjects.** For example, you could compare different models of SUV's or different models of mid-sized sedans, but don't compare SUV's to mid-sized sedans, an "apples to oranges" comparison. You could compare different brands of pianos or different brands of keyboards, but don't compare pianos to keyboards, another dissimilar comparison.

5. **Consider a number of different areas where you could find comparative subjects: school, jobs, products, music, politics, sports, technology, etc.** Scan a range of potential subjects before deciding on the best comparison for your essay.

Take your time deciding on a topic you'd like to write on, and ultimately, choose a comparison that you feel your readers could learn something from.

Sample topic: Comparing different electric cars

Preparation

Once you have selected your topic, you can decide on the criteria by which to evaluate your subjects. Your criteria might change somewhat as you write your first draft, adding a comparative point that you hadn't previously considered or deleting one that you decide isn't that important. Your initial criteria, however, will help you begin to compare subjects and, if necessary, do some targeted research.

Writing Assignment 6.2

Decide on the criteria for your essay: the main points of comparison that you want to develop. Include every comparative point that you feel readers would have an interest in and that would help to distinguish between the subjects.

Example:

Topic: Comparing the Chevy Volt and Nissan Leaf

Criteria: Cost and savings
           How they work
           Range (driving distance between recharges)
           Size
           Looks
           Performance
           Relative "greenness" (how environmentally friendly)

Writing Assignment 6.3

After you develop your criteria, decide on a potential order for presenting your comparative points. What do you think should come first, second, and so on in your essay? There may be a logical progression of points, you might put them in descending or ascending order of importance, or you might begin and end with the most important points. Order your comparative points in a way that you feel would be most effective for readers.

Example:

Topic: Comparing the Chevy Volt and Nissan Leaf

Ordered comparison: How they work
                         Range (driving distance between recharges)
                         Performance
                         Size

Looks
Relative "greenness" (how environmentally friendly)
Cost and savings

Researching Subjects

Do you need to find out more about your subjects to write a well-informed essay? If you are writing about subjects that you need to learn more about, decide the best way to get information and proceed from there. To research your subjects, if necessary, consider these suggestions.

1. **Find *objective* information on your subjects.** For example, if you are comparing Sony and Toshiba camcorders, pamphlets put out by Sony and Toshiba would probably provide the most favorable, least objective information. Look for websites, periodicals, and experts who would evaluate the products objectively, such as *Consumer Report*, *Today's Electronics* or a local expert on camcorders.

2. **Use your criteria to find relevant information.** Look specifically for information that compares your subjects in the areas you have decided on. You might also find some *new criteria* based on what you learn about your subjects.

3. **Use whatever credible sources you can find.** You might get information online, in books or periodicals in the library, or from local "experts" on the topic. The most important consideration is that the information is accurate and up-to-date.

Writing Assignment 6.4

If necessary, do some research on your topic, taking notes on any information that you may use in your essay to help compare subjects.

Audience and Purpose

By now, you may have a good idea on the best reading audience for your essay: readers who would have the most interest in it. It may be people who are looking for a good used car, deciding on what college to transfer to, deciding which political talk show to watch on television, or wondering which tax-reduction proposition to vote for in the upcoming state election. Choose a reading audience that you feel would be interested in your topic, that would learn something from it, and that might benefit from reading about it.

Your writing purpose for this essay depends on your subject. If you are comparing the Great Depression to the Great Recession, your purpose may be to educate readers to the differences and similarities. If you are comparing two musical groups, your purpose may be to recommend to readers which group's concert to attend in your city. If you are comparing three candidates for mayor, your purpose may be to encourage readers to vote for none of them and instead support a "write-in" candidate of your choice. If you are comparing different brands of HD 35-inch televisions, your purpose may be to help readers decide which brand to buy if they are shopping for a TV.

Writing Assignment 6.5

Decide on a tentative audience for your comparative essay and your purpose in writing to them.

Example:

Topic: Comparing the Chevy Volt and Nissan Leaf

Audience: Anyone who is interested in electric cars and may consider buying one now or in the future.

Purpose: To help readers decide which electric car would be the best choice for them.

Drafting

As you progress through the lessons, each drafting experience presents some new and some familiar considerations. For your current comparative essay, the new considerations include doing a point-by-point comparison of similar subjects and drawing conclusions for readers based on your comparison. The familiar considerations include providing an interesting topic introduction in the opening, developing your main points in the middle paragraphs, providing a strong conclusion, and keeping your reading audience and purpose in mind.

Each previous drafting experience will, in some way, influence how you write your current draft. From your writing experience, you have learned something about writing effective openings and conclusions, developing an idea fully in a paragraph, explaining something clearly for readers, or providing a good example. You also probably have a greater sense of when some aspect of your draft *isn't* going that well, and you work to make it better. As writers, much of our improvement comes from building on our previous writing experiences.

Organizing a Comparative Essay

There are two basic ways that writers organize most comparative essays. The organizational method that you decide on depends on how you believe you can present your comparisons most effectively to readers.

One way to organize your essay is to compare the subjects point-by-point throughout the essay. For example, let's say that you are comparing organically and non-organically grown fruit, and your criteria include looks, size, taste, cost, and environmental impact. After your opening, your essay organization may look like this:

Paragraph one: Compare the looks of your two subjects.
Paragraph two: Compare their size.
Paragraph three: Compare their taste.
Paragraph four: Compare their cost.
Paragraph five: Compare their environmental impact.

Look at the first draft of "Comparing Electric Cars" in Writing Assignment 6.8, which follows the point-by-point comparison.

A second way to organize your essay is to take one subject at a time, cover all of the criteria for that subject, and then do the same for the next subject. For example, with the same fruit comparison, your organization may look like this:

Paragraph one: Present the looks and size of organically grown fruit.
Paragraph two: Present the taste and cost of organically grown fruit.
Paragraph three: Present the environmental impact of organically grown fruit.

Paragraph four: Present the looks and size of non-organically grown fruit.
Paragraph five: Present the taste and cost of non-organically grown fruit.
Paragraph six: Present the environmental impact of non-organically grown fruit.

An advantage of this organizational method is that you get all of the information on a subject at one time. A disadvantage is that you don't get a "side-by-side" comparison of the two subjects and may have to read back and forth to see how they compare.

   Most comparative essays lend themselves best to a "side-by-side" comparison of subjects on each point. However, there can be exceptions, such as comparing the health care systems in two countries or comparing two famous Civil War generals, which may be more effectively presented one subject at a time.

Writing Assignment 6.6

Decide on the best organization for your comparative essay based on your topic, purpose, and reading audience.

Sample organization:

Topic: Comparing Electric Cars

Organization: Comparing subjects together point by point

Reason: Readers can get the best sense of the differences and similarities between the two cars if I compare them together on each point.

Drawing Conclusions

In the opening of your draft, you introduce your subjects for comparison. In the middle paragraphs, you compare them in a number of different areas. What remains in the ending is to draw conclusions for readers based on your evaluation of the subjects. Based on your subjects and how they compare, you might draw any of the following conclusions:

1. **Clear-cut conclusion.** With a "clear-cut" conclusion, you have one recommendation to make for all readers: vote for Dominguez, lease an apartment rather than rent it monthly, take Dr. Cheney for Biology II. If one subject stands out over the other(s), you may single it out for readers.

2. **Qualified conclusion.** With a "qualified" conclusion, rather than make a single recommendation, you may make recommendations based on a reader's circumstances or preferences. For example, with the organic/non-organic fruit comparison, a writer might conclude, "If price or looks of the fruit are your most

important considerations, buy non-organic fruit. If you are concerned about the environment and the effects of chemical fertilizers and pesticides used in non-organic farming, you should buy organic fruit. For another example of a "qualified" conclusion, read the ending of the upcoming "Comparing Electric Cars" draft.

3. **Either-or conclusion.** If in evaluating the subjects you don't see a great difference between or among them, your conclusion should reflect that opinion. For example, if you find that the top three brands of 52" HD televisions are comparable in price, picture clarity, looks, and warranty length, you might conclude that readers can't go wrong with any brand. On the other hand, if neither gubernatorial candidate in your state measures up in your evaluation, you might conclude that readers could send a message by voting for a write-in candidate.

Writing Activity 6.7

Considering your subjects and reading audience, what type of conclusion are you most likely to draw? If you might write a qualified conclusion, think of the readers' circumstances and preferences that could influence your recommendations.

Sample Conclusion:

Topic: Comparing electric cars

Conclusion: Qualified

Reason: Which electric car a reader might buy depends on different factors: what they can afford, how far they drive every day, how much seating room they need, how important looks are, and how "green" they want their car to be. I'll make different recommendations based on people's circumstances.

Drafting Suggestions

As you write the first draft of your essay, consider the following suggestions:

1. **In your opening, introduce your subjects and give readers an idea of why you are comparing them and why they may be interested in the comparison.** How might readers benefit from reading this essay?

2. **If you need to provide some background or explanatory information about your subjects, include it after the opening.** For example, the writer of the "Comparing Electric Cars" draft explained to readers the kind of electric cars he was comparing in his second paragraph.

3. **In the middle paragraphs, present your points of comparison in the most effective order, and make sure to compare both (or three or four) subjects on each point.** In general, develop each comparative point in a separate paragraph, with its first sentence indicating the point of comparison. (See the middle paragraphs of the "Comparing Electric Cars" draft.)

4. **End your draft by drawing a conclusion for readers based on your evaluation of subjects.** Your conclusion should take in mind your reading audience and your purpose in writing to them, and should follow logically from the comparative information you have provided on the subjects.

5. **As you write, be open to including new ideas that may come to you: a new point of comparison, the explanation of a particular term, a different conclusion than you had planned on.** The drafting process is a thinking process, which can lead to new, sometimes critical discoveries. No matter how much preparation you do for a draft, new connections and insights may come to you as you write.

Writing Activity 6.8

Read the following first draft "Comparing Electric Cars," noting its introduction of subjects, explanation of what electric cars are in the second paragraph, points of comparison in the middle paragraphs, including details provided to make the comparisons, and the "qualified" conclusion that takes into account the reader's circumstances and preferences. Then write the first draft of your essay, keeping the five drafting considerations in mind.

Sample First Draft

Comparing Electric Cars

Reading audience: Anyone who is interested in electric cars and may consider purchasing one at some time.

With the price of gasoline constantly rising and auto emissions contributing significantly to global warming, more Americans are seriously looking into buying electric cars. Many companies are beginning to come out with electric car models, but two models stand out at this time: the Chevy Volt and the Nissan Leaf. The Tesla Roadster is a third electric vehicle that is getting a lot of attention, but with a price tag of $110,000, it is not in a price range that most people can afford.

Unlike hybrid vehicles such as the Prius and Ford Focus, which use electric and gasoline power in combination to improve gasoline mileage, the Volt and Leaf are electricity-first cars. The Leaf is a pure electric car with no gasoline engine and has a 100 mile driving range. The Volt is an electricity-first, gasoline-second vehicle which has a 40 mile electric driving range, after which its gasoline engine kicks in and can extend the range to 400 miles. However, each time the electric engine is recharged, it powers the car for 40 miles. In other words, the gas engine is a "safety valve" for longer drives between recharges. Both the Leaf and Volt can be recharged in a few hours by simply plugging into a 120 volt wall plug in a garage.

Both the Leaf and Volt are 5-door hatchbacks, but the Leaf holds five passengers while the Volt holds four. The interior and seating space in both is similar to most compact cars, with comfortable front-seat space and a little tight sitting in the back. Both cars also have the same technological dash features of most autos today, including GPS navigation and blue tooth phone systems.

As far as performance, the Volt is smooth and quiet, it rides well, and it has good acceleration. There is little difference between the Volt's performance and that of gas-powered compacts. The Leaf, which is not as quick as the Volt, also has a quiet, smooth, pleasant drive. As far as performance, there is little to choose between the two. Both cars handle well and possess similar safety features to gas-powered compacts.

If you are into looks, you'll probably find the Volt more pleasing to the eye. It has a sleek, sedan-like look despite being a hatchback while the Leaf definitely looks like a hatchback with its boxy rear end. The Leaf also has a higher top, accentuating its boxiness and giving it a mini-SUV look.

When it comes to price, the Leaf definitely has the Volt beat, which may explain why it has outsold the Volt two-to-one in the last year. The Leaf's base price is $33,000 while the Volt's is $41,000. It's duel-engine set-up may contribute to the higher price than the Leaf's single electric engine. As sales and production go up in the future for both cars, their prices will undoubtedly fall nearer the price of comparable gas-powered compacts.

There is no question that both the Volt and Leaf outperform all hybrids when it comes to gas consumption and emissions. The Leaf uses no gasoline and the Volt only uses gas when it's 40-mile electric range is exceeded, which may seldom occur during daily around-town driving. While the price of the Volt and Leaf exceeds that of comparable gas-powered compacts, the savings in annual gas cost can be in the $2000-$4000 range. Since the cost of running a car on electricity is a small fraction of the cost of gasoline, the savings is significant when factoring in the cost of electricity.

Whether the Volt or the Leaf is the best choice depends on your situation. For a family of five, the five-seated Leaf obviously seems the best choice. For someone whose commute exceeds 100 miles, the Volt with its gas-powered engine that kicks in after 40 electrical miles makes the most sense. For looks-conscious drivers, the Volt is also the sleeker-looking car. For someone wanting the "greenest" car, the Leaf is a clear choice since it burns no gasoline and emits no carbon dioxide into the atmosphere. If cost is a big consideration, the Leaf is also about $8,000 less expensive. Whichever car you may consider buying, the prices could come down appreciably in the future, putting them on the radar for more prospective buyers. There may also be more electric car models in production, but for now, the Volt and Leaf are the best choices on the market.

Revision

Each draft that you write has some revision considerations specific to that essay and some broader considerations that apply to most essays you write. For example, with your current comparative essay, the specific considerations include evaluating the criteria that you used for your comparison, the effectiveness of each point of comparison, and the appropriateness of your conclusion based on your comparison.

The broader revision considerations include improving your sentence wording, evaluating your paragraphing and organization, considering what you might add to strengthen the essay, checking your use of transitional wording, and determining how you might improve your opening or ending. By this time, most of these considerations are probably built into to your revision process as you become increasingly adept at revising your drafts.

Revision Suggestions

To revise your current draft, consider the following suggestions:

1. **Read your entire draft once to get an overall sense of its strengths and possible weaknesses.** You may notice that you have spent too much time on some areas of comparison and too little on others, buried one comparison in an overly long paragraph, or left readers unclear as to which subject was superior or the better option. Keep such concerns in mind as you begin revising your draft.

2. **Check your opening to see how effectively you introduced your topic and created interest for readers.** Make any changes that will pique readers' interest in the topic.

3. **Check to see whether you have provided explanations for anything your readers might not understand.** For example, the writer of the "Comparing Electric Cars" draft explained what an electric car and a hybrid car were so readers would understand the difference. Check for any terms or concepts in your draft that may require some explanation for your readers' understanding.

4. **Check your criteria - the points of comparison you presented - to see whether you have covered the most important comparisons and ordered them effectively.** If a new point of comparison comes to mind, you may want to include it. If a point in your draft seems rather minor, you may want to delete it. In addition, evaluate the order in which you presented your criteria, and determine whether a different order may be more effective.

5. **Check your use of details and examples to develop each comparison between subjects.** What might you add to make a particular comparison clearer or show a

sharper distinction between subjects?

6. **Check the wording of each sentence.** Delete unnecessary words or phrases, reword awkward or vague sentences, and replace questionable word choices.

7. **Check your use of transitional wording to tie thoughts together and help readers navigate your paper.** Since you are presenting a number of different comparative points, you might find use for transitions such as "first," "next," "another," or "lastly," as well as transitions that show different relationships such as "however," "nevertheless," "therefore," or "consequently."

8. **Check your conclusion to see whether it follows logically from the comparisons you made and takes into account your reading audience.** Does your conclusion make the most sense based on your evaluation of subjects? Does it take into account the different circumstances or preferences that your readers may have? Your comparative points lead to what may interest readers the most: the recommendations that you make in the conclusion..

9. **Evaluate how well you achieved your writing purpose.** Viewing your draft from a reader's perspective, what changes might you make to ensure that your purpose is clear and that you have accomplished it successfully?

Readers' Perspective Tips

While the text suggests viewing a draft through a "reader's perspective," that isn't necessarily easy. Stepping outside yourself and into your readers' mind may be a difficult metamorphosis.

In revising your current comparative draft, try this approach. Set the draft aside for awhile and then read it as if you are the intended reader: someone interested in the comparative subjects who may want some help in deciding what to do (or what to buy, where to transfer to, whom to vote for, or what instructor or class to take).

Rather than reading the draft from a reader's perspective, become that reader yourself, wanting to know everything you can about the subjects, how they compare, and what the writer would recommend. Does the draft include everything that you need to make a well-informed decision? What else do you want to know? What isn't clear to you?

By becoming that engaged reader that you would like reading your draft, you might make the most objective, constructive evaluation.

Writing Activity 6.9

Look at the revisions below for the "Comparing Electric Cars" draft, noting how the changes improve each paragraph. Then revise your own draft, keeping the previous revision suggestions in mind. For the best results, you may want to read your draft several times, covering one or two revision areas at a time.

Sample Draft Revisions

Comparing Electric Cars   (Deletions crossed out; additions in bold)

First two paragraphs:

With the price of gasoline constantly rising and auto emissions contributing significantly to global warming, **many** Americans are ~~seriously looking into~~ **considering for the first time** buying **an** electric ~~cars~~. Many companies are beginning to ~~come out with~~ **introduce** electric car models, but two models stand out at this time: the Chevy Volt and the Nissan Leaf. The Tesla Roadster, ~~is~~ a third electric vehicle ~~that is~~ getting a lot of attention, **is out of most people's price range at $110,000.** ~~but with a price tag of $110,000, it is not in a price range that most people can afford.~~ **However, the Volt and Leaf give drivers two reasonable electric car options to consider.**

Unlike hybrid vehicles such as the Prius and Ford Focus, which use **a combination of** electric and gasoline power ~~in combination to improve gasoline mileage~~, the Volt and Leaf are electricity-first cars. The Leaf is a pure electric car with no gasoline engine and has a 100 mile driving range **between charges.** The Volt is an electricity-first **car** ~~gasoline-second vehicle~~ which has a 40 mile ~~electric~~ driving range **between charges**, after which its gasoline engine kicks in and ~~can~~ extend**s** the range to 400 miles. ~~However, each time~~ **Once** the electric engine is recharged, it **again** powers the car, ~~for 40 miles. In other words~~ the gas engine ~~is being~~ **being** a "safety valve" for longer drives between recharges. Both the Leaf and Volt can be recharged in a few hours by ~~simply~~ plugging **them** into a 120 volt wall plug ~~in the garage.~~

Final paragraph:

Whether the Volt or the Leaf is the best choice depends on your situation. ~~For a family of five, the five-seated Leaf obviously seems the best choice.~~ For someone whose commute or regular travel exceeds 100 miles **daily**, the Volt with its **"safety valve"** gas-powered engine ~~that kicks in after 40 electrical miles~~ makes the most sense. For looks-conscious drivers, the Volt is also the sleeker-looking car. For someone ~~wanting the "greenest" car, **and**~~ whose daily driving remains under 100 miles, the Leaf is a clear choice since it burns no gasoline. **It is the "greenest," most environmentally friendly car, emitting no carbon dioxide into the atmosphere.** ~~and emits no carbon dioxide into the atmosphere.~~ **For a family of five, the five-seated Leaf also seems the best choice.**   If cost is a big consideration, the Leaf is about $8,000 less expensive.

Whichever car you may consider buying, the prices could come down appreciably in the next couple years, ~~putting them on the radar for a lot more prospective buyers~~, **making them more affordable**.   There may also be more electric car models in production by then, but for now, the Volt and Leaf are the best choices on the market **and the first viable electric car options that Americans have had.**

Writing Activity 6.10

Exchange drafts with a classmate or two to get some reader feedback. Ask questions about anything that you don't understand or would like more information on, including additional areas of comparison. Make any revision suggestions that you feel would improve the draft for readers. Then based on your classmate's feedback, make any revisions that you feel would further improve your essay.

Editing

Now that you have revised your draft, you are ready to correct any errors to produce a final error-free essay for your readers' consumption. While error correction is your top priority, to some degree, writers are always in the "revision mode," and if you notice a way to improve your paper while you are proofreading for errors, make the revision.

By now, you probably have a good idea of the types of errors you tend to make, which should be your primary proofreading focus. You needn't spend much time looking for errors that you seldom make, whether run-on sentences, fragments, or subject pronouns. Finally, it is worthwhile to check for the types of errors that any writer can occasionally slip up on: subject-verb agreement, pronoun-antecedent agreement, frequently confused words, or comma usage.

In this lesson, you are first introduced to apostrophe usage in possessive words and contractions. Then you do a review activity covering the grammatical and punctuation areas from previous lessons. Finally, you proofread your draft for errors to complete the writing process.

Apostrophe Usage

Apostrophes are used in possessive words to indicate "ownership" and in contractions to replace the letters that are omitted when the two words forming the contraction are combined (you + are = you're). Omitting an apostrophe in a possessive word is a fairly common error, usually caused by the writer not recognizing the possessive form of a word. For example, in writing the sentence, "Todays weather is supposed to be much milder than yesterdays," a writer may pay little attention to the possessive words "todays" and "yesterdays" and omit the required apostrophes: Today's weather is supposed to be much milder than yesterday's. Most writers see the problem when it is brought to their attention and correctly insert apostrophes when they focus their proofreading on possessive words.

Using apostrophes correctly in contractions is less of a problem for most writers since most contractions look rather "naked" without their apostrophe. For example, a contraction such as "haven't" or "I'm" doesn't look right to most writers without its apostrophe: "havent" or "Im." You may have little problem with contractions and if so, needn't spend much time on them.

To use apostrophes correctly in possessive words and contractions, follow these basic rules and suggestions:

Possessive Words

1. **A possessive word shows *ownership* - something *belongs* to a person or thing: cat's instinct, rainbow's colors, Bernadette's wig, freedom's power.**

2. **If a *singular* word is possessive, it ends in *apostrophe* + "*s*" ('s): car's windshield, Malcolm's toothbrush, tomorrow's headline. If a *plural* word is**

possessive, it ends in *"s" + apostrophe* (s'): several cities' budget deficits, thirty students' math scores, boxes' lids.

(Exception: If a word forms its plural without adding "s" (children, geese, men, women), its possessive form ends in *apostrophe + "s:"* children's books, geese's pond, men's clothing, women's prerogative.)

3. **Apostrophes are not used in possessive pronouns such as *his, hers, theirs, yours, ours.*** However, apostrophes are used in *indefinite* possessive pronouns: someone's umbrella, everybody's business, no one's fault; somebody's coat.

4. **A possessive word may *follow* the word it possesses:** That credit car is Fran's That newspaper is yesterday's. The coat I borrowed is my mother's.

Contractions

1. **A *contraction* is a word formed by combining two words:**

   I + am = I'm   you + are = you're
   has + not = hasn't   they + are = they're
   will + not = won't   we + are = we're
   you + have = you've   he + will = he'll

2. **An apostrophe replaces the letters that are omitted when the words are combined:**

   you're (apostrophe replaces "a" in "are")
   they'll (apostrophe replaces "wi" in "will")
   she's (apostrophe replaces "i" in "is")

3. **Contraction problems occur most frequently with the follow word mix-ups:**

   Its time to change the calendar in the kitchen. (*Its* is a possessive pronoun.)
   Correct:
   It's time to change the calendar in the kitchen.

   I don't think *were* going to the concert. (*Were* is a past tense verb.)
   Correct:
   I don't think *we're* going to the concert.

   Amal hopes that *your* not angry with him. (*Your* is a possessive pronoun.)

   Correct:

Amal hopes that *you're* not angry with him.

Theirs no better debater than Therese. (*Theirs* is a possessive pronoun.)

Correct:
There's no better debater than Therese.

Writing Activity 6.11

The following paragraph contains some possessive words and contractions in need of apostrophes and some incorrect words that need to be replaced with contractions. Insert apostrophes where they are needed and replace the incorrect words with contractions.

Example:

The Italian cruise ship rammed into a reef and turned onto its side. Theres reason to suspect that the captain steered too close to the port islands reef before turning into its harbor. Many of the ships lifeboats were incapacitated, so hundreds of island residents boats anchored in the harbor sailed to the sinking ship to rescue the 4,000 passengers and ships crew. Its the first major cruise ship disaster in over fifty years.

Corrected:

The Italian cruise ship rammed into a reef and turned onto its side. *There's* reason to suspect that the captain steered too close to the port *island's* reef before turning into its harbor. Many of the *ship's* lifeboats were incapacitated, so hundreds of island *residents'* boats anchored in the harbor sailed to the sinking ship to rescue the 4,000 passengers and *ship's* crew. *It's* the first major cruise ship disaster in over fifty years.

Science Experiment

Amalias science project didnt turn out the way she had hoped. She and a friend collaborated on an experiment to try and prove that greenhouse gases, most notably CO_2, were responsible for climate change. They built a large, rectangular plastic box with a hole in its side for inserting a rubber hose into the box. The boxs dimensions were three-feet long, two-feet wide, and two-feet high.   The rubber hoses outside end was attached to a pump that theyd borrowed from the chemistry lab. The pumps chamber was filled with CO_2 gas, and when they turned on the pump, the boxs interior filled with the gas. As the CO_2 gas trapped heat inside the box, they theorized that the temperature inside the box should increase, as a thermostat placed inside the box would indicate. They awaited anxiously for the thermostats red bubble to begin to rise.

Its clear that their experiment had a significant flaw, however. CO_2 traps heat in the earths atmosphere which would otherwise escape into space. The gas acts like a giant lid that retains more heat in the atmosphere and consequently warms the air. And theres the problem with the experiment. The "atmosphere" inside Amalia and her friends plastic box already had a lid on it, allowing no heat to escape. Therefore, whatever heat was inside the box was already trapped, so adding CO2 to the box had no effect.

Rather than abandoning the experiment, their looking into ways to allow heat to escape from the box, such as drilling some holes in its lid, to try and duplicate the heat loss in the earths atmosphere. Theyve put a lot of time and effort into the experiment, and theyd love to be able to provide a working model of mankinds contribution to global warming.

Writing Activity 6.12

Proofread your paper focusing specifically on possessive words and contractions, and insert any apostrophes you may have omitted.

Writing Activity 6.13

This review activity provides some proofreading practice involving run-on and comma-splice sentences, sentence fragments, subject-verb agreement, subject pronouns, pronoun-antecedent agreement, and comma usage. Proofread the follow paragraphs for errors and make the necessary corrections.

Example:

The parking pass validation rules at the shopping mall is tricky. Which means that you need to read the fine print. First a shopper can only get their parking pass validated if they spend at least $20 in a store. Second only certain stores on the mall accepts parking validations, you need to check the list of participating stores. Finally, if you leave your parking pass in the car which is very easy to do you are out of luck.

Corrected:

The parking pass validation rules at the shopping mall ~~is~~ *are* tricky, *which* means that you need to read the fine print. First, ~~a shopper~~ *shoppers* can only get their parking pass validated if they spend at least $20 in a store. Second, only certain stores on the mall ~~accepts~~ *accept* parking validations. *You* need to check the list of participating stores. Finally, if you leave your parking pass in the car, which is very easy to do, you are out of luck.

Campus Maze

Not one of the internal campus roads get you from one side of the campus to the other. Each road in the structural maze dead-end at some point, you are forced to turn around and try a different route. Which is a waste of precious time when you're trying to get to class. In addition, most of the roads are one-way. It is sometimes difficult to find a

road going the direction you want, a student can literally get stuck mid-campus trying to navigate their way across the college. Me and my friends have given up on using the campus roads to get to class and I think that is the intent of the college's crazy road maze. If college officials wanted students on the roads they would have devised a more workable system. In my opinion the college trustees and president wants to maintain the roads primarily for faculty, campus security staff, and administrative use.
It prefers that students walk or ride bikes around campus instead of driving. Making it difficult to get to class on time if your next class is across the campus.

Writing Activity 6.14

Proofread your draft for errors, focusing on the types of errors you most frequently make and the common problem areas covered in the text. Make sure to run the spell-check on your word processing program, and also check for spelling errors involving similar-sounding words the spell-check may not catch: their/they're/there, know/no, to/too/two, affect/effect, then/than, your/you're, its/it's.

Communicating with Readers

With your instructor's help, decide on the best way to get your essay to your reading audience or representatives. In addition, since you are providing readers with a comparison of subjects and drawing some conclusions which may help them make a decision, figure out a way to get some feedback from readers. Essay writing is often a two-way communication from writer to reader to writer, and most writers are interested in getting some idea of how their essay was received by readers.

Lesson Seven: Comparative Support

Objective: To write a thesis-based essay using comparative evidence to support the thesis.

Purpose: Writer's choice

Audience: Writer's choice

In Lesson Six, you compared subjects in your essay to reveal their differences and similarities, evaluate their relative quality or value, and draw conclusions for readers. Writers also use comparisons to support their viewpoint in thesis-based essays, which you will do in this lesson. Using comparisons is among the most effective and common ways that writers clarify their ideas and convince readers of their validity.

For example, a writer wrote an essay in support of a high-speed rail system that would zip travelers from one end of the state to the other. She used the following comparisons to help support her viewpoint:

1. Compared the state high-speed rail project to successful high-speed rail systems in Spain, Germany, China, and Japan, showing that high-speed rail can be an effective, cost-efficient transportation system and not the novel, "far out" idea that opponents claim.

2. Compared the differences between automobile and high-speed rail travel, emphasizing the superiority of high-speed train travel: three times as fast, uses no gasoline, doesn't pollute the air with emissions, reduces rather than adds traffic to congested freeways.

3. Compared the cost of building a high-speed rail system to constructing more freeways and renovating existing ones to accommodate growing population. Comparison would show that building the rail system would be no more costly than building more freeways.

4. Compared the state economy if the rail system was built and if it wasn't. If it was built, it would add thousands of new jobs for constructing and later operating and maintaining the system, generate greater tax revenues from rail-system profits, and provide an economic boost for the state. If it isn't built, the state's unemployment rate would remain high, its tax coffers would remain depleted, and the economy would continue to stagnate.

5. Compared the building of the high-speed rail to other historical transportation breakthroughs that also faced opposition: the first automobiles, the first passenger airplanes, the intercontinental railroad, the Erie Canal.

6. Used an *analogy* - a comparison of dissimilar things to make a point - to show the two options that the state has:

   One elementary teacher uses the Smart Board in her classroom, a writing board with computer and video components that allow students and teachers to access the Internet, create and show multi-media presentations, and develop interactive assignments. Another teacher, leery of technological advancements and stuck in her ways, stays with the same old green chalkboard, ignoring the educational opportunities the Smart Board presents. In accepting or rejecting the high-speed rail system, our state has the choice of sticking with the old green chalkboard or grasping the opportunity that the Smart Board provides. We can remain stuck in the past or embrace the future.

As you can see, the writer used a number of different comparisons to support the creation of a high-speed rail system: her state's proposed rail system compared to successful high-speed rail systems in other countries; traveling by high-speed train compared to traveling by automobile; the cost of constructing the high-speed rail system compared to the cost of adding new freeways and renovating existing ones; the effects on the state economy if the high-speed rail system was built and if it wasn't built; the high-speed rail system compared to other historical transportation breakthroughs; and building the high-speed rail system compared to embracing the new Smart Board educational technology. The writer gave readers a number of relevant comparisons to think about, all of which furthered her purpose: to convince readers to support the high-speed rail project.

Making Comparisons

Using comparisons to make a point can have a powerful impact on readers. It can help them understand a topic better, view it from a different perspective, or see its value or reasonableness. For example, from the prior comparisons used in an essay supporting a high-speed rail system, readers realized that successful high-speed systems were already operating, that it would cost no more than building new freeways, that it would help the state's economy, and that it would reduce pollution and traffic. Readers were also provided perspectives on the high speed rail that they probably hadn't considered: its place among other historical transportation breakthroughs in the country, and its similarity to other technological advances that forward-thinking people are grasping, such as the educational Smart Board.

   To use comparisons most effectively in your upcoming essay and future writing, consider these suggestions:

1. **To support your viewpoint, think of the most relevant comparisons you can make.** For example, let's say that you are supporting the creation of a downtown walking mall on a two-block section of main street. You think it would attract more shoppers downtown, beautify the downtown area, help the current downtown stores, and attract new businesses. What comparisons might you make to convince people that you are right?

    If you could compare successful downtown malls in similar-sized cities to your own, you might convince readers that a mall could be a good idea. If you took a couple of the cities with malls and compared their downtown business today to what it was *before* the mall was created, you might further strengthen your point. If you made the analogy that the downtown area is a priceless gem that simply needs some polishing to regain its luster, you might change some readers' perspective.

2. **Consider using different *types* of comparisons to support your thesis.** For example, the writer who supported the creation of a high-speed rail system used a direct comparison of the state's high-speed rail project to other high-speed rail systems, similar comparisons of high-speed train and automobile travel and high-speed rail and freeway construction costs, a "future-projection" comparison of the state's economy with and without the high-speed rail system, and a dissimilar comparison of the high-speed rail and the Smart Board, using an *analogy* to show how each represented important technological advancement.

3. **Use comparisons that help readers see the *logic* of your viewpoint.** For example, a writer defending the huge salaries that professional athletes are paid compared them to the huge salaries of top-paid movie and television actors, which people seldom question. A writer whose thesis was that rap music is a musical genre that is here to stay compared it to rock 'n roll music in the '50, which many people also viewed as a passing fad. A writer who believed that the U.S. military should leave Afghanistan compared the futility of the war to the Soviet Union's failed ten-year military campaign in Afghanistan. Such comparisons can provide a different perspective for readers, reveal the logic of the writer's viewpoint, and help convince them of its validity.

4. **Use comparisons that readers can relate to and that are easy to understand.** For example, if a writer was urging readers not waste their money playing the state lottery, which comparison would be the most effective: "You have as great a chance of winning the state lottery as you do of picking the number I am thinking of between 1 and 10,0000,000," or, "You have as great a chance of winning the state lottery as you do solving Fermat's Last Theorem, which went unsolved for 300 years." Clearly, the first comparison is easier for readers to relate to and understand unless they are theoretical mathematicians.

Writing Activity 7.1

To support the thesis for any three of the following topics, decide on some relevant comparisons that you might make. Consider different types of comparisons, including using an analogy.

Examples:

Topic: Proposed increase in the college's parking fee for students

Thesis: The parking fee for students shouldn't be increased.

Comparisons: Compare cost of parking fee to comparable colleges' fee.
                Compare how the college covered parking lot maintenance costs in the past without raising the fee.
                Analogy: Increasing the fee without student approval is the same as taxation without representation.

Topic: Burning wood in fireplaces in winter

Thesis: To reduce pollution, burning wood in fireplaces in winter months should be banned in the county.

Comparisons: Compare the different pollution levels during wood-burning and non-wood burning periods of the year.
                Compare incidence of asthma and respiratory ailments in the county to areas of the state with lower pollution levels.
                Compare projected pollution levels in the county during winter months with and without the burning of wood in fireplaces.
                Analogy: People who burn wood in fireplaces are like smokers subjecting others to second-hand smoke. They both harm other people.

1. Topic: Declining students enrollment at the college.

   Thesis: The college needs to take action to increase student enrollment.

   Comparisons:

2. Topic: Legal drinking age

   Thesis: The legal drinking age should be lowered to 18.

   Comparisons:

3. Topic: Beer at on-campus pizza restaurant

   Thesis: No alcoholic beverage should be sold on campus.

   Comparisons:

4. Topic: Higher salaries for teachers

   Thesis: K-12 teachers should earn higher salaries for the invaluable contribution they make to our children's futures.

   Comparisons:

5. Topic: Pre-school education

   Thesis: Pre-school is critical to a child's educational success.

   Comparisons:

6. Topic: U.S. health care

   Thesis: The high cost of health care in the U.S. is indefensible.

   Comparisons:

Writing Activity 7.2

For practice using analogies, try coming up with an analogy for some of the following topics, or for other topics of your choice.

Examples:

Topic: not going to the dentist regularly (the negative results)

Analogy: Not going to the dentist regularly is like not doing regular maintenance on your car. In the long run, you'll end up having more problems and spending more money.

Topic: eating too much fried, fatty foods (the negative results)

Analogy: Eating too much fried, fatty foods can clog your arteries like overloading your computer with software can clog your computer. Eventually your system will fail you.

Topic: watching too much television (negative results)

Analogy: Watching too much television is as mentally stimulating as staring
           all day at a water cooler.

1. Topic: Dropping out of high school (the negative results)

   Analogy:

2. Topic: Voting in presidential elections (the positive results)

   Analogy:

3. Topic: Getting the weeds out of your lawn (positive results)

   Analogy:

4. Topic: Driving without your seat belt on (negative results)

   Analogy:

5. Topic: Taking too many classes in one semester (negative results)

   Analogy:

6. Topic: Driving an electric car (positive results)

Writing Assignment

For this lesson's writing assignment, you will choose a topic that people have differing opinions on, decide on a thesis that expresses your viewpoint, and support your thesis primarily through the use of comparisons. To help decide on a writing topic, consider these suggestions:

1. **Select a topic that attracts differing viewpoints.** Think of current issues that people don't agree on. They may involve your college, community, state, or country, and they may come from any field: education, foreign affairs, music, technology, business, the environment, transportation, health and fitness, and so on.

2. **Select a topic whose thesis you could support through comparisons.** When you consider a topic, think of the types of comparisons you might use to support a thesis. If no possible comparisons come to mind, consider other topics.

3. **Select a topic that you are interested in, that may interest readers, and that you can cover effectively in an essay.** Choose a topic that is specific enough to do justice to in an essay - e.g. "America's Effective Iranian Policy" as opposed to "American Foreign Policy Problems in the Middle East and Europe" - and that you would like to write about.

As with many possible writing topics, our interest often exceeds our knowledge. If that is the case with the topic that you select, you can do whatever research and investigation that may be required to write knowledgeably on the issue. For example, the writer who wrote the upcoming first draft "Decriminalizing Marijuana Usage" felt that the current U.S. laws regarding marijuana usage needed changing, but it wasn't until she began reading comparisons between the U.S. policy and other countries' that she had the evidence to support her viewpoint. Learning more about your topic may help you decide on a thesis and generate some comparative evidence to support it, or it may alter your viewpoint on the topic.

Writing Activity 7.3

Keeping the suggestions for topic selection in mind, choose a topic for your upcoming essay. Consider a number of different issues, perhaps do some preliminary research, and ultimately select the topic that you are most interested in and that you can use comparisons to support a thesis.

Preparation

Once you have selected a topic, you can do whatever prewriting preparation you feel will help you write the first draft of your essay. Each "Preparation" section provides some prewriting suggestions that you might find useful, perhaps supplementing other strategies that you employ. A primary consideration will be to marshal some comparisons to help support your thesis.

Thesis

In this lesson, you are writing a thesis-based essay where you present and support your viewpoint on an issue, relying primarily on comparative evidence. To decide on a thesis for your essay, consider the following suggestions:

1. **Pose the question that your thesis will answer.** A thesis statement often answers the central question related to a particular issue: Should a high-speed rail system be built in the state? Is it necessary for the college to raise tuition for the next school year? Is pollution endangering the health of children living in your city? Should a new performing arts theater be built on campus? Should products purchased on the Internet be taxed just like products bought in stores? Should condoms be available at

the college health center? Ask yourself the question that is central to your particular issue, and decide on the best answer, which may be your thesis for the essay.

2. **Decide on a thesis that expresses your personal viewpoint and that you feel is the fairest, most reasonable, or most valid position to take on the issue.** Look at both or all sides of the issue before deciding on your thesis, and generate a thesis that you feel reflects the "right" thing to do or to believe.

3. **If you need to learn more about your topic, don't decide on a thesis until you feel knowledgeable enough to have an informed opinion.** For example, the writer who wrote the upcoming first draft "Decriminalizing Marijuana Usage" wasn't certain about her thesis until she had done considerable comparative research on the topic.

Writing Activity 7.4

Decide on a thesis for your essay, and generate a potential thesis statement to include in your opening. If you need to learn more about your topic, do some research before deciding on your thesis.

Sample thesis:

Topic: Marijuana usage

Thesis statement: Marijuana usage should be decriminalized in the U.S. as it has been done successfully in other countries.

Comparative Evidence

Since the emphasis in this lesson is on using comparisons to help support your thesis, take some time to think of possible comparisons for your particular topic. To help generate some possible comparisons, consider these suggestions:

1. **Consider any types of comparisons that would help readers to see the logic, reasonableness, or fairness of your thesis.** For example, if your thesis were, "Americans pay too much for health insurance," you might compare health care costs in the U.S. to other countries; the percentage of their paycheck for average Americans that goes towards health insurance payments today compared to twenty years ago; the rate of overall inflation for the past ten years compared to the rate of inflation for health insurance; the rate that other types of insurance - automobile, homeowners, life - has increased compared to health insurance rates; and a possible analogy: Increasing health insurance rates are like a growing cancer. They eat away larger and larger chunks of people's paychecks until it becomes difficult to survive.

2. **For each type of comparison you consider, determine what you are trying to show readers with the comparison.** For example, with the health insurance comparisons in 1., the writer would be trying to show how unfair high health insurance rates are in America compared to other countries, to earlier times in America, and to other types of insurance, and to show the negative effects of the higher rates on Americans.

3. **Use the most logical, appropriate comparisons to convince readers.** For example, if a writer's thesis is, "Dropping out of high school can have devastating effects for the rest of a young person's life," the writer might compare high school dropouts to high school graduates in a number of areas: rates of employment, comparative salaries, drug use, percentage on welfare, percentage incarcerated, percentage living in poverty. She might also use an analogy such as, "Dropping out of high school is like running a long race without any preparation. The farther you run, the farther behind you get until you finally give up." Use comparisons that you feel will support your thesis in ways that readers will find relevant.

Writing Activity 7.5

Come up with as many possible comparisons as you can to support your thesis, and determine what you want to show readers with each comparison. Think of different types of comparisons you might use, and include an analogy or two. If you are going to research your topic, you may find more comparisons through your reading.

Example:

Topic: Marijuana Use

Thesis: Marijuana usage should be decriminalized in the U.S. as it has been
          done successfully in other countries.

Comparisons:

> Compare level of marijuana usage in countries where marijuana has been decriminalized to the U.S. to show that countries where marijuana usage isn't a felony don't have higher levels of usage.

> Compare level of usage in countries before and after they decriminalized marijuana to show that decriminalization didn't increase usage.

> Compare level of usage in states that have decriminalized marijuana or reduced penalties to states that have punitive anti-marijuana laws to show that usage in states where marijuana has been decriminalized isn't greater.

Compare level of usage in states before and after they decriminalized marijuana to show that the level of usage didn't increase.

Compare the cost to taxpayers today with the U.S.' current marijuana laws to the cost if marijuana were decriminalized nationwide.

Compare marijuana usage to beer drinking to show that marijuana is no more of a "gateway" drug to cocaine and heroin than beer.

Analogy: Treating marijuana and heroin users alike under the law is like treating parking ticket offenders the same as drunk drivers. It makes no sense and is unfair.

Research

If you need to learn more about your subject to write about it knowledgeably, to decide on a thesis for your topic, or to find some potential comparative material, do the necessary investigation. This may include talking to some local experts, getting some information from on-campus or city sources, locating online information on your topic, or browsing your library for periodical or newspaper articles or books on the topic.

As you research you topic, consider the following suggestions:

1. **Research your topic with a purpose.** For example, you may want to find some explanatory information to help readers clearly understand the issue and some comparative information to support your thesis. Focus on sources that may provide the necessary information.

2. **As you research, write down any information you may include in your essay**. Later you can decide what information is worth including and how best to use it.

3. **Write down the source for each piece of information, such as the author's name, title of the article, and the periodical or online site where it appeared.** You will provide such reference material in your essay to indicate to readers the sources of the information that you use. (See the source references in the upcoming first draft of "Decriminalizing Marijuana Usage.")

4. **Research with an open mind.** In researching your topic, you may learn some things that alter your viewpoint on the issue or discover some comparisons that you hadn't considered.

Writing Activity 7.6

Following the suggestions presented, do the necessary research in preparation for writing your first draft. Make sure to write down the source for each piece of information you might use in your essay.

Audience and Purpose

Writers write essays for different purposes. A writer may write a particular essay, which may be a newspaper editorial or a periodical article, to enlighten readers on a particular topic, to persuade readers to think or act a certain way, to help solve a problem, to give advice, or to entertain and amuse. Of course, an essay can be enlightening, entertaining, and persuasive at the same time, but the writer's purpose is focused primarily on the impact he wants to make on readers.

Your purpose in writing a particular essay is usually determined by its topic and the audience you want to reach. If you are writing about an issue at the college, your audience may be your fellow students or the board of trustees. Depending on the audience, your purpose may differ. You may want students to take action against a proposal that on-campus security officers carry guns, and you may want the board of trustees to reject the proposal made by the administration. The essays that you write to those two audiences may differ significantly in content.

To decide on the audience and purpose for your current essay, consider the following questions:

1. **Whom would I like to read this essay?** Who would find it interesting, who could benefit from reading it, whose mind would I like to change on the issue, or who could help make a difference regarding the future of the issue? Depending on your topic, your audience may be your fellow students, women in general, the city council, high school students, or the general public.

2. **What would my purpose be in writing to this audience?** Do you want to persuade readers to believe as you do about the topic? To take a particular action? To better understand an often misunderstood issue?

3. **How can I best accomplish my purpose?** What are the most important things that you need to do in your essay to have the desired impact on readers? No matter how strongly you believe in your thesis, how you choose to support it will determine its impact on readers.

Writing Activity 7.7

To decide on an audience and purpose for your essay, answer the three preceding questions in the "Audience and Purpose" section.

Example:

Topic: Decriminalizing marijuana usage

1. I think this is a topic for the general public. Most people know little about marijuana laws in other countries or their impact on usage. To change the laws in this country, people have to be more knowledgeable.

2. My purpose is for readers to see how our punitive marijuana usage laws are unfair and costly to enforce. My ultimate purpose is to have marijuana usage decriminalized, and to do that, public opinion needs to change.

3. To accomplish my purpose, the most important things for people to understand are that decriminalizing marijuana usage won't lead to increased usage, will solve the problem of overcrowded prisons and unnecessary expenses for taxpayers, and will free police to focus on serious crime. I think those are three things I need to emphasize.

Drafting

The writing emphasis for this lesson is on using comparisons to support your thesis. The purpose of your comparisons is to show readers why your viewpoint on the essay's topic is the most sensible, reasonable, or fairest. What you learn about using comparisons in an essay can apply to much of your future writing.

Of course, a writer isn't limited to one type of thesis support such as comparative evidence. While most of the thesis support for your current essay is devoted to comparisons, you may have other points that you want to make. For example, while the writer of the "Decriminalizing Marijuana Usage" draft in Writing Activity 7.9 used a number of comparisons to support her thesis, she also provided statistics showing that marijuana possession caused a high percentage of drug-related incarcerations, which could be reduced dramatically if marijuana usage were decriminalized. If you have a powerful supportive point or two that don't involve comparisons, feel free to use them in your essay.

Incorporating Sources

When writers use material in an essay that came from another source such as a book, article, editorial, or individual, they let readers know what the source was. They do this to acknowledge their sources, to lend credibility to the information provided, and to distinguish their own thoughts from any "borrowed" material in order to avoid *plagiarism*: passing off someone else's material as their own. You find source references - According to meteorologist Issac Freeman, In her book *White Collar Criminals*, In the December 12th edition of *Time*, According to the latest Gallop Poll, - in many newspaper editorials, periodical articles, online articles, books, and essay collections.

If you are using material from research sources in your essay, you need to provide source references for that material. If you didn't need to research your topic, you obviously won't use such references but will not doubt do so in future essays. To provide clear source references in your essays, follow these suggestions:

1. **Whenever you introduce material from a source, provide a clear reference for readers.** You might include the author's name and title of her book (In Nora Ashley's book *Wall Street Meltdown*,), the title of an article and the online site or periodical where it was found (The article "The Asthma-Pollution Connection" in *Science Today* confirmed . . .), the name of a particular study (The British Health Department's four-year study on obese children found . . .), or the name of a particular expert (Renown pediatrist Dr. Patricia Fernandez recommended . . .).

2. **When you use the same source later in an essay, refer back to the original**

reference. While you needn't provide the entire source reference again, provide enough information so readers know what source you are referring to: Ashley also contends that . . ., The "Asthma-Pollution" article goes on to suggest . . ., The British Health Department's study concludes . . ., Dr. Fernandez argues that . . . .

3. **Use the most current, credible sources available.** In most cases, the more recent the article or book you are referencing, the more relevant readers will find it. For example, a book on Islamic political influence in the Middle East written in 2000 would not provide a clear or accurate picture of the political landscape today.

   The most credible sources are those that readers would tend to believe. For example, a *National Inquirer* article on UFO's would carry little weight for most readers compared to an article in *Science Digest*, and a politician's opinion on global warming would not rival that of a leading climatologist.

4. **Source referencing in articles, editorials, and essays is different than in formal research papers.** A research paper follows a prescribed format, identifies sources through parenthetical references, and includes a "Works Cited" section, all of which you will learn more about in Lesson Twelve. Source referencing in articles and essays provides a more informal way for readers to distinguish between "borrowed" material and your own ideas.

Writing Activity 7.8

Read the first draft of "Decriminalizing Marijuana Usage" in Writing Activity 7.9, noting the way the writer uses source references to introduce and identify all research material. You may use this essay as a guideline for incorporating research material in your first draft.

Drafting Suggestions

As you write the first draft of your essay, consider the following suggestions:

1. **In the opening, introduce your topic in a way that creates reader interest.** Give readers a sense of why the topic is important or how it may affect them. You can either present your thesis statement in the opening or save it for the conclusion after you have presented your comparative evidence, as the writer of "Decriminalizing Marijuana Usage" did. (See the opening paragraph of the essay.)

2. **Present your comparisons in support of your thesis in the middle paragraphs.** Make sure that readers know what you are trying to show with each comparison, i.e. how the comparison relates to your thesis. You may also include other supportive points that don't involve comparisons.

3. **If you incorporate research material in your draft, provide a source reference for each "borrowed" piece of information.** Put the research material in your own words (*paraphrase*), and when you want to use a direct quote, use quotation marks (" ") and introduce the "speaker." (See the quoted material in the "Decriminalizing Marijuana Usage" draft.)

4. **Paragraph your draft, changing paragraphs as you move to different comparisons or different parts of your paper (opening to middle, middle to conclusion).** Consider using topic sentences to introduce paragraphs that have a definite main idea. (See topic sentences that begin paragraphs 3, 4, 6, 7, and 8 of the "Decriminalizing Marijuana Usage" draft.)

5. **Conclude your essay in a way that reinforces your thesis, provides something new for readers, and leaves them with a clear sense of your purpose: what you hope to accomplish in writing to them.** If you have saved your thesis for the conclusion (as the author of "Decriminalizing Marijuana Usage" did), make your viewpoint clear to readers, perhaps showing how the comparative evidence led inevitably to your thesis.

6. **Keep your audience and purpose in mind.** Since your essay is aimed at a particular audience for a definite purpose, the decisions you make as you write the draft - what to include, what to emphasize, how to word your ideas - can be made with your readers in mind.

Writing Activity 7.9

Read the first draft "Decriminalizing Marijuana Usage," noting its opening, its use of comparative evidence, its referencing of sources, the inclusion of supportive points not involving comparisons, and its four-paragraph conclusion, which summarizes the comparative evidence and makes the essay's thesis and purpose clear. Then write the first draft of your essay, keeping in mind the drafting suggestions.

Sample first draft

Decriminalizing Marijuana Usage

(audience: general public)

Should marijuana usage be decriminalized in the U.S.? Millions of marijuana users certainly think so, claiming that smoking marijuana is no different than drinking alcohol. What would happen if marijuana usage was decriminalized in the U.S.? Would usage, particularly among younger Americans, increase dramatically? Looking at what has happened in states and countries that don't put people in jail for using marijuana gives us some indication.

Although recreational marijuana usage is illegal in the U.S., in 1973, Oregon became the first state to decriminalize cannabis possession, according to Wikipedia. By 1978, Alaska, California, Colorado, Mississippi, New York, Nebraska, North Carolina, and Maine had some form of cannabis decriminalization, meaning that possessing small amounts of marijuana, one ounce being the most common maximum, was not a misdemeanor or felony. At worst, the possession of marijuana, if detected by police, would result in a fine.

What impact did the decriminalization of marijuana have on usage rates in states where the fear of arrests and prison sentences for users no longer existed? According to Wikipedia, studies conducted in California, Oregon, and Maine within a few years of decriminalization found little increase in cannabis use compared to the rest of the country. In 1997, the Connecticut Law Revision Commission examined states that had decriminalized cannabis and found any increase in cannabis usage was *less* than the increase in states that had not decriminalized cannabis, and that the largest proportionate increase of marijuana use occurred in those states with the most severe penalties. The Commission recommended that Connecticut decriminalize the possession of one ounce or less of marijuana for adults 21 years and older.

Enough countries in different parts of the world have decriminalized marijuana usage to give a good picture of the impact of decriminalization. In South Australia, marijuana usage has been decriminalized, and Australians who are caught in possession either receive a warning or pay a small fine. In Western Australia, however, marijuana possession remains a felony and jail sentences are the norm. A two-year study conducted by the Drug and Alcohol Council of South Australia found no difference in levels of marijuana use between Western Australia with its harsh anti-marijuana laws and South Australia with its decriminalization of marijuana usage.

The Netherlands is known for the most liberal marijuana laws in the world, where people can actually smoke marijuana legally in "shops" around the city of Amsterdam. However, according to a 2010 study by The European School Survey Project on Alcohol and Other Drugs (ESPAD), marijuana use among teens in the Netherlands is actually lower than in the United States. The survey found 28% of Dutch teens have smoked marijuana as compared with 41% of American teens, and 23% of American teens have experimented with other illicit drugs as compared with only 6% of Netherlands' teens.

According to American decriminalization advocate Kevin Zeese of Common Sense for Drug Policy, the lure of the "forbidden" attracts American teens to marijuana. Zeese added, "It is worth pointing out that the Dutch, when they made marijuana available for purchase, said one reason they were doing so was to make marijuana boring." The Netherlands eliminated the forbidden lure of marijuana usage that Zeese contends attracts American teens, who are in the most rebellious, risk-taking phase of their lives.

According to a *Times Science* article "Drugs in Portugal: Did Decriminalization Work?" decriminalization has been a great success. Following decriminalization, according to a Cato Institute Report, Portugal had the lowest rate of lifetime marijuana use in people over 15 years of age in Europe: 10%. The most comparable figure in

America is in people over 12 years of age: 39.8%. In fact, proportionally, more Americans have used cocaine than Portuguese have used marijuana. Might decriminalization of marijuana in the U.S. lead to similar positive effects? Mark Kleiman, director of the drug policy analysis program at UCLA says, "I think we can learn that we should stop being reflexively opposed when someone else does decriminalize and should take seriously the possibility that anti-user enforcement isn't having much influence on our drug consumption."

In the article "The Drug Problem: Europe Tolerance vs. U.S. Criminalization," world-travel expert and author Rick Steves offers some compelling anecdotal evidence. Steves talked with locals, researched European drug policies and visited marijuana "coffee shops" in Amsterdam, getting a close look at the alternative to America's war on drugs. "While the Netherlands' policies are the most liberal," says Steves, "across Europe no one is locked away for discreetly smoking a joint. The priority is on reducing abuse of such hard drugs as heroin and cocaine. The only reference to marijuana I found among the pages of the European Union's drug policy was a reference to counseling for 'problem cannabis use.'"

Meanwhile, according to FBI statistics, in recent years about 40 per cent of the roughly 80,000 annual drug arrests in the U.S. were for marijuana, and the majority - 80 per cent - were for possession. Treating marijuana users the same as hard drug users is like treating parking ticket offenders like drunk drivers. It just doesn't make a lot of sense.

Comparisons between states in the U.S. that have decriminalized marijuana usage and those that haven't and between countries where marijuana possession has been decriminalized and the U.S. appear to confirm that decriminalization doesn't lead to increased marijuana usage and that it may even cause a decrease in use. But is the fact that decriminalizing marijuana possession doesn't lead to increased usage enough to warrant changing America's punitive marijuana laws? Perhaps not by itself.

However, consider the other effects if America decriminalized marijuana. The 64,000 drug arrests for marijuana possession in recent years would not have occurred. The millions of dollars and tremendous amount of police time spent on the arrest and prosecution of recreational marijuana users could have been much better spent on reducing the usage of hard drugs such as heroin and cocaine. The millions of taxpayer dollars wasted on incarcerating marijuana users could have been spent on much more important concerns. Our prisons would not be overcrowded with marijuana users, and the continual need to build more prisons would disappear.

It is clear that America's criminal drug law against marijuana usage doesn't work. Marijuana is used as much if not more in states where possession is a felony than in states where users receive a small fine. Despite its punitive marijuana law, marijuana usage in America is significantly higher than in European countries, where no one is arrested for possession. It is also clear that the tremendous amount of time and money spent on busting and prosecuting marijuana users could be put to much better use, and that America's huge prison population would diminish significantly, as would the great expense to incarcerate marijuana users.

If marijuana usage did in fact lead conclusively to harder drug use, that would be a concern in its decriminalization, but no credible study has ever proven marijuana to be a "gateway" drug to heroin, cocaine, or other dangerous drugs. Apparently, marijuana smokers are no more apt to use cocaine or heroin than beer drinkers, and anyone can see the ludicrousness of criminalizing beer drinking. There are some very good reasons for decriminalizing marijuana usage in America and little reason for maintaining the current unworkable law. If enough states lead the way in decriminalizing marijuana possession, the Federal government will eventually follow. That appears to be the only way that America will one day have a sensible nationwide law that doesn't treat recreational marijuana users like hard drug users.

Revision

Once you have completed your first draft, set it aside for awhile before beginning the revision process. When writers distance themselves from their writing for some time, they often see things more clearly, evaluate their writing more objectively, and better understand the changes they need to make to improve the draft. On rereading a draft, those awkward or wordy sentences often stand out, organizational flaws become more evident, needlessly repetitive ideas appear obvious, and a weak ending reveals itself. At the same time, writers can see more clearly what they have done well and where the strengths of the paper lie.

Revision Suggestions

Since your revision considerations do not vary greatly from essay to essay, most of the following suggestions serve as reminders of those basic elements that may need some attention. How you address them during revision - one element at a time, two or three similar elements together, or all elements simultaneously - depends on what approach works best for you.

1. **Read your entire draft once to get a sense of its strengths and weaknesses.** You may find some parts of your draft that clearly need more work and others that you are satisfied with. Keep in mind the areas of concern as you begin your revision.

2. **Check the effectiveness of your opening.** Do you introduce your topic in a way that will interest readers? Have you included your thesis statement or saved it for the end after you have presented your comparative evidence? What might you add or change to help readers see the importance of the topic or how it may affect them?

3. **Check to see whether you have provided explanations for any concepts or terms that readers may not understand.** Read through the draft as someone who is unfamiliar with the topic and determine whether you have explained everything necessary to help his understanding.

4. **Check your use of comparative evidence.** Is each comparison you make relevant and appropriate for the topic? Do readers know what you are trying to show with each comparison and how it supports your thesis? Have you used different comparisons to make different points? Have you included an analogy or two that might help readers understand or see the logic of your viewpoint? As you read your draft, can you think of other comparisons that might be effective?

5. **Check your use of other supportive evidence.** While the writing emphasis is on providing comparisons, do you include other supportive points for your thesis?

Evaluate other supportive evidence you have used besides comparisons, and make revisions that will strengthen the support, including adding new points.

6. **Check your paragraphing and organization.** Do you change paragraphs as you move to different comparisons or different supportive points? Are there any overly long paragraphs that need dividing or short paragraphs that could be combined or developed further? Are your comparisons paragraphed in the most effective order? Could any paragraph(s) be relocated to improve the overall organization?

7. **Check the wording of each sentence.** Revise wordy sentences by eliminating unnecessary or repetitive words, smooth out awkward sentences, replace questionable word choices, and clarifying vague sentences. In addition, check your use of *transitional wording* (*first, next, also, in addition, therefore, however, finally, meanwhile,* etc.) to tie paragraphs together and show relationships between thoughts.

8. **Check your source references.** If you included research material, did you provide source references for all material (According to Dr. Rutger Hallaway, A recent Mayo Clinic study found . . ., The article "Our Polluted Drinking Water" claimed . . .,)? Did you *paraphrase* - put into your own words - most research material and provide quotations and a source introduction for quoted statements?

9. **Evaluate the effectiveness of your conclusion.** What exactly are you trying to accomplish in your conclusion, and how well did you do it? Did you reinforce your thesis in some manner, summarize your main supportive points, or clarify your writing purpose? What do you want readers to bring away from your conclusion?

10. **Read your draft with your purpose in mind.** Evaluate each aspect of your draft in respect to how it furthers your writing purpose, and make any changes that will help accomplish that purpose.

Writing Activity 7.10

For revision practice, reread the first draft of "Decriminalizing Marijuana Usage" in Writing Activity 7.9. With a classmate or two, apply the revision considerations and come up with some specific suggestions for improving the paper.

Writing Activity 7.11

Since sentence-wording improvement is a common goal for most writers, sentence revision activities are provided in different lessons. Revise the following first draft sentences to eliminate wordiness, improve word choice, and smooth out awkward sentences. You may add, delete, replace, and move words and phrases around.

Example:

One of the problems associated with dropping classes is that a student may lose his or her financial aid standing if he or she drops below a certain number of units.

Revised:

One ~~of the~~ problems ~~associated~~ with dropping classes is that ~~a~~ students may lose ~~his~~ **their** financial aid ~~standing~~ if ~~he~~ **they** ~~drops~~ below a certain number of units.

1. Looking at what has happened in states and countries that don't put people in jail for using marijuana gives us some indication of what the impact would be in the U.S. if marijuana were decriminalized.

2. Enough countries in different parts of the world have decriminalized marijuana usage to give a good picture to us of the impact of decriminalization.

3. In 1997, the Connecticut Law Revision Commission examined states that had decriminalized cannabis and found any increase in cannabis usage was *less* than the increase in states that had not decriminalized cannabis, and that the largest proportionate increase of marijuana use occurred in those states with the most severe penalties.

4. It is also clear that the tremendous amount of time and money spent on busting and prosecuting marijuana users could be put to much better use, and that America's huge prison population would diminish significantly, as would the great expense to incarcerate marijuana users.

5. The millions of dollars and tremendous amount of police time spent on the arrest and prosecution of recreational marijuana users could have been much better spent on reducing the usage of hard drugs such as heroin and cocaine.

Writing Activity 7.12

Keeping the revision suggestions in mind, revise your first draft, making any changes you feel would improve the paper and help accomplish your writing purpose.

Writing Activity 7.13

Exchange drafts with a classmate(s) and provide any feedback that would help the writer improve her draft. From your classmate's feedback, make any additional revisions that you feel would improve your paper.

Editing

By this time in the course, your proofreading process is probably quite proficient, resulting in detecting and correcting most errors. You know what to look for regarding your personal error tendencies as well as the more common problem areas such as run-on and comma splice sentences, subject-verb agreement, pronoun-antecedent agreement, and comma usage. You have no doubt developed a proofreading process that works well for weeding out errors, and you also are probably making fewer errors as you have worked on eliminating your error tendencies.

As your proofreading competency grows, new editing considerations are added in each lesson. In this lesson, you work with three punctuation marks - the semi-colon, colon, and dash - that you may not currently use much in your writing. However, as you become more familiar with their functions, you may find greater use for them. (Notice the inclusion of dashes (-) in the second sentence of this paragraph to set off the three new punctuation marks.)

Semi-Colons, Colons, and Dashes

Semi-colons, colons, and dashes all have specific purposes that help writers communicate more effectively with readers. They set off and highlight certain words in sentences and show relationships between thoughts. Many writers use semi-colons, colons, and dashes regularly in their writing to good effect. In this lesson, you will learn more about their functions, practice using them in sentences, and see how you might incorporate them in your current essay.

The following rules and suggestions will help you use these punctuation marks correctly in your writing:

1. **A semi-colon (;) is most commonly used to connect two complete sentences that are related in meaning.** When you want to tie the ideas in two sentences together rather than separate them with a period (.), you can use a semi-colon:

   Flocks of migrating geese often fly in a "V" formation; this aerodynamic formation reduces air resistance and helps the birds fly more effortlessly.

2. **Semi-colons are frequently used when the second sentence begins with a transition such as "therefore" or "however:"**

   Today's cars burn less oil than their predecessors; *however*, it is still wise to get a new car serviced at least every 5,000 miles.

3. **Semi-colons can also be used in place of commas in series of three or more longer groups of words to separate them more distinctly:**

The glider that took off from Kettleman City stalled in the air when it hit a dead spot; rose on a current of warm air moving upward; caught a westward-moving current heading towards Paso Robles; and continued on a smooth flight for the next thirty miles.

4. **A colon (:) is most commonly used towards the end of a sentence to set off and emphasize a particular idea or a group of related elements:**

There is one thing that distinguishes successful entrepreneurs from others: persistence.

Anyone planning to scale Rock Mountain needs the following: rock-climbing experience, a trusted climbing companion, courage, and the proper equipment.

3. **A dash (-) functions similarly to a colon but is most frequently used in *pairs* to set off an idea or a group of elements *within* the sentence:**

Grady's most noticeable shortcoming - his lackadaisical attitude - was responsible for his difficulty finding employment.

I don't like shopping on Black Friday - the big crowds, long lines, and discourteous people - and prefer waiting until the weekend.

Writing Activity 7.14

Insert semi-colons (;) , colons (:) , and dashes (-) in the following paragraphs where they are needed.

Example:

Luong enjoys attending college basketball games on campus. He usually goes with a group of friends; they stand the entire time at their seats behind the basket. They are there primarily for one reason: to shake up the opposing players. They use a variety of methods - huge posters of bikini-clad women, bright red body paint, noise makers, taunting chants - to distract the visiting team. They have a lot of fun, but since the local team seldom wins, their antics apparently have little effect.

Poverty in America

A recent government study concluded that nearly half of all Americans live at or below the poverty line, meaning that their annual income is $20,000 or less. This is an astonishing and troubling finding the U.S., after all, is known as the richest country in the world. How could half of its citizens live in poverty?

The reasons for the current situation the recession, the outsourcing of millions of good jobs, the shrinking middle class, the huge number of minimum wage jobs in our "service" economy are fairly obvious. However, there is one thing that doesn't appear to be evident the solution. The job losses through outsourcing may be permanent in fact, the outsourcing of jobs could get even worse. The business trend towards huge chain discount stores and fast food franchises, which are responsible for millions of minimum wage jobs, isn't going to change. There are signs that the recession is easing such as reduced unemployment, improved house sales, and rising stock market prices however, most of the new employment is in lower-end jobs.

   Another factor contributes significantly to the current situation political gridlock. Republicans and Democrats can agree on nothing to help turn around the economy and create better-paying jobs. Their antithetical positions on many issues tax reform, government investment, entitlement programs, stimulating the economy don't bode well for compromise or action. Many Americans have given up on the government doing anything to help rebuild the middle class and get people out of poverty.

Writing Activity 7.15

For practice, write nine original sentences: three with semi-colons, three with colons, and three with dashes.

Examples:

The unseasonably cool May weather should end by Wednesday; the latest report has temperatures back in the mid-80's.

Students need to bring the following items to the geometry test on Tuesday: a protractor, a #2 pencil, and some graph paper.

The advantages of leasing a car - a small down payment, lower monthly payments, driving a new car - outweigh the disadvantages for many drivers.

Writing Activity 7.16

Read your draft to see whether you might revise some sentences to incorporate semi-colons, colons, or dashes effectively. If you have already used some semi-colons, colons, or dashes in your draft, check to make sure you have used them correctly, and make any necessary corrections.

Writing Activity 7.17

For proofreading practice, correct any errors in the following paragraph involving run-on or comma splice sentences, fragments, subject-verb agreement, pronoun-antecedent agreement, comma usage, frequently confused words (there/their/they're, know/no, to/too/two, effect/affect), or apostrophes in possessions or contractions.

Campus Construction

Our college campus seems like one large construction site, the sound of hammers, power saws, and building cranes fill the air from morning until dark. There is fences of yellow tape everywhere to cordon off most construction areas and a cyclone fence has been erected around the new high-rise dormitory which has risen half way to its eight-story height. The old rows of dormitory barracks are being torn down. Because they will no longer be needed. The sixty-year old 50-meter swimming pool which was built when the campus was still a military base has been filled in, and will be paved over for parking. A new pool currently being built at the southeast corner of campus. With construction on a new performing arts building beginning next month there appear to be no end to the building projects or the noise. The states commitment to renovating older college campuses is finally being realized so todays students are going to have get used to living in construction zones.

Writing Activity 7.18

Proofread your draft for errors, focusing on the types of errors you most frequently make as well as the common problem areas: run-ons and comma splices, comma usage, subject-verb agreement, pronoun-antecedent agreement, fragments, apostrophes in possessive and contractions, and frequently confused words (their/there/they're, to/too/two, your/you're, know/no, affect/effect, then/than, its/it's). After you have made your corrections, exchange drafts with a classmate and proofread each other's paper. Make additional corrections, if necessary, and note the kinds of errors you had overlooked.

Communicating with Readers

When your essay is in final-draft form, find the best way to share it with its intended audience or representatives, whether they be college students, the board of trustees, the city council, the state legislature, high school students, or the general public. Your instructor may have some ideas for reaching your particular audience.

Lesson Eight: Using Factual Support

Objective: To write a thesis-based essay with an emphasis on providing factual support.

Audience: Writer's choice

Purpose: Writer's choice

In the classic television crime show "Dragnet," when Sergeant Joe Friday would interview a female witness to a crime, he would always say, "Just the facts, ma'am." Friday would follow a trail of facts that helped him "get his guy" every time, courtesy of television scripting. Writers likewise often provide a "trail of facts" to lead readers to an inevitable conclusion. Factual evidence is one of the strongest types of evidence that writers use to support their viewpoints.

In a recent television debate on a cable news show, a retired general said that a Senate proposal to reduce the military budget would "gut our military strength and make us vulnerable to attack." The show's host said, "Wait a minute. Let's look at the facts. The Senate proposal would reduce military spending by 1.5% of the current budget, close three military bases world-wide out of the 737 U.S. bases, and adjust the current military pension to reduce costs. There are no cuts in the size of our military force, our nuclear arms, or our conventional weaponry. Our military would not be weakened at all." The general could not dispute the host's facts, and the ludicrousness of his initial contention was exposed. The host had wisely heeded the wisdom, "When you go into a battle of words, arm yourself with the best facts."

For most readers, factual evidence carries significant weight because it gets at the truth. For example, someone can say, "Pre-school education greatly enhances a child's chances for educational success." Someone else can say, "Pre-school education plays little role in a child's educational success." Which statement, if either, is correct? Do the facts show that children with pre-school education score better on standardized tests, have a lower drop-out rate, or have a lower absence rate than children without a pre-school education? Whatever the truth is regarding the impact of pre-school on children, a factual analysis is the best way of finding it.

In this lesson, you will write a thesis-based essay with the emphasis on providing factual support. What you learn will be of value for much of the writing that you do, for supporting any viewpoints you may have, for getting at the "truth' of a particular issue, or for evaluating the writing of others. While there are always biased readers who don't want to be "bothered" by the facts, the majority of readers prefer basing their opinions on what is known to be true. These are the readers that you will address in your upcoming essay.

Providing Factual Support

Factual evidence can provide a writer with the strongest support for her thesis. Facts are difficult to dispute and can expose the weakness of opinions based on emotions, misconceptions, or bias. For example, opponents of gun control adamantly contend that people who own guns are safer in their homes. Facts show, however, that family members are far more likely to shoot another member by mistake than an intruder. Death penalty proponents claim that the death penalty serves as a deterrent against murder. Facts show, however, that the imposition of the death penalty does not reduce the murder rate and that there is no correlation between the rise and fall of murder rates and the death penalty. While such factual evidence may not sway people who adamantly oppose gun control or who believe in "an eye for an eye" justice, it can influence readers who consider such issues with some degree of objectivity.

Of course, that a writer presents something as a fact doesn't necessarily make it so, and sometimes writers try to pass off opinions as if they were facts. To use factual support most effectively in your writing, you need to convince readers that your facts are both valid and relevant to your thesis. To that end, consider the following suggestions:

1. **Be aware of the difference between stating opinions and providing facts.** For example, a writer believes that the college showing movies on Friday nights at the student union is a good idea, her *opinion* on the topic. She provides *factual evidence* to support her opinion: the large number of students who attend the Friday-night movies, the positive results of a student survey on whether the college should show Friday-night movies, and the reduced number of on-campus disturbances on Fridays when movies are shown. A writer's thesis often reveals her opinion on a topic, which she supports with factual evidence.

2. **Be as certain as possible that the facts you provide are valid.** For example, if a team of leading oceanographers found that over 50% of the Great Barrier Reef has been irreparably damaged by pollution, most readers would accept the findings as fact. If you find out from the college admissions' office that over 40% of incoming freshmen drop out of school during their first year, most readers would trust that figure. If a Honda dealership pamphlet claims that the Honda Civic gets the best gas mileage of any compact car on the road, you might question the objectivity of the claim.

3. **Provide evidence for any "alleged" fact that you present.** For example, if you allege that students who "cram" before an exam do better than students who study regularly for a week, many readers would doubt the claim. If you cite a university cognitive-learning experiment where the test group of students who crammed for an exam performed significantly better on the exam than the test group who studied regularly for a week, you have provided evidence supporting your factual claim which may convince readers. When you present a fact that readers might question, i.e. that isn't universally accepted as fact, provide the best evidence

available to verify the fact.

4. **Provide the strongest factual evidence to support your thesis.** For example, let's say that you are against the college's proposal to "arm" the school's security officers. What facts might you use to support your opinion? You might seek out factual answers to the following questions: How many violent crimes, if any, were committed on campus in the last year? How many comparable colleges in the state have "armed" security officers? What would a student survey on the advisability of arming security officers indicate? What is the crime rate at comparable colleges with armed security officers and those with unarmed officers?

5. **Don't "cherry pick" your facts.** Don't use facts that support your thesis and ignore others that don't, providing an inaccurate picture for readers. For example, if you found from number 4. that colleges with armed officers have a lower on-campus crime rate than those that don't, you shouldn't ignore the fact. It may cause you to reexamine your viewpoint, or you may present the fact and explain to readers why you still are against arming security officers.

6. **Determine the best way to find the facts for a particular topic.** Depending on the topic, you might get factual information from your own first-hand knowledge, from on-campus sources, from city officials, from local experts, from online or periodical articles, or from studies done on the topic. Use sources that will provide the most credible factual information for a particular topic.

Writing Activity 8.1

For three or four of the following topic questions, list four or five types of factual information that would help you answer the question in an essay.

Examples:

Topic: Is teenage pregnancy a serious problem?

Facts: Find out the percentage of teen girls who become pregnant in high school.
              Find out the percentage of pregnant girls who don't finish high school.
              Find out the percentage of girls who don't attend college after
              having babies.
              Find out the percentage of teenage mothers living in poverty.

Topic: Is urban air pollution a serious health problem for children?

Facts: Find out the pollution level in various major cities.
              Compare the incidence of asthma and other respiratory ailments in
              children in highly polluted cities compared to other areas of country.

Find out whether there is a definite correlation between pollution and respiratory ailments in children.
Find out how frequently children can't play outside at school on "bad air days" in polluted cities compared to ten years ago.
Find out other health problems in children that high levels of pollution contribute to.

1. Topic: Do private schools do a good job of educating students?

    Facts:

2. Topic: Do community college transfer students do well in four-year colleges?

    Facts:

3. Topic: Are adults who graduate from college better off financially than those who don't?

    Facts:

4. Topic: Is the quality of health care better in the U.S. than in other industrialized countries?

    Facts:

5. Topic: What were the results of the Federal government's "bailout" of American automobile manufacturers at the beginning of the recession?

    Facts:

6. Topic: For single people, is owning a pet good for your health?

    Facts:

7. Topic: Who is the best NFL quarterback of all time?

    Facts:

Writing Activity 8.2

Decide which of the following topics could best be developed through factual evidence, which could not, and why.

1.   Topic: Summer is typically the highest crime season of the year.

2.   Topic: Sweden is the most socialistic government in Europe.

3.   Topic: Is there a God?

4.   Topic: Football is a better spectator sport than baseball.

5.   Topic: Legalized gambling has been an economic boon for some states.

6.   Topic: With all of the nuclear weapons in the world, an eventual nuclear war is inevitable.

Writing Assignment

In this lesson, you will write an essay on a topic of your choice and support your thesis primarily with factual evidence. You may have to research your topic to learn more about it, to gather some facts on the issue, and to decide on a thesis for your essay.
    To help you decide what to write about, consider these suggestions:

1. **For your topic, select an issue that interests you and that may interest a particular reading audience.** Your topic may come from any field - education, health, the environment, music, fashion, law enforcement, sports, employment, etc. - and may be local, state-wide, national, or international in scope.

2. **Select a topic that you can find factual information on.** When considering a particular topic, think about the kinds of factual information that might be available. For example, you could probably find factual evidence for topics such as "The negative effects of dropping out of high school," "The value of parental support in a child's education success," or "The impact of gang violence on inner-city youth." Even an ethical issue such as "Should people be able to download music for free off the Internet?" could include factual elements: the impact of free downloading on CD sales, the Federal law covering the legal downloading of music, the lawsuits that the music industry has brought against free downloading sites, and the online sites where people can legally download music for a reasonable price.

3. **Consider topics that you are knowledgeable about or have some experience with.** Writers themselves can be a source of factual information. For example, a writer who worked at a Montessori school witnessed time and again the great enthusiasm with which young students performed "hands on" learning tasks. She presented this factual information, along with evidence from other sources, to support her thesis, "For educating young children, 'hands on' learning experiences are the best."

While you shouldn't *rely* on factual evidence gleaned from personal experience, you can use it to provide "real life" examples that may have an impact on readers. For example, a writer who presented a psychological study on the traumatic effects on children living in gang "war zones" revealed his own childhood experiences to provide a "real life" example that helped validate the study.

Writing Activity 8.3

Keeping the topic-selection suggestions in mind, decide on a writing topic for your essay. Consider a range of issues and choose one that interests you, that may interest some group of readers, and that you can find factual information on.

Sample Topic: Global Warming

Preparation

Preparing for the first draft of your essay will undoubtedly include some research, whether it be talking with college officials, local police, or experts on your topic, searching the Internet, or visiting your college library. Your goal is to find the most credible factual information on the topic, which will ultimately provide the best support for your thesis. While you may already have a viewpoint on your topic, you can see how well it "squares" with the facts as you do your research.

Researching Your Topic

To research your topic most efficiently and effectively, consider the following suggestions:

1. **Know the types of factual information you are looking for, and focus your search on that information.** For example, if your topic were "The Effects of Obesity on Children," your factual search might focus on health issues associated with obesity, social adjustment issues, self-esteem issues, and later-life issues. If your topic were, "The Effects of Divorce on Children," your factual search might focus on physical effects, psychological effects, behavioral effects, attitudinal effects, and later-life effects. As you research, also be open to other types of factual information that you hadn't considered.

2. **Whenever possible, find out *how* a particular fact was arrived at.** For example, a leading sport's medicine physician stated that steroid use causes abnormal outbursts of rage among high school athletes. He reached this factual conclusion by observing the behavior of a large number of athletes, through studies comparing the behavior of steroid users to non-users, and through the self-reporting of steroid users who

experienced the abnormal rage.

An article in *Education Digest* contended that college students who choose a major their freshman year graduate on average earlier than students who choose a major later. The article cited a study that tracked full-time students in ten colleges, half who declared majors their freshmen year and half who didn't, and compared their dates of graduation. By providing the evidence that *led* to the factual conclusion, you help substantiate the claim for readers.

3. **Use the most credible sources available for your factual information.**   Do the facts come from experts in the field? Do they come from objective sources that hold no biases? Do they come from reputable publications, organizations, or institutions? In general, the more believable the source, the more believable the fact.

4. **As you research, look for "corroborating" factual evidence.**   If you find the same fact repeated by different credible sources, the validity of the fact is strengthened. For example, if several medical experts agree that childhood obesity is a cause of Type 2 diabetes in children, you can feel comfortable presenting their finding as fact.

5. **Don't rely on one or two sources for your factual information.** When you only use one or two sources for your information, you may leave readers with the impression that you didn't do much research, that you relied too heavily on a source, or that you only used sources that supported your thesis. Using different sources reveals the breadth of your research and shows that your thesis is based on a thorough investigation of the topic.

Writing Activity 8.4

Research your topic to learn more about it and to gather factual information for your essay. Take notes on any information that you might use, and include the source for each piece of information to reference in your essay.

When you complete your research, separate the different facts you have on the topic, evaluate their relevance and importance, and consider how you might use them in your upcoming essay.

Thesis

As you know, your thesis for an essay expresses your viewpoint on the topic. Your essay is written in support of your thesis, explaining to readers *why* you believe as you do. The thesis provides direction for the writer and a viewpoint on the topic for readers to consider and evaluate.

As you decide on your thesis for the upcoming essay, consider these suggestions:

1. **Decide on a thesis that clearly reflects your viewpoint on the topic.** If you believe strongly in your thesis, you will write with a conviction and enthusiasm that won't be lost on readers.

2. **Decide on a thesis that the facts support.** Since the writing emphasis in this lesson is on providing factual support for your thesis, make sure that your thesis is supported by the facts that you present. Your factual findings should lead you to your thesis.

3. **Your thesis may be an opinion or a factual statement.** For example, the thesis statement, "Deer hunting should be restricted in the Western Rockies" is an opinion that a writer might support with factual evidence: the dwindling deer population in the area, the large number of out-of-state hunters who flood the area, the rash of hunting accidents that have occurred.

   The thesis statement, "Child abuse affects many children their entire lives" is an alleged fact - a claim the writer is making - that she might support with factual evidence: the frequency with which abused children become abusers themselves, the low self-esteem that characterizes many abused children, the difficulty of abused children to form relationships as adults, the rate of alcoholism among adults who were abused as children. Whether your thesis is an opinion or an alleged fact, you can use factual evidence to support it.

Writing Activity 8.5

Generate a thesis statement for your essay based on your factual findings.

Sample thesis statement:

Topic: Global warming

Thesis: The negative effects of man-made global warming are revealing themselves in a variety of ways.

Audience and Purpose

Your reading audience and writing purpose are important considerations when writing your essay. You want people to read your essay who may have an interest in your topic, who may be affected by it, or who may influence its future direction. Your purpose in writing to this audience depends on both the audience and the topic. For example, if you are writing to people who support your viewpoint that the college should not require students to pay an activity fee, your purpose may be to muster their support against it. If you are writing to people who have the power to change the requirement, your purpose may be to get them to make the fee optional. How you write your essay and what you include in it are influenced by both your audience and purpose.

To decide on the best audience and purpose for your upcoming essay, consider these suggestions:

1. **Whom would you most like to reach with this essay?** People who have a similar interest to yourself? People who are most affected by the issue? People who can influence an outcome regarding the issue? People who disagree with your thesis? People who would value factual evidence and be persuaded by it?

2. **What is your purpose in writing to this audience?** Are you interested in getting the "facts" out to people who may have misconceptions on the issue, in alerting people who are more affected by the topic than they realize, in getting people to act on the issue who may influence its future, or in shedding light on an issue that doesn't get enough attention? Given the audience you decide on, what do you hope to accomplish?

Writing Activity 8.6

Decide on a potential reading audience and purpose for your upcoming essay.

Sample audience and purpose:

Topic: Global Warming

Audience: general public

Purpose: I want people to understand that made-made global warming is a reality, that it has serious consequences, and that we all need to support policies and do what we can individually to reduce its causes.

Drafting

Now that you have selected your topic, decided on a thesis, gathered some supportive facts, and decided on your reading audience and purpose, you are ready to write the first draft of your essay. After having written several essays, you have probably become more comfortable and confident with the drafting process, and your ability to write engaging openings, strong supportive paragraphs, and effective conclusions has undoubtedly grown. As with any skill that you develop, the more essay writing that you do, the more proficient and effective you become.

Organizing Your Facts

Before you begin your draft, consider how you might organize your facts to have the greatest impact on readers. What are you trying to show with each fact, and how might it relate to other facts you are using? What might be the most logical or effective order to present your factual evidence?

For example, a writer whose thesis was, "The city needs to make the apartment area west of campus safe for students" had gathered the following facts:

Drug trafficking occurs every weekend. (Personal observation and observation of other students)
Police have successfully "cleaned up" other areas of city with similar problems. (Newspaper reports)
Several apartment break-ins occurred in the last two months. (Based on police reports)
Students are afraid to walk alone at night. (Based on student survey)
Three shootings, one resulting in a student's death, occurred this semester. (Confirmed by police and newspaper reports)
Because of the dangers, the student turn-over rate in the apartments is high. (Confirmed by landlords and personal observation)
Drugs and violence go hand-in-hand in the area. (Police statistics showing the highest incidence of violence occurring in drug-trafficking neighborhoods)

The writer decided to present her facts in the following order:

> I'll start with the shootings and murder since those are the most frightening examples of what's happening in the area. Then I'll present the two drug-trafficking facts to show the tie-in between the drugs and violence. Then I'll present the apartment break-ins to show another serious problem. Then I'll show the effects on students: the high turn-over rate in the apartments and students being afraid to walk alone at night. Finally, I'll show how police have cleaned up other areas of the city, meaning they could do the same for this area.

As the writer did for the apartment safety essay, consider the best way to present your facts based on what you are trying to show with each fact and how they may be related.

Drafting Suggestions

As you write the first draft of your essay, consider the following suggestions:

1. **In the opening, introduce your topic in a way that engages your readers' interest.** Give them a reason for reading further. You can either present your thesis statement at or near the end of your opening (as the writer did in the "Man-made Global Warming" draft in Writing Activity 8.7) or save your thesis for the conclusion after you have presented the factual evidence that leads to it.

2. **If necessary, follow your opening with any definitions or explanations that will help readers understand your topic.** For example, in her second paragraph, the writer of the "Man-made Global Warming" draft defined the term "man-made global warming" and explained how it occurs.

3. **Present your factual evidence in the middle paragraphs to support your thesis.** Present each fact in a separate paragraph and make clear to readers what you are trying to show with that fact. Present your facts in the most logical, effective order and provide any available evidence to validate each fact. You may also supplement your factual evidence with any logical or anecdotal evidence to support your thesis.

4. **Paraphrase - put into your own words - most of your source material, and use direct quotes (" ") to capture the more vivid or emphatic statements.** Most of the source material should read like your own writing, distinguished from it by a source reference for each "borrowed" piece of information.

5. **Provide the source for each researched fact to show readers where it came from, to enhance its credibility, and to distinguish source material from your own ideas.** (See how the writer introduces her sources in the "Man-made Global Warming" draft.)

6. **Conclude your draft by reinforcing your thesis in some manner, by including something "new" for readers, and by helping to accomplish your writing purpose.** Decide what you want readers to take from your ending.

7. **Keep your audience and purpose in mind as you write: the readers you want to reach and your reason for writing to them.**

Writing Activity 8.7

Read the first draft of "Man-made Global Warming," noting its opening, including the thesis statement, its explanatory second paragraph, its presentation of facts in the middle paragraphs, its introduction of sources for the researched information, its use of quotations, and its conclusion, which emphasizes the writer's purpose for readers. Then write the first draft of your essay.

Sample First Draft

Man-made Global Warming

(Audience: general public)

The existence of man-created climate change is an established fact within the scientific community. However, some politicians and corporate oil spokesmen continue to portray such climate change as a debatable issue of inconclusive findings. Nothing, it seems, could be further from the truth, and the negative effects of an ever-warming environment are revealing themselves in a variety of ways.

Man-made global warming is an average increase in temperatures near the Earth's surface and in the lowest layer of the atmosphere caused by man's activities, chiefly the burning of fossil fuels that release CO_2 emissions into the atmosphere. Such increases in temperatures in our Earth's atmosphere can also contribute to changes in global climate patterns, according to the U.S. Environmental Protection Agency.

When NASA (National Aeronautics and Space Administration), the IPCC (Intergovernmental Panel on Climate Change), and the Geological Society of America all agree unequivocally that the earth's atmosphere is warming due to man-created carbon dioxide emissions, there should be few doubters. Add to this the fact that 191 countries have signed the Kyoto Protocol, an international agreement which aims at substantially reducing greenhouse gas emissions in industrialized countries to combat global warming. Under former President George Bush, the United States was the only industrialized nation in the world that refused to sign the protocol.

According to the IPCC, "Scientific evidence for the warming of the climate system is unequivocal. The current warming trend is of particular significance because most of it is very likely human-induced and proceeding at a rate that is unprecedented in the past 1,300 years." NASA provides the following evidence of rapid world-wide climate change:

- Sea level rise: Global sea levels rose about 6.7 inches in the last century. The rate of the last decade, however, is nearly double that of the last century, meaning the sea level rose twice as much in the last 10 years than it did in the last 100 years.

- Global temperature rise: The 20 warmest years in history have occurred since 1981, and the 10 warmest years ever have occurred within the last 12 years.

- Shrinking ice formations. Greenland and Antarctic ice sheets have decreased dramatically in the 2000's, the extent and thickness of Arctic sea ice has declined rapidly, and glaciers are retreating almost everywhere around the world.

- The number of record high temperatures in the U.S. has been increasing while the number of record low temperatures has been decreasing since 1950. The U.S. has also witnessed increasing numbers of intense rainfall events.

- Ocean acidification. Since the beginning of the Industrial Revolution, the acidity of surface ocean waters has increased by 30%. The increase is the result of humans emitting more carbon dioxide into the atmosphere and more being absorbed into the oceans. The amount of carbon dioxide absorbed by the upper layer of the oceans is increasing by about 2 billion tons per year.

Clearly, the evidence is overwhelming that the warming of the earth's atmosphere is causing unprecedented climatological and surface changes across the earth, but are human-created carbon dioxide emissions definitely the culprit? Without doubt. A NASA graph showing amounts of carbon dioxide in the atmosphere at different historical times provides dramatic evidence. For 650,000 years, atmospheric carbon dioxide never exceeded 300 parts per million. Then from 1950 on, the graph line goes up dramatically, showing a current-day level of 380 parts per million. Due to modern-day world-wide industrialization, the atmospheric carbon dioxide level has increased more in the last 60 years than it did in the previous 650,000 years!

Regarding man's role in atmospheric warming, the Geological Society of America released this clear statement: "The Geological Society of America (GSA) concurs with assessments by the National Academies of Science (2005), the National Research Council (2006), and the Intergovernmental Panel on Climate Change (IPCC, 2007) that global climate has warmed and that human activities (mainly greenhouse-gas emissions) account for most of the warming since the middle 1900s." The Geological Society also debunks the notion that the warming of the atmosphere and its earthly effects could be caused by natural changes: "Given the knowledge gained from paleoclimatic studies, long-term causes of the current warming trend can be eliminated. Changes in Earth's tectonism and its orbit are far too slow to have played a significant role in a rapidly changing 150-year trend."

According to the Geological Society, greenhouse gases, mainly carbon dioxide, and solar fluctuations must account for the unprecedented atmospheric warming. Since a 2007 IPCC report concluded that changes in solar irradiance account for less than 10% of the warming of the last 150 years, man-created greenhouse gases remain as the major explanation. The greater the level of greenhouse gases in the atmosphere, the more of the sun's infrared radiation is trapped and held, and the higher the temperatures on earth rise. The correlation between the dramatic increase in carbon dioxide levels in the atmosphere in the last 60 years and the world-wide warming trend is undeniable.

That the earth's atmosphere is warming and that man is responsible are indisputable. The question remains, "Why should you and I care?" According to the Geological Society, the projected changes involve risk to humans and other species which should concern us all:

- Continued shrinking of Arctic sea ice with effects on native cultures and ice-dependent plants and animals.

- Less snow accumulation and earlier melt in mountains, with reductions in spring and summer runoff for agricultural and municipal water use.

- Increased evaporation from farmland soils and greater stress on crops.

- Greater soil erosion due to increases in heavy summer rainfall.

- Longer fire seasons and increases in fire frequency.

- Severe insect outbreaks in vulnerable forests.

- Fundamental changes in the composition and biodiversity of many terrestrial and marine ecosystems.

- Melting of Greenland and West Antarctic ice along with thermal expansion of seawater and melting of mountain glaciers and small ice caps, causing substantial future sea-level rise along densely populated coastal regions, inundating farmland and dislocating large populations.

- Carbon-climate model simulations indicating that 10–20% of the man-emitted CO_2 could stay in the atmosphere for thousands of years, extending the duration of fossil-fuel warming and its effects on humans and other species.

Clearly, we are doing our planet, ourselves, and all life and plant forms no good by creating an ever-warmer atmosphere. Why, you may ask, would anyone oppose measures to reduce greenhouse gas emissions and reverse the warming effects? That only one geological organization - the American Association of Petroleum Geologists - disputes the existence of man-made global warming provides the answer.

The rich, powerful oil industry wants to prevent anything from occurring that would reduce their profits and compel Americans to pump less gasoline, a major contributor to carbon dioxide emissions. Some major industrial corporations also line up against reducing greenhouse gases because they want no emission control restrictions on their factories. Politicians who owe their careers to oil-industry connections spread the misconception that man-made global warming has not been conclusively proven.

In short, only those who feel they have something to lose try to cast doubts about man-made global warming and stymy governmental attempts to reduce emissions. But what can the average citizen do to make sure that greed doesn't win out over the health of our planet and the devastating impacts of global warming? First, we can support all initiatives and legislation aimed at reducing greenhouse gases in a responsible manner. Second, we can make sure to vote only for political candidates who believe in man-made global warming and want to reduce it. Third, we can do our individual parts to emit less carbon dioxide into the environment by driving electric and hybrid autos which burn significantly less gasoline, by walking and riding bicycles, and by taking public transportation. We can help win the "war" against global warming.

Revision

While the specific revisions that you make in a draft are unique to that essay, most of *types* of revisions that you make vary little from one draft to another: adding a new thought, improving your opening, changing the wording of a sentence, dividing an overly long paragraph, adding an omitted source reference, moving some information to a better location, or beefing up a weakly developed paragraph. After having revised several drafts in previous lessons, you have probably made most of the types of revisions common to writers. Your growing familiarity with the revision process and how best to improve each individual draft has undoubtedly led to an increasingly efficient and productive process.

Sentence Variety

Writers sometimes get into the habit of relying on similarly structured sentences and a few reliable joining words. Such structural and wording limitations can become monotonous for readers and make it difficult for writers to express more complex ideas and relationships.   For example, read the following paragraphs, which have little variation in sentence structures and wording.

We tend to equate heart problems with being overweight, but being thin is not a guarantee of a healthy respiratory system. There are the shocking examples of thin, physically fit joggers who drop dead of a heart attack while running. There are the thin, healthy-appearing people who are rushed into emergency and onto the operating table for quadruple by-pass surgery. There are the thin individuals who are on Lipitor to drive down excessively high blood pressure, a major culprit in strokes.

Heredity and diet play a role in everyone's lives, including the thin. You may have a history of heart problems in your family, and cholesterol may be clogging up your arteries. You may not exercise, eat too much salt, or drink too much alcohol, and you may develop high blood pressure no matter your body type. Your diet may consist of fatty foods and lots of carbohydrates, and your "bad" cholesterol count can skyrocket whether you are thin or obese. Being thin certainly reduces your chances of contracting a number of diseases, but it is not a "free pass" to having a healthy heart. Eating well and exercising regularly are still important, and regular heart exams and stress tests are a must for anyone with hereditary family heart problems.

As you can see, the sentence structures consist mainly of "There are" beginnings and *compound sentences* joined by "but" or "and," and some of the same words - e.g. "thin" and "may" - are repeated to distraction. Now read the same paragraphs revised to provide some sentence and wording variety:

While we tend to equate heart problems with being overweight, being thin is not a guarantee of a healthy respiratory system. There are the shocking examples of trim, physically fit joggers who drop dead of a heart attack while running. You also hear of slender, healthy-appearing people who are rushed into emergency and onto the operating table for quadruple by-pass surgery. In addition, it is not uncommon for trim individuals to be on Lipitor to drive down excessively high blood pressure, a major culprit in strokes.

Heredity and diet play a role in everyone's lives, including the thin. If you have a history of heart problems in your family, cholesterol may be clogging up your arteries. People who don't exercise, eat too much salt, or drink too much alcohol may develop high blood pressure no matter their body type. When your diet consists of fatty foods and lots of carbohydrates, your "bad" cholesterol count can skyrocket whether you are thin or obese. While being thin certainly reduces your chances of contracting a number of diseases, it is not a "free pass" to having a healthy heart. Eating well and exercising regularly are still important, and regular heart exams and stress tests are a must for anyone with hereditary family heart problems.

The revised sentences contain more sentence and wording variety and are more interesting to read. When the sentences in a paragraph are adequately varied in structure and wording, readers aren't even aware of the structures and concentrate on the content. When the sentences are monotonously similar, the structures and wording can become a distraction to readers.

To vary your sentence structures and wording effectively in your writing, consider these suggestions:

1. **Don't over-rely on simple and compound sentence structures.** Writers who have problems with sentence "sameness" tend to rely on *simple sentences* - those containing a single subject and verb - and *compound sentences* - those containing two *independent clauses* (complete sentences) joined most frequently by "and" or "but." Try to avoid writing strings of short, simple sentences or compound sentences joined by "and" or "but."

2. **Use complex sentences to show a range of relationships among thoughts.** *Complex sentences* contain an *independent clause* and a *dependent clause* beginning with a *subordinate conjunction* such as *while, when, as, if, before, because, unless, whether* or *until*. Writers find them useful for connecting ideas in a variety of ways: time associations (*when, before, after*) , cause/effect (*because, since*), conditional situations (*if, unless, until*), and contrasting situations (*although, whether*).

3. **Vary your sentence beginnings.** Writers have a variety of options for opening sentences:

    Prepositional phrases*:*
    During the commercial break, I fed the dog.

Subordinate clauses:
Before you decide whether to attend the seminar, check on the cost.

Infinitives:
To run in Saturday's half-marathon, you need to check in at 8:00 a.m.

Participial phrases:
Working on her manuscript late at night, Samantha finally gave in to fatigue.
Considered the best chess player on the team, Madison always drew the opposing
college's best player.

Adverbs:
Determinedly, Felicia scaled the granite face of Half Dome.
Unfortunately, the last bus to Tewksbury left an hour ago.

Transitions:
However, test scores are but one indication of a student's ability.
Despite the evidence, the defendant was cleared of all charges.
As you can see, there are many ways to cook asparagus.

4.   **Consider the variety of "joining words" at your disposal**. For example, you
have coordinate conjunctions (*and, but, or, so, for, yet*), subordinate conjunctions
(*before, after, while, meanwhile, if, unless, until, because, since, when, whether*)
relative pronouns (*who, whose, which, that*), and transitions (*however, nevertheless,
therefore, consequently*). All of these words can help you express your thoughts
and vary your sentence structures and wording.

Writing Activity 8.8

Revise the following paragraph to improve its sentence variety. You may move words
and phrases around, add words, replace words, insert transitions, and combine
sentences with joining words.

Example:

Online registration is proving to be the best way for students to enroll in classes at the
college. Students don't have to wait in lines at the school to enroll. They can go to the
online registration site and click on the classes they want to enroll in. A student sees
that a class is open. He clicks the "add" button. A class section is full, and a "class
full" message flashes on. The student looks for another section. Sometimes a
"disallowed" message appears, and a student has exceeded eighteen units of enrollment.
Eighteen units is the maximum for enrolling online. Students go to the final "check-
out" stop, and they can pay for their classes with a credit card, and the process is
complete.

Revised:

Online registration is proving to be the best way for students to enroll in classes at the college. *Instead of waiting in lines at the school to enroll*, students can go to the online registration site and click on the classes they want to enroll in. *If a class is open*, the student clicks the "add" button. *When a class section is* full, a "class full" message flashes on and the student looks for another section. A "disallowed" message appears *if* a student exceeds eighteen units of enrollment, *which is* the maximum for enrolling online. *At the final "check-out" stop*, students can pay for their classes with a credit card to complete the process.

A popular uprising against a government occurs in a Middle Eastern country, and the U.S. response can be problematical. Hosni Mubarak was president of Egypt for thirty years. Egypt was an American ally and had friendly relations with Israel. Mubarak was viewed as a dictator by many Egyptians, and no one was allowed to run against him in presidential "elections." The U.S. is the "beacon for democracy" in the world, and the U.S. could not deny the democratic aspirations of the people of Egypt. The overthrow of Mubarak could ultimately lead to a democratically elected hard-line government, and it could be less friendly to both the U.S. and Israel. The U.S. cannot determine the political destiny of another country. Its response to democratic uprisings in other countries registers around the world.

Writing Activity 8.9

Read your current draft and evaluate the variety of its sentence structures. Look in particular for frequently repeated sentence structures and joining words and for pairs of shorter sentences that could be combined effectively. Make any changes that will improve your sentence structure and wording variety, including using a greater variety of joining words and introductory phrases and clauses.

Revision Suggestions

Although most revision considerations don't vary greatly from essay to essay, writers can still benefit from an occasional reminder of what to focus on, which each lesson provides. Use the following suggestions as a "checklist" for revising your draft.

1. **Read through your entire draft once see what you have done well and what you might do better.** Make note of anything that jumps out at you - a paragraph that seems out of place, an omitted source reference, a questionable piece of factual evidence, a boring opening - and address each problem at some point in the revision process.

2. **Evaluate your opening to determine how well you introduced your topic and created interest for readers.** Is there anything in the opening that would "grab" a

reader's attention? Is your thesis statement clearly worded and obvious to readers? What changes might you make to improve your opening?

3. **Evaluate the effectiveness of each fact presented in the middle paragraphs to support your thesis.** Do readers clearly understand what you are showing with each fact? Do they see how the fact is related to your thesis? Is each fact presented in a way that makes it most believable to readers, including verifying facts with evidence? Do you include any other types of thesis support besides factual?

4. **Check your inclusion of source introductions and your wording of research material.** Have you referenced the source for each researched fact in a way that strengthens its credibility? Have you *paraphrased* - put into your own words - most of the research material and used quotation marks (" ") and a source introduction for any direct quotations?

5. **Check the effectiveness of your paragraphing.** Do you change paragraphs as you introduce different factual evidence? Do your paragraphs containing a main idea begin with a topic sentence? Are there overly long paragraphs that need dividing or short paragraphs that can be developed further? (See Writing Activity 8.10.)

6. **Check the organization of your draft.** Evaluate the order in which you present your facts. As you read your draft, does any information seem out of place that could be relocated more logically elsewhere? Make any organizational changes that will improve your draft.

7. **Check the wording of each sentence.** Shorten overly long sentences by deleting unnecessary or repeated words, smooth out awkward sentences, replace questionable word choices, and clarify any vague sentences. Also check your use of *transitional wording* to tie paragraphs together and show relationships among ideas (e.g. *first, second, next, finally, however, therefore, as you can see, in the meantime*).

8. **Evaluate the effectiveness of your conclusion.** Do you reinforce your thesis in some manner? Do you provide something new for readers? Do you make your purpose clear? What might you change to make your ending stronger or more memorable?

9. **Evaluate how well you have accomplished your purpose.** Read your draft with your purpose in mind and make any changes that will make your purpose clearer or help you accomplish it.

Writing Activity 8.10

Effective paragraphing helps readers navigate an essay with the greatest understanding. For some paragraphing practice, read the following draft and divide it into paragraphs.

Mark off the first sentence of each new paragraph of the essay, most of which begin with topic sentences. Then compare your paragraphing decisions to a classmate's.

Overweight America

There is little question that Americans in general have a weight problem. According to the Gallup-Healthways Well-Being Index in 2010, 63% of American adults were overweight, and almost half of those were obese. But one doesn't need any statistical confirmation that Americans are overweight. Just sit in a mall for a half hour and watch people walk by, notice the people in a fast-food restaurant or "all you can eat" buffet restaurant, or watch elementary school children on the playground at recess. We have become a nation of overweight overeaters, and the amounts of food served at restaurants are a big part of the problem. Food portions in restaurants today are often twice as large as they were fifty years ago, according to nutritionist Beverly Gainer. The size of everything is larger: the plates, the cuts of meat, the mound of mashed potatoes, the portion of vegetables, the hamburgers, the servings of fries, the plate of chow mein, the pasta. When people eat out, they are consuming nearly twice as much food as Americans consumed while eating out in the 50's and 60's. It is no wonder that the average American today is much heavier than his predecessors. In addition, Americans eat out much more frequently today than in the past. It is not unusual for a family to eat out two or three times a week, and some of those stay-at-home meals are restaurant take-outs. With women working outside the home in almost as large a number as men, it is not surprising that home-cooked meals have become less frequent. So not only are restaurants serving much larger portions than in the past, Americans are eating out in greater numbers, compounding the weight problem further. Drinks are also coming in larger quantities, adding significantly to the problem. Today's "small drink" in a fast-food restaurant or movie theater, according to marketing professor Janet Swartz, was yesterday's "large" drink. In the 50's and 60's, a "large" drink was sixteen ounces. Today's large drink is often thirty-two ounces. Of course, movie-goers need that large drink to wash down a huge bucket of popcorn, more than three times the amount of popcorn that past movie-goers ate. The size of drinks has grown steadily with the increased size of food portions, packing more and more pounds on America's soda-guzzling population. Of course, the latest calorie-exploding advance by fast-food restaurants is the "super-sized" meal. Remember when the quarter pounder used to be a really big hamburger? It feels like a light snack today to many Americans. Now there's Carl Jrs. half-pound Six Dollar Burger, McDonald's half-pound Big New-York Burger, Wendy's half-pound square burger, and Burger King's Double Whopper. And if you "supersize" your fries and drink, you can enjoy a nice 2000-calorie meal, an adult's average calorie requirement for an entire day! There is no question that the larger and larger portions that restaurants serve are contributing significantly to America's weight problem. Restaurants are in frenzied competition to serve you more food than their competitors, and there seems to be no end to the outrageous-sized portions that they will come up with. It is also clear that restaurants don't care whether they are contributing to the weight and health problems of Americans. As long as we are willing to eat triple-paddy cheeseburgers with bacon, restaurants will serve them up.

Americans have to look at themselves in the mirror and admit, "I'm too fat and I eat too much."   Parents have to look at themselves in the mirror and say, "What am I doing to my children with our eating habits?" Everyone knows what they need to do: eat less, eat healthier, and exercise more. But that is more easily said than done, given that each generation of Americans grows fatter. The good news is that overweight adults and their overweight children don't have to change their eating habits dramatically. Don't eat out quite as much, never "supersize" a meal, only eat hamburgers or chicken nuggets and fries once rather than three or four times a week, pay attention to yours and your children's calorie intake, take half of your food home from the big-portion restaurants for left-overs, keep the "all you can eat" buffet dining to a minimum, and cut down on the desserts and sweet snacks. If you do those things, there is no question that your weight and that of your overweight children will drop. You will be eating just a little less of everything without drastically changing your diet. Finally, don't let the big-portion restaurants control your food mentality. These restaurants try to make you believe that abnormal, glutinous eating is really normal. They want you to relish that full rack of ribs, potatoes the size of footballs, a heaping plate of spaghetti, or a burger so big you can't get it in your mouth. Deep down, we know we shouldn't be eating so much.   If we just get back to normal eating, Americans will no longer be the fattest people on earth, and we will raise more slender, healthier children.

Writing Activity 8.11

Keeping the revision suggestions in mind, make any changes in your draft that you feel will improve it. Be open to new ideas and connections that may come to you as you read your draft, and don't hesitate to add anything new that will strengthen your essay: a new supporting point, an example, some clarifying information, or a final thought for readers.

Writing Activity 8.12

After you have revised your draft, exchange drafts with a classmate or two and provide some reader feedback. Ask questions regarding anything you don't understand clearly, would like more information on, or question the factual credibility of. Make any suggestions that you feel would improve the draft. Then make any final changes in your own draft based on your classmate's feedback. Make note of any suggestions that your classmate(s) makes that may help you revise future drafts.

Editing

The final step in preparing your essay for readers is to correct any errors you may find. In each "Editing" section you are introduced to a new editing consideration, review some of the common problems presented in previous lessons, and proofread your latest draft for errors, making the corrections that will produce an error-free final essay.

Misplaced and Dangling Modifiers

Two common types of writing problems involve faulty sentence structures: *misplaced and dangling modifiers*. While they aren't considered "errors" in the same sense as a misspelled word or a run-on sentence, they nonetheless are problems that can distract readers and weaken any essay's impact. Although they are both sentence revision *and* editing concerns, misplaced and dangling modifiers are frequently identified and corrected in the final proofreading stage of the writing process.

The following guidelines will help you identify and correct any problems with misplaced or dangling modifiers in your writing:

1. **A misplaced modifier is most typically a phrase or clause located some distance from the word it modifies. It can create an awkward sentence with ambiguous meaning:**

   The woman works at the "return" counter of Home Depot *in the green plaid leisure suit*. (The phrase *in the green plaid leisure suit* is too far from the word it modifies: "woman").

   I prefer sitting where I can see the facial expressions of the actors *in the front row of a playhouse*. (The phrase *in the front row of a playhouse* is too far from the word it modifies, "sitting," and could mistakenly refer to the actors.)

   The chemistry instructor is no longer teaching in the evening *whose class you had hoped to enroll in*. (The clause *whose class you had hoped to enroll in* is too far from the word it modifies, "instructor," creating an awkward sentence.)

2. **To correct a misplaced modifier, move the modifying phrase or clause close to the word it modifies, most typically directly after it:**

   The woman *in the green plaid leisure suit* works at the "return" counter of Home Depot.

   I prefer sitting *in the front row of a playhouse* where I can see the facial expressions of the actors.

The chemistry instructor *whose class you had hoped to enroll in* is no longer teaching in the evening.

3.   **A dangling modifier is most typically an introductory participial phrase followed by a subject that it doesn't modify.** The modifier "dangles" because it doesn't clearly modify a particular word in the sentence:

Driving in the countryside, the orchards were clothed in pink, white, and red blossoms. (Orchards can't drive. Who does the participial phrase modify?)

Frightened by the size of the needle, the nurse assured the young patient that he would barely feel the shot. (The nurse isn't frightened by the needle.)

Studying late into the night, the formula for photosynthesis became an indecipherable mass of numbers and letters to Rhonda. (A formula can't study late into the night.)

4.   **To correct a dangling modifier, either make the modified word the subject of the sentence or change the participial phrase to a dependent clause, the modified word becoming the subject of the clause:**

Driving in the countryside, *I* saw the orchards clothed in pink, white, and red blossoms. (*Driving in the countryside* correctly modifies the subject "I.")
While *I* was driving in the countryside, the orchards were clothed in pink, white, and red blossoms. ("I" is the subject of the introductory dependent clause.)

Frightened by the size of the needle, *the young patient* was assured by the nurse that he would barely feel the shot. (*Frightened by the needle* correctly modifies the subject "the young patient.")
Because *the young patient* was frightened by the size of the needle, the nurse assured him that he would barely feel the shot. ("The young patient" becomes the subject of the introductory dependent clause.)

Studying late into the night, *Rhonda* viewed the formula for photosynthesis as an indecipherable mass of numbers and letters. (*Studying late into the night* correctly modifies the subject "Rhonda.")
As *Rhonda* studied late into the night, the formula for photosynthesis became an indecipherable mass of numbers and letters. ("Rhonda" becomes the subject of the introductory dependent clause.)

Writing Activity 8.13

The following paragraph contains some problems with misplaced and dangling modifiers. Move misplaced modifiers directly after the word they modify and correct dangling modifiers by either making the subject of the sentence the modified word or by creating an introductory dependent clause with the modified word its subject.

Example:

The owners of the strawberry field picked on the plants the remaining berries. Coming in from the north, the next night there were dark clouds gathering ominously. That morning, rain poured on the field, by late afternoon leaving it flooded.

Corrected:

The owners of the strawberry field picked the remaining berries *on the plants*. Coming in from the north, *dark clouds* gathered ominously the next night. That morning, rain poured on the field, leaving it flooded *by late afternoon*.

Animal Bonding

Remarkably, animals of very different species can bond. For example, one family had a dog and a duck which shared a backyard that they had rescued. It's difficult to think of two animal species more different than birds and canines. However, after a few days staying at arm's length from one another, they became fast friends. They would chase each other playfully, eat together, and sleep together from the same bowl. If the family brought the dog into the house or put the duck in a pen, the other would act forlorn and just sit around. Returning to the back yard, the play would commence immediately, each animal obviously happy to see the other. When an animal doesn't have one of its own kind to interact with, it can form cross-specie bonds that are good for both animals of lifetime duration. Studying the interaction of different kinds of animals, the universal desire for companionship among all species is confirmed time and again by biologists.

Writing Activity 8.14

Proofread each sentence of your draft for any problems involving misplaced or dangling modifiers. If you find a modifying phrase that seems awkwardly placed, move it closer to the word it modifies. If you find a dangling modifier, either make the subject the correctly modified word or change the participial phrase to a dependent clause, its subject the modified word.

Writing Activity 8.15

The following activity provides some proofreading practice involving run-on and comma-splice sentences, subject-verb agreement, pronoun-antecedent agreement, comma usage, fragments, apostrophes in possessives and contractions, semi-colons, colons, and dashes, and frequently confused words (their/there/they're, its/it's, whose/who's, to/too/two, effect/affect, then/than, no/know, etc.). Proofread the following paragraphs and make the necessary corrections.

The Swinging Educational Pendulum

The extreme emphasis on standardized testing in grade schools, appear to be swinging back to a more moderate position. States and school districts are recognizing that memory-based testing where students are tested primarily on what they remember doesnt address important learning functions such as critical thinking, problem solving, and collaborative learning. While memory learning is certainly an important part of a childs education. Most educators agree that it should not be emphasized at the expense of a critical educational component developing a childs thinking and reasoning skills. Many states are moving towards less standardized testing, they are also developing testing models that requires more from students then memory recall. The educational pendulum which often swings from one extreme to another now appear to be moving towards a moderate middle where the importance of memory learning, thinking and reasoning skills, and creativity are all nurtured. Many on the learning forefront classroom teachers, learning coordinators, educational researchers, and site principals have advocated such a change for some time.

Writing Activity 8.16

Proofread your draft for errors, focusing on the types of errors you are most prone to make and the common problem areas covered in the text. Afterwards, if you feel the need, exchange drafts with a classmate and proofread each other's essays, pointing out any errors that you find. Make any additional corrections, noting the types of errors that you overlooked in your draft.

Communicating with Readers

When your essay is in final "publishable" form, share it with your reading audience or representatives in the most viable way. Talk with your instructor about ways of getting the essay to your readers and perhaps receiving some feedback.

Lesson Nine: Addressing Opposing Arguments

Objective: To write a thesis-based essay with an emphasis on addressing opposing arguments.

Audience: Writer's choice

Purpose: Writer's choice

One of the greater challenges for writers is to change readers' minds or their perspective on a particular topic. Often, readers have a deeply ingrained opinion on an issue, and to get them change that viewpoint, or even to consider a different one, can be difficult. However, the written word is a powerful instrument for change, and when readers are confronted with the faulty or shaky premises on which their viewpoint may be based, they might reconsider it.

No matter how effectively a writer presents supportive evidence for her thesis, skeptical readers may cling to their own unchallenged arguments. For example, a writer who proposed that the local school board undertake a plan to reduce the high school drop-out rate presented the devastating effects that dropping out can have on students and laid out a plan for the school district to follow. However, she didn't touch on the arguments of skeptics who oppose more district involvement: that it is the parents, not the school district's, responsibility; that the problems are societal and beyond the reach of schools; and that there are higher priorities for district funds, like bringing back art and music programs. As long as such arguments remained unchallenged, many skeptics would find no reason to reconsider them or support the plan.

However, if the writer were to show how parental involvement is a critical part of the plan she is proposing, how other districts have succeeded despite the societal influences at play, and how keeping significantly more students in school would generate enough state funding to bring back the art and music programs, she would have addressed the opposing arguments in ways that may change some minds. In "persuasive" writing, addressing opposing arguments can be the most effective way to move readers off of their contrary position.

In this lesson, you will write a thesis-based essay with an emphasis on addressing opposing arguments in ways that will get readers to reconsider their viewpoint. Your reading audience will be people who don't agree with your thesis, who are skeptical of it, or who don't have a clear position on the topic. Your purpose will depend on your topic and what you hope to accomplish with a particular reading audience. What you learn about identifying and responding to opposing arguments will be beneficial for much of your writing as well as for analyzing and evaluating the writing of others.

Addressing Opposing Arguments

A mistake that writers sometimes make is being so focused on supporting their thesis that they don't consider contrary positions. They may simply ignore opposing arguments or not even be aware of them. The first step in addressing the concerns of skeptics is to find out what their concerns are. The next step is to figure out the best way to respond to them.

To address opposing arguments effectively in your upcoming essay, consider the following suggestions:

1. **Determine the opposition's position on the issue.** Sometimes readers will be directly opposed to your thesis: you believe that a new bookstore should be built on campus and your readers believe it shouldn't. Other times readers may have a different approach than yours to an issue: you believe the city should build a large water feature to revitalize the downtown area while your readers feel that building a local history museum would be a greater attraction. Sometimes the readers' viewpoint on an issue may vary in degree to your own: you believe that all hand-guns and assault weapons should be banned while your readers believe that assault weapons, but not handguns, should be banned. Before considering opposing arguments, know the primary opinion that most of your readers hold on the topic.

2. **To identify opposing arguments, ask yourself, "What are the reasons that readers believe as they do?** Just as you consider your own reasons in support of your thesis, find out the reasons behind your readers' viewpoint. Why are they opposed to a new on-campus bookstore? Why do they favor a local history museum over a downtown water feature? Why do they support a ban on assault weapons but not on hand guns? You may have to do some research - reading articles or editorials or talking to people - to find out what drives the opposition's viewpoint.

3. **Once you have determined the opposing arguments, focus on the most critical ones.** What are the arguments that you hear or read about most often? What arguments seem to be the strongest? Focus on those arguments - perhaps two or three of them - that are central to the opposing position.

4. **Consider how you can best address the arguments in your essay.** If an argument is factually inaccurate, you should point that out. If an argument has no factual basis, you might emphasize that. If an argument flies in the face of reason, you might provide a reasonable option. If a claim is made in an argument that is simply not true, you might point out what *is* true.

5. **Be respectful of your readers' viewpoint.** Most readers don't appreciate being insulted or condescended to or having their viewpoint belittled. When you show readers and their opinions the same respect that you want them to show yours, you will have the best chance of getting their attention.

6. **While you refute opposing arguments, also look for areas of agreement to help "connect" with readers.** For example, the writer whose readers disagreed on the city building a water feature downtown pointed out this commonality: "We all agree that the downtown needs revitalizing and that something bold needs to be done. Let's look at the best way to accomplish our goal." A writer who was pro-choice on the abortion issue wrote to his right-to-life readers, "You are absolutely right that human life is precious and that abortion is a tragic act; however, if abortions were illegal, the unspeakable horrors of back-alley abortions would reappear, and the government would be controlling what women can do with their bodies." Look for areas of agreement that might break down barriers without diminishing support for your thesis.

Writing Activity 9.1

Generate two or three opposing arguments that some readers might raise against each of the following thesis statements.

Examples:

Topic: School bond election

Thesis: Voters should support the bond election that would fund a new elementary school in the district.

Possible opposing arguments:

> Residents are already taxed enough. No more taxes!
> District can do without another elementary school.
> Wait for matching funds from the state before trying to build a new school.

Topic: Afghanistan war

Thesis: All American troops should withdraw from Afghanistan immediately.

Possible opposing arguments:

> American withdrawal would embolden and strengthen the Taliban.
> Anti-American terrorist training camps would reappear.
> America would not have accomplished its mission.

1. Topic: Term limits for state legislators

    Thesis: State legislators should have a four-year term limit, after which they would not be allowed to run for the legislature again.

Possible opposing arguments:

2. Topic: Pay for teachers

    Thesis: Teachers should be paid as much as other professionals like doctors and lawyers.

    Possible opposing arguments:

3. Topic: Dropping elementary school art and music programs

    Thesis: Despite the need for budget cuts, the school district should not drop the art and music programs in the elementary schools.

    Possible opposing arguments:

4. Topic: Trying juveniles as adults

    Thesis: Minors fifteen and under who commit violent crimes should never be tried as adults.

    Possible opposing arguments:

5. Topic: College activity fee

    Thesis: Students who do not attend school activities should not be required to pay an activity fee.

    Possible opposing arguments:

6. Topic: Condom distribution at the health center

    Thesis: Condoms should be distributed to students on request at the college health center.

Writing Activity 9.2

For three of the topics in Writing Activity 9.1, consider how you might address each opposing argument in a way that would influence readers who agree with those arguments. In addition, come up with one area of agreement you might have with readers opposed to the thesis to help "connect" with them.

Example:

Topic: School bond election

Thesis: Voters should support the bond election that would fund a new elementary school in the district.

Responses to opposing arguments (in parentheses):

Residents are already taxed enough. No more taxes! (This is a small tax - two cents on the dollar - and a one-time tax to build the school. It is not an on-going tax.)

District can do without another elementary school. (This simply isn't true. The current elementary schools are badly overcrowded, class sizes are too large, and students are suffering educationally as a result.)

Wait for matching funds from the state before trying to build a new school. (The need is immediate; we need to build the school this year. Waiting for matching state funds can take years as there is a waiting list for such funding.)

Area of agreement:

We all want quality schools where our children can get the best education possible, and nobody likes to pay more taxes. However, paying this small, *one-time* tax to provide quality education for our children is a worthwhile investment, and we know exactly what our tax dollars are paying for.

Writing Assignment

For this lesson, you will write a thesis-based essay with an emphasis on addressing opposing arguments to help support your thesis and influence readers who have an opposing viewpoint. In deciding on a topic for your essay, consider these suggestions:

1. **Select a topic on which people have differing opinions.** Consider topics that can be framed as a question beginning with "should:" Should people be allowed to download music free off the Internet? Should the school year for U.S. K-12 students be lengthened? Should college health centers provide "day-after" birth control pills? Should recreational marijuana usage be decriminalized? Should silent prayer be allowed in public schools? Should same-sex marriage be legalized? Should minors who commit violent crimes be tried as adults? Should Roe vs. Wade be repealed? Should students attending K-12 private schools be given government-provided vouchers to cover costs?

2. **Select a topic that interests you and that would be of interest to some audience of readers.** Your topic can come from any field - education, health, music, sports, technology, law enforcement, the environment, politics, etc. - and be of local, state, national, or international concern.

3. **Consider topical issues that are on people's minds.** Readers will take the most interest in topics that are currently being debated and that may have an impact on their lives.

4. **Select a topic that is substantial enough to generate reader interest and specific enough to cover effectively in an essay.** For example, a topic such as "Should grade-school children be allowed to wear knee-length shorts in warmer weather?" falls short on substance while a topic such as, "Should the U.S. change its foreign policy towards South American nations?" is overly broad to tackle in an essay-length paper.

5. **Select a topic on which you need to change people's minds to affect a desired outcome.** For example, if you are against the proposal before the college school board to raise the student parking fee by 50%, you may have to change some board members' minds to keep the increase from going into effect. If you support the legislative term limit initiative on the November ballot, you may have to change some people's minds who are skeptical about term limits to get the initiative passed.

Writing Activity 9.3

Keeping the topic-selection suggestions in mind, choose a topic for your upcoming essay. Consider a range of topics and settle on one that you would most like to write on.

Sample topic:

Constructing a high-speed rail system in the state

Preparation

In preparing to write the first draft of your essay, the usual considerations from previous essays apply: What research may you need to do to learn more about your topic? What will your thesis be? How might you support your thesis? Whom might your primary reading audience be, and what is your writing purpose? In addition, there is the new consideration for this essay: What are some opposing arguments to your thesis, and how might you address them?

After having prepared for several essays in previous lessons, you have probably developed a pre-writing routine that you find productive. Some writers like to do most of the preparation in their heads, beginning with general ideas that they flesh out as they write their draft. Others prefer writing out their ideas, planning their drafts in some detail before writing. At this point, how you prepare for writing your draft depends on what works best for you. Make use of the suggestions in the "Preparation" section in ways that you find most useful.

Researching Your Topic

As with some of your previous writing assignments, you may have to do some research on your topic to become more knowledgeable. Through your research, you may gain a deeper understanding of the topic, decide on a thesis statement, find some supportive evidence for your thesis, and identify some opposing arguments to address.

If you need to do some research on your topic, consider these suggestions:

1. **Use a range of research sources - online articles, periodical and newspaper articles, local experts, books - to explore your topic in depth.** Relying on one or two sources may not provide enough information or variance in viewpoints to give readers a comprehensive picture.

2. **Formulate your thesis based on the evidence that you find.** You may already have a viewpoint on the topic which your research findings may validate, call into question, or not support. Ultimately, your thesis should be supported by the best evidence you can provide, some of which may come from your research.

3. **Find opposing arguments to your thesis.** The emphasis for this essay is to present and address some opposing arguments to your thesis that readers may have, which you may find through your research. Seek out articles that provide opposing viewpoints. In addition, find evidence you could use to support your thesis.

4. **As you research, take notes on anything that you may use in your essay.** Err on the side of including more material than you may use, deciding later what may be most relevant. Write down the source for each piece of information to provide source references in your essay as you have done previously.

5. **Look for corroborative evidence as you research.** When you find the same facts, studies, statistics, or arguments appearing in different sources, you may give them greater credence than to an isolated fact or statistic found in only one source.

6. **Research the most credible and current sources available on your topic.** Using dated material or sources whose objectivity or verisimilitude is suspect can weaken your essay.

Writing Activity 9.4

If necessary, do some research to learn more about your topic, decide on a thesis, find some supportive evidence, and identify some opposing arguments, taking notes on anything you may use in your essay and including a source reference for each piece of information.

Thesis

As you know from previous essays, your thesis presents your viewpoint on the topic: what you think or believe to be true, reasonable, or fair. Your job as a writer is to convince readers of the validity of your thesis by both providing supportive evidence and addressing opposing arguments that readers may have.

To decide on a thesis for your topic, if you haven't already done so, consider the following suggestions:

1. **Generate a thesis that is both consistent with your belief on the topic and with the best evidence available.** Clearly, your thesis and the supportive evidence you provide go hand in hand. If the best evidence doesn't support your belief, you will have a difficult time convincing readers.

2. **Provide a clear thesis statement in your essay.** A writer may know what his thesis is but not convey it clearly to readers. By the end of the essay readers may still be uncertain what the writer believes. Whether you state your thesis in the opening or save it for the conclusion, express it in a way that leaves readers with a clear understanding of where you stand on the issue.

3. **Write your thesis statement with skeptical readers in mind.** Since you are writing this essay for readers who may oppose your viewpoint, generate a thesis that states your belief in a way that may have the greatest impact on skeptics. For example, a writer opposed the 50% parking fee increase proposal before the college board of trustees. Her thesis was, "Despite the need to re-pave the college parking lots, putting the cost on the back of students is both unfair and unnecessary." The thesis statement acknowledges the need to re-pave the parking lots, which fee-increase supporters agree with, but not by making students pay the bill.

Writing Activity 9.5

Generate a thesis statement for your upcoming draft that reflects your belief on the topic and that you can support in an essay.

Sample thesis statement:

Topic: Constructing a high-speed rail system in the state

Thesis: Building a high-speed rail system will solve both transportation and
environmental problems in the state and boost the flagging economy.

Opposing Arguments

As you know, an emphasis for your upcoming essay is to present and respond to
opposing arguments to your thesis. How you address your readers' arguments may have
a greater impact than how you present your own evidence. To respond effectively to
opposing arguments, consider these suggestions:

1. **Address the most prevalent arguments: those that opponents or skeptics lean
   on most heavily to support their viewpoint.** Identify two or three major
   arguments and focus on them in your essay.

2. **Decide on the best way to respond to each argument.** Take each argument and
   decide how you can refute it: By showing that it is factually flawed? By showing
   that it is illogical? By drawing relevant comparisons? By showing that it isn't
   supported by the vast majority? Respond to opposing arguments in ways that will
   best undermine their credibility with readers.

Writing Activity 9.6

Decide on two or three opposing arguments to present and respond to in your essay.
Then consider how you can best address each argument.

Sample arguments and responses (responses in parentheses):

Topic: Constructing a high-speed rail system in the state

Thesis: Building a high-speed rail system will solve both transportation and
environmental problems in the state and boost the flagging economy.

Opposing arguments:

> High-speed rail is a risky, "far-out" venture. (Eight European and Asian
> nations have had high-speed rails operating successfully for years.)
>
> Building a high-speed rail is too expensive. (Other countries with smaller
> economies than our state have built them. It is no more expensive than
> renovating and building more freeways, and it will boost the state economy,
> providing more state funding for the project.)

It won't attract enough passengers. (This has not been the case in countries where high-speed rail is successful, and Department of Transportation "ridership" studies have shown that enough people will take the high-speed trains for the system to be cost effective.)

Supportive Evidence

While the emphasis in this lesson is on responding to opposing arguments to your thesis, you will also include your own supportive evidence as you have done in previous essays. Some of your thesis support may come through your responses to opposing arguments. For example, in countering opposing arguments to the construction of a high-speed rail system, the writer provided her own supportive evidence for its construction: many countries already have high-speed rail systems; the cost of construction is no greater than the cost of renovating and building more freeways; the system would be an economic boon to the state.

Beyond that, the writer went on to provide additional support in her essay (first draft, Activity 9.9). The high-speed rail would lower pollution in the state, reduce traffic on its clogged freeways, make freeway driving safer and easier for motorists and truck drivers, and make trans-state travel three times faster than car travel and less expensive than flying. The most effective persuasive essays both provide strong supportive evidence for the thesis and effectively counter opposing arguments.

To include supportive evidence in your essay, consider these suggestions:

1. **What evidence for your thesis do you provide through countering opposing arguments?** As you respond to each argument, what supportive points might you make in the process? Make a list of points you might include as you address these arguments.

2. **What additional evidence might you provide?** Make a list of the reasons that you believe as you do, and consider what factual evidence, comparisons, and examples you might use to make your points. Some of your supportive evidence may come from your research.

Writing Activity 9.7

Make a list of supportive points for your thesis, some of which you might use to counter opposing arguments and others that you can present in direct support.

Sample thesis support:

Topic: Constructing a high-speed rail system in the state

Thesis: Building a high-speed rail system will solve both transportation and environmental problems in the state and boost the flagging economy.

Support:	Other countries have successful rail systems.
	The system would be cost effective.
	It is no more expensive to build than renovating and building more freeways.
	It would cut down considerably on the state's pollution.
	It would make trans-state travel much faster.
	It would reduce traffic on freeways and make them safer.
	It would provide jobs for construction, maintenance, and operation.
	It would be a boon to the state's flagging economy.
	It would be great for business people who have to travel regularly.

Audience and Purpose

Since you are addressing opposing arguments to your thesis, your readers will include people who either agree with those arguments or who may be influenced by them. Decide on that group of readers whose minds you would like to change on the issue: people who view it differently than yourself. For example, the writer of the "high-speed rail" essay wrote to the people who could "derail" the project: state legislators who currently opposed it.

Your writing purpose depends on your topic, your audience, and what you hope to accomplish. Your purpose may be to encourage people to support a particular proposal or to oppose something that you feel is unfair or unnecessary. If you are writing to readers with strongly entrenched viewpoints, your purpose may be, at the least, to open their minds to a different perspective. The writer of the "high-speed rail" essay had a clear purpose: to convince skeptical legislators to get onboard the project.

Writing Activity 9.8

Decide on the most appropriate reading audience for your essay, including people who disagree with your viewpoint, and your purpose in writing to them.

Sample audience and purpose:

Topic:	Constructing a high-speed rail system
Thesis:	Building a high-speed rail system will solve both transportation and environmental problems in the state and boost the flagging economy.
Audience:	State legislators who oppose or are skeptical of the project.
Purpose:	To convince legislators that they should support the construction of a high-speed rail system.

Drafting

While your essay for each lesson involves a different writing emphasis, what you have learned from previous lessons carries over. For example, in previous essays you have generated and supported your thesis, provided details and examples to clarify your ideas, included explanations to help readers understand the topic, used comparisons to make your points, provided factual evidence to support your thesis, and included source references to identify research material and enhance its credibility. Much that you have done in previous essays is applicable to your current essay, and in writing your draft, you can draw from your previous writing experiences.

The new challenge for this draft is presenting and responding to opposing arguments to your thesis. What is the best way to respond to each argument to have the desired impact on readers? You have already given that some thought, and when you actually get those responses on paper, you can evaluate the effectiveness of each response. That, of course, is the purpose of the drafting process: to get your ideas on paper to evaluate how they may resonate with readers.

For example, the writer who wrote the essay "High-Speed Rail System" realized on reading her draft that in some places she had been quite harsh with readers whose arguments she was refuting. She didn't want to alienate the very readers that she was trying to persuade, so as she revised, she softened her tone in some places.

Drafting Suggestions

As you write your first draft, consider the following suggestions:

1. **Create an opening that catches the readers' attention and reveals the topic's importance.** Why is this an issue that people should take an interest in? What is a creative way to present the topic? Include your thesis statement at or near the end of your opening.

2. **Include any explanatory information or definitions that readers may need to understand your topic clearly.** Follow your opening with any information that may be important to help readers understand the issue. (See the second paragraph of the "High-speed Rail" draft in Activity 9.9, which explains what high-speed rail is.)

3. **Following the opening, you may either present and address the opposing arguments first or present your own supportive points.** Sometimes writers lead with their own supportive evidence and other times with the opposing arguments. The writer of the "High-speed Rail" paper first presented and addressed the opposing arguments, followed by the supportive evidence for her thesis. Decide which order you think would be most effective or logical for your topic. Also consider including any areas of agreement you may have with readers that could

create a connection and help open readers' minds.

4. **Conclude your draft in a way that reinforces your thesis and makes your purpose clear to readers.** What final thoughts do you want to leave with your readers? How can you make the strongest final impact? Writers often don't know how they are going to conclude an essay until they reach that point in the draft. Since the conclusion is predicated on everything you have written, reserve judgment on the best way to end your essay until you get there.

5. **As you write, be open to new ideas that may come to you.** While your prewriting preparation no doubt gave you some good ideas, the drafting process may trigger new ideas and connections you hadn't considered. You may think of a new example, a better way to address an opposing argument, or another reason that readers should embrace your thesis. As you write, continually consider how you might add to your initial ideas.

6. **Keep your readers in mind.** For this essay, you are writing for a different type of audience: people whose viewpoint on the topic differs from yours. Present your ideas in ways that you feel will get the best response from such readers.

Writing Activity 9.9

Read the first draft "High-speed Rail System," noting its opening, including the thesis statement; the explanatory information and definition of "magnetic levitation" in the second paragraph; the presentation and response to opposing arguments in the third, fourth, and fifth paragraphs; the direct thesis support in the sixth paragraph; the source references throughout the draft; and the two-paragraph conclusion, which clarifies the writer's purpose and in the last paragraph, reveals areas of agreement among readers and writer. Then write the first draft of your essay, keeping in mind the drafting suggestions.

First Draft

High-speed Rail System

(audience: legislators)

Imagine high-speed passenger trains running the length of the state connecting Southern California and the Bay Area. Trains traveling up to 200 miles/hour could zip passengers from Los Angeles to San Francisco in less than two hours. Residents in the central part of the state could reach Disneyland or Fisherman's Wharf in about an hour. High-speed trains could revolutionize travel in California, provide a model for other states, and benefit Californians in many ways.

A high-speed rail system is a passenger train system that would connect the Northern and Southern population centers of the state and run down its middle. It would make few stops, only at the larger cities on its route, and get passengers to their destination as quickly as possible. Trains would run regularly throughout the day and evening, providing transportation for thousands of passengers daily. The system would be modeled most closely on the German Transrapid system that uses magnetic levitation, or "Maglev," a system of transportation that suspends, guides and propels trains rapidly and safely.

Skeptics depict high-speed rail as some risky, futuristic gamble. In fact, Japan's high-speed rail, the "bullet" train, has been around for over thirty years, and today high-speed passenger train systems also operate in China, Taiwan, France, Germany, Spain, Italy, and the UK. Rather than being some "far out" venture, high speed rail is a common, viable form of transportation in many countries.

Skeptics also point to the multi-billion dollar price tag for building a high-speed rail system. However, the cost of building didn't keep Japan, China, Taiwan, France, Germany, Spain, Italy, or the UK from building their high-speed rail systems, and according to the Department of Commerce, California has the eighth largest economy in the world compared to entire countries. In addition, the state's High-Speed Rail Department points to the thousands of jobs that the construction project will create, adding to the state's economic growth. It also contends that building the high-speed rail system would cost no more than renovating and expanding the current freeway system. Beyond that, as with all construction work, the longer that California waits, the more expensive the project will become.

What if California builds a high-speed passenger train system and no passengers show up? Skeptics question whether car-crazy Californians will leave their cars at home to jump on a high-speed train. However, the California High Speed Rail Department conducted an extensive two-year "ridership" study that projected a level of usage that would make the operation of the system cost effective. There is also the fact that the level of usage in the eight countries that operate high-speed rail systems has proven cost effective. Of course, opponents question the ridership study, as they do the amount that the project will cost and the number of jobs it will create, but they have produced no alternative studies that contradict the Department's findings.

The advantages of having a high-speed rail system are tremendous, something that skeptics tend to ignore. First, it would reduce statewide travel time dramatically for the vast majority of people who traverse the state, or parts of it, by car. This would be particularly beneficial for the hundreds of thousands of Californians whose business takes them to different parts of the state. Second, it would remove thousands of cars from California's vehicle-choked freeways, providing safer, faster, and more convenient travel for those car drivers traveling shorter distances and for California's commercial truckers. Third, it would significantly reduce the unhealthy level of pollution throughout the state, getting thousands of emission-spewing cars off the freeways. Finally, it would be a permanent boost to the economy and California's employment situation, creating thousands of construction, operating, and maintenance jobs.

Of course there is some risk to building a high-speed rail system since it has never been done in the U.S. However, the benefits greatly outweigh the risk, and all great construction projects have had their risks and their skeptics: the Erie Canal, the U.S.

transcontinental railway, Hoover Dam, California's statewide waterway system, the great subway systems of our Eastern cities. There are always people who are fearful of progress and the unknowns that come with it. It is when we overcome those fears that we accomplish great things, and building the high-speed rail system will be one of the state's greatest accomplishments, one that all Californians will benefit from.

There are some things we can all agree that our state needs: more jobs, a stronger economy, less pollution, fewer cars clogging the freeways, lower gas prices. While the high-speed rail may not be a magic bullet, it can help out tremendously in all of these areas. Please support current legislation for the construction of the high-speed rail. The longer we wait, the more expensive the project gets, the more polluted and unhealthy our air becomes, the more clogged and unsafe our freeways grow, and the more the economy and employment lag. The time to build is now, and you can help make the greatest transportation advancement in California's history a reality.

Revision

Now that you have revised a number of drafts in previous essays, you no doubt have developed a revision process that works best for you. Some writers prefer to deal with one revision consideration at a time, whether it be improving their sentence wording, evaluating the organization of their draft, seeing how their paragraphing may be improved, or considering what they might add or delete to improve the paper. Others may deal with related considerations simultaneously such as paragraphing and organization; sentence wording, structural variety, and transitional wording; or incorporated research material, sources references, paraphrasing, and quotations. Still others deal with all revision considerations simultaneously, making changes whenever they find something to improve.

Whether you prefer to focus on one revision area at a time, evaluate related areas together, or make changes as you see the need, the important thing is to give all revision considerations some attention. As you read the following revision suggestions, apply them to your revision process in ways that work best for you.

Revision Suggestions

As you revise your draft, consider the following suggestions.

1. **Read your entire once to get an overall sense of its strengths and weaknesses.**
    As you read, some things may catch your attention that need work, you can see how the different parts of your essay fit together, you may notice some organizational glitches, and you may get a sense of how readers might respond to what you have written. Then as revise your essay sentence by sentence, paragraph by paragraph, you will already know some of the concerns you want to address.

2. **Evaluate your opening.** Does it catch your readers' attention? Does it introduce your topic and show its importance in some way? Does it include a thesis statement that makes your viewpoint on the topic clear? Make any changes that will strengthen your opening and its impact on skeptical readers.

3. **Evaluate your responses to opposing arguments.** Have you presented the main arguments against your thesis that readers may have? Have you responded to each argument by refuting it in the most effective way to influence skeptical readers? Have you presented any areas of agreement between writer and readers to help make a connection? Can you think of other things you might add to counter a particular argument? Can you think of other arguments that you should address? Make any changes that will get readers to reconsider the credibility of their arguments.

4. **Evaluate the supportive evidence for your thesis.** Beyond responding to opposing arguments, what reasons have you given to support your thesis? What

factual evidence have you provided, what comparisons have you made, and what examples have you given to clarify your supportive points? Make any changes that will strengthen the support for your thesis.

5. **Evaluate the wording of each sentence.** Make any changes to eliminate wordiness, smooth out awkward sentences, replace questionable word choices, or clarify vague sentences. In addition, check your sentence variety to make sure you aren't over-relying on the same sentence structures or joining words, and make changes to add more variety. Finally, check your use of transitional words to tie paragraphs together and show the relationship between thoughts, and add transitions that will help readers navigate your paper.

6. **Evaluate your incorporated research material.** If you used research material, make sure that you have referenced each source of material (According to paleontologist Dr. Inez Suarez, A study by the Benet Diabetes Institute, A recent *Time* article indicated . . .), paraphrased most research material, and used quotation marks (" ") and sources introductions for any quoted material.

7. **Evaluate your paragraphing.** Have you changed paragraphs as you moved to different opposing arguments or supporting points? Do your paragraphs centered on one main idea begin with a topic sentence? Are there any overly long paragraphs that need dividing or very short paragraphs that need combining or developing further? Make any paragraphing changes that will help readers follow your ideas most clearly.

8. **Evaluate your organization.** Whether you presented the opposing arguments or your own supportive evidence first, consider whether "flipping" the order would have a greater impact on readers. In general, are there paragraphs that would fit better in a different location? Are there sentences that appear out of place in certain paragraphs? Make any organizational changes - moving paragraphs or sentences to better locations - that would produce a more logical, clearer organization for readers.

9. **Evaluate your conclusion.** Does your conclusion follow logically from what has come before it? Does it reinforce your thesis in some manner, provide some new thoughts for readers, and make your purpose clear? What do you want to accomplish in your conclusion, and what changes might you make to help accomplish it?

10. **Read your draft from your readers' perspective.** Consider how your readers - people who don't agree with your thesis - will react to everything you have written. Since your purpose is to persuade them to change, or reconsider, their viewpoint, what changes might you make to influence their thinking?

Writing Activity 9.10

The following sentence-revision activity is for anyone who could use the practice. Since sentence-wording improvement is a revision constant for most writers, if you find such practice beneficial for improving your own sentences, take the time.

Revise the following sentences by eliminating wordiness, smoothing out awkward sentences, and improving some word choices. You may add, delete, replace, or move words or phrases around.

Example:

There are some things we can all agree that our state needs: more jobs, a stronger economy, less pollution, fewer cars clogging the freeways, lower gas prices.

Revised:

~~There are some things~~ **W**e can all agree that our state needs more jobs, a stronger economy, less pollution, fewer cars clogging the freeways, **and** lower gas prices.

1. It is when we overcome our fears that we accomplish great things, and building the high-speed rail system will be one of the state's greatest accomplishments, one that all Californians will benefit from.

2. First, high-speed rail would reduce statewide travel time dramatically for the vast majority of people who traverse the state, or parts of it, by car.

3. There is also the fact that the level of ridership in the eight countries that operate high-speed rail systems has proven cost effective for those countries.

4. The trains would make few stops, only at the larger cities on their route, and get passengers to their point of destination as quickly as humanly possible.

5. However, the California High Speed Rail Department conducted an extensive two-year "ridership" study that projected a level of usage among Californians that would make the operation of the system cost effective for the state.

6. The longer we wait to build the high-speed rail system, the more expensive the project gets to be, the more polluted and unhealthy our air quality becomes, the more clogged and the more unsafe our freeways become, and the more our economy and our employment lag behind.

Writing Activity 9.11

Revise your current draft, keeping the drafting suggestions in mind, and make any changes that you feel will strengthen its impact on readers: people who oppose or are skeptical of your viewpoint.

Sample Revisions:

From "High-speed Rail System" draft, paragraphs one, two, and three

Imagine high-speed passenger trains running the length of the state connecting Southern California and the Bay Area. ~~Trains~~ **You could be** traveling up to 200 miles/hour ~~could~~, zip**ping** ~~passengers~~ from Los Angeles to San Francisco in less than two hours. ~~Residents~~ **If you live** in the central part of the state, **you** could reach Disneyland or Fisherman's Wharf in about an hour. **Your car could remain in the garage, not burning fuel, polluting the air, or clogging the freeways.** High-speed trains could revolutionize travel in California, provide a model for other states, and benefit Californians in many ways.
 ~~A~~ High-speed rail ~~system~~ is a passenger train system that would connect the Northern and Southern population centers of ~~the state~~ **California** and run ~~down~~ **through** its middle. It would ~~make few~~ stops only at the larger cities on its route, ~~and~~ get**ting** passengers to their destination**s** as quickly as possible. Trains would run regularly throughout the day and evening, providing transportation for thousands of passengers ~~daily~~. The system ~~would~~ **will** be modeled most closely on the German Transrapid system that, **like most high-speed systems,** uses magnetic levitation, or "Maglev," a system of transportation **using magnetic coils, rather than fossil fuels, to create a magnetic field** that suspends, guides and propels trains rapidly and safely.
 Many skeptics depict high-speed rail as some risky, futuristic gamble. In fact, Japan's high-speed rail, the "bullet" train, has been ~~around~~ **in operation** for over thirty years, and today ~~high-speed passenger train systems also operate in~~ China, Taiwan, France, Germany, Spain, Italy, and the UK **all have high-speed rail systems**. Rather than being some "far out" venture, high speed rail is a common, viable form of transportation ~~in many countries~~. **There is no reason why it can't be successful in California.**

Writing Activity 9.12

Exchange drafts with a classmate or two and provide some reader feedback. Make any suggestions that you feel would improve the paper. Then make any further revisions to your own draft based on your classmate's feedback.

Editing

For most writers, the final step in the writing process is to proofread their essay for errors before turning it over to readers. Professional writers often have copy editors at publishing companies to proofread their drafts. For most writers, however, the task falls on themselves to ferret out those niggling errors that may annoy readers and tarnish an otherwise excellent essay.

At this point, your proofreading skills are probably quite good, and your task has no doubt become easier as you have eliminated errors that you made earlier in the course. As writers progress, most of their proofreading involves catching the inadvertent "mind-slip" mistakes and "typos" rather than entrenched, fundamental errors. You may well be at this stage in your writing, fully capable of producing an error-free final essay.

In this lesson, you are introduced to the new editing consideration of *comparative* and *superlative adjectives,* review editing concerns from previous lessons, and proofread and correct your latest draft to get your essay in "publishable" form.   When you set your draft aside for awhile before proofreading, errors that you might otherwise overlook sometimes leap off the page.

Comparative and Superlative Adjectives

Since writers often use comparisons to make their points and show the differences and similarities among subjects, they frequently use *comparative* and *superlative adjectives*. The following paragraph comparing candidates for the office of county supervisor contains a number of comparative and superlative adjectives in italics.

> Glenna Ramirez is the *most experienced* candidate for county supervisor, having served on the county planning commission for years. She is far *more experienced* than Isaac Johnston, who has never held a civic office or served on county committees. Faye Iwanaga, however, is perhaps *most knowledgeable* of the problems of rural county residents. She has farmed with her brother for over twenty years and has a *better* understanding of farm-related issues than any candidate. Marcus Young is the *youngest* candidate at twenty-one years of age, and Valerie Crumb is the *oldest* at age seventy-eight. Vanessa Pang, who represents the large Hmong population in the county, may be the *most electable* with her sizable voting block. County officials are predicting a *larger* voter turnout than in 2008 because of the land-use issue that has put farmers and commercial developers at odds.

As you will learn, some of the adjectives in the paragraph are *comparative* and some are *superlative.* In addition, some comparisons use two words - e.g. *most experienced*, *most electable* - and some use one - e.g. *larger*, *oldest*. Knowing the difference between comparative and superlative adjectives and when a comparison requires two words or one will help you use them correctly in your writing.

To use the correct comparative and superlative adjective forms in your writing, follow these guidelines:

1. *Comparative adjectives* **compare two things and often use the word "than" to make the comparison.**

   Examples: Joshua is *taller* than his older brother.
   I am *more appreciative* of my parents than I used to be.
   Hawthorne Beach is *more eroded* than Heath Beach.
   Amanda's job prospects are *bleaker* than Maria's.

2. **One-syllable comparative adjectives end in "er" while two-or-more syllable comparative adjectives begin with "more."**

   Examples: The state of Washington is *larger* than Oregon.
   Sherise is much *slimmer* than she was a year ago.
   In Paris, it is much *warmer* in August than in July.
   Arelia is a *more precise* figure skater than Addison.
   I am *more interested* in photography than my brother.
   The Tann River is *more difficult* to navigate than the Kings River.

   (Exceptions: Two-syllable words ending in "y" or "ow" add "er" when used as comparative adjectives: It is *noisier* in the kitchen than the den. Norton Fry is a *funnier* comedian than Alice Noyes. The linoleum in the bathroom is *yellower* than in the hallway.)

3. *Superlative adjectives* **compare three or more things.**

   Examples: Joshua is the *tallest* of three brothers.
   Of my siblings, I am the *most appreciative* of my parents.
   Hawthorne Beach is the *most eroded* beach on the coast.
   Amanda's job prospects are the *bleakest* among the applicants.

4. **One-syllable superlative adjectives end in "est" while two-or-more syllable superlative adjectives begin with "most."**

   Examples: Washington is the *largest* of the northwestern states.
   Sherise is the *slimmest* of the sisters.
   In Paris, the *warmest* month is August.
   Arelia is the *most precise* figure skater on the team.
   I am the *most interested* in photography of my family.
   The Tann River is the *most difficult* river to navigate in the valley.

   (Exceptions: Two-syllable words ending in "y" or "ow" add "est" when used as superlative adjectives: The kitchen is the *noisest* room in the apartment. Norton Fry is the *funniest* comedian on the circuit. The linoleum in the bathroom is the *yellowest* in the house.)

Writing Activity 9.13

Use the correct comparative or superlative form for each word in parentheses.

Examples:

(modest) You are the <u>most modest</u> person that I know.

(kind)   Freda seems much <u>kinder</u> to young children than her cousin.

1. (hungry)   Every day I am the _____ around 9:00 p.m.

2. (ridiculous)   That was the _____ movie I've seen.

3. (cool)   The breeze seemed _____ this morning than now.

4. (short)   Madison has a _____ temper than her twin brother.

5. (sincere)   Fran is the _____ person that I know.

6. (frequent)   Derrick is the _____ museum visitor in his class.

7. (anxious)   I am _____ to finish the semester than Jerome.

8. (sharp)   Thaddeus has the _____ wit of anyone I know.

9. (pleasing)   The willow tree is _____ to the eye than the elm.

10. (reluctant)   Fluffy is the _____ of the kittens to go outside.

Writing Activity 9.14

Proofread your latest draft for any errors involving comparative or superlative adjectives and make the necessary corrections.

Writing Activity 9.15

For punctuation practice, correct any run-on or comma-splice sentences by inserting periods, semi-colons, or joining words; correct any fragments by deleting periods that create the fragments; and insert commas, colons, dashes, and apostrophes where they are needed.

Example:

At a local elementary school three ten-year old students two boys and a girl put rat poison in their fifth-grade teachers coffee. In a pang of conscience one of the students tipped over the cup at the last second, the teacher never drank the coffee. Which could have killed her. Shocking as the incident was it is also a sign of our disturbingly troubled times. Where some children commit unthinkable acts of violence.

Corrected:

At a local elementary school, three ten-year old students - two boys and a girl - put rat poison in their fifth-grade teacher's coffee. In a pang of conscience, one of the students tipped over the cup at the last second, **so** the teacher never drank the coffee, which could have killed her. Shocking as the incident was, it is also a sign of our disturbingly troubled times, where some children commit unthinkable acts of violence.

Attendance at football games

Attendance at our community colleges football games is terrible. The team plays at one of the high schools in town, the stands are usually about one-quarter full for games. Which doesnt provide much motivation for players. First the high school stadium is old, the parking is poor, and the wooden bleachers have splinters creating an uninviting venue. In addition most of the players are recruited from out of the area so local people dont relate well to them. Perhaps the biggest problem is the teams record 6 wins, 28 losses in the last three years, people get tired of seeing the team lose. Those three negative factors the run-down stadium, the out-of-area players, the lousy record are enough in themselves to discourage attendance. A fourth factor however may be the biggest problem the price of tickets. To make up revenue from the poor attendance the college has raised ticket prices to $20. Which adds to the problem rather than solves it. Our colleges students who you would think would get a discount have to pay the same as the general public. Needless to say there arent many college students who are going to pay $20 to see a game.

Writing Activity 9.16

If you could use some additional revision practice, correct any errors in the following paragraph involving subject-verb agreement, pronoun-antecedent agreement, misplaced modifiers, dangling modifiers, or frequently confused words (their/there/they're, effect/affect, no/know, its/it's, etc.).

Example:

Jackie Evanko, an eleven year-old who on the television show "America's Got Talent" demonstrated her amazing operatic singing skills, perform at the Saroyan Theater on Saturday. Evanko was first discovered on You Tube, where her singing video drew over a half million "hits." Today she performs in concerts and on television specials throughout the country. She also attends school full-time, and her parents and voice coach makes certain she doesn't overuse her vocal chords. Sitting in the audience at a concert, Evanko's voice elicits a hushed awe from concert goers.

Revised:

Jackie Evanko, an eleven year-old who ~~on the television show "America's Got Talent"~~ demonstrated her amazing operatic singing skills **on the television show "America's Got Talent,"** perform**s** at the Saroyan Theater on Saturday. Evanko was first discovered on You Tube, where her singing video drew over a half million "hits." Today she performs in concerts **throughout the country** and on television specials ~~throughout the country~~. She also attends school full-time, and her parents and voice coach **make** certain she doesn't overuse her vocal chords. Sitting in the audience at a concert, ~~Evanko's voice elicits a hushed awe from concert goers.~~ **concert goers sit in awed hush elicited by Evanko's voice.**

Destination Imagination

Students in the school districts of Topanga County receives recognition for more than excelling in sports. Students from second grade through high school who's creative ability exceeds there athletic skill participates in Destination Imagination (DI) competition. Teams of students create skits based on a particular criteria. For this year, for example, teams created movie trailers from different schools that included the integration of any two cultures. In addition, at the competition each team does a short skit it hasn't seen beforehand on a topic to show their extemporaneous skills. Judging from the looks on their faces, the competition is fun for all the students, and the winning teams from throughout the County receives the same recognition as the sports' teams.

Writing Activity 9.17

Proofread your draft for errors and make corrections as needed. Focus on your personal error tendencies and the common problems covered in the lessons: run-on and comma splice sentences, fragments, subject-verb agreement, pronoun-antecedent agreement, comma usage, colon, semi-colon, and dash usage, apostrophes in contractions and possessive words, misplaced and dangling modifiers, and frequently confused words.

If you still tend to overlook a few errors during proofreading, exchange drafts with a classmate, proofread one another's drafts, and make any additional corrections.

Communicating with Readers

Since your essay was created with a particular reading audience and purpose in mind, share your essay with those readers or representatives in the most viable form. Consult with your instructor in deciding on the best way to reach your audience and perhaps get some feedback.

Lesson Ten: Analyzing Cause

Objective: To write an essay that analyzes the causes of a particular problem, occurrence or condition and draws conclusions based on that analysis.

Audience: Writer's choice

Purpose: Writer's choice

Writers frequently examine the causes of a particular problem or occurrence to determine exactly why something happened or is happening. In some cases the writer's purpose is to suggest a possible solution to a problem based on its causes. For example, if the causes for forty per cent of community college freshmen dropping out are identified, a solution can be fashioned that addresses those causes.

Other times the writer's purpose may be to explain why something is happening to give readers a better understanding. For example, scientific studies indicate that girls are going through puberty at earlier ages on average than their predecessors. The main reason, it appears, is that because of today's eating habits, girls have more body fat, which leads to an earlier onset of puberty. This knowledge may not change the trend, but it provides a cause/effect relationship that helps people understand why it is occurring.

In this lesson, you will write an essay examining the causes of a particular problem or occurrence and draw conclusions based on your analysis. Your essay will answer the "what " or "why" question that causal analysis answers: What were the causes of the French Revolution? Why has the violent crime rate dropped in the U.S. in the past five years? What is causing the extreme weather events that are occurring worldwide? Why have the wing spans of migratory birds increased in the past ten years? Why is there a performance gap in science and math between boys and girls beginning in the middle school years?

Analyzing cause and drawing conclusions provides a valuable step in your writing development. Too often people treat the symptoms of a problem rather than its causes. For example, the high school drop-out rate remains persistently high despite efforts to keep students in school because a major underlying reason for a student dropping out - years of failure in the school system - is seldom addressed at its roots: a child's elementary school years. In addition, people often rely on faulty cause/effect relationships to form opinions. For example, some U.S. politicians are quick to blame the expensive "welfare state" programs of European nations for their current economic woes when in reality, the countries who spend the most on providing services for their citizens - Sweden and Denmark - are experiencing the fewest problems. Finding the legitimate causes of a problem and drawing the most rationale conclusions will further both your analytical and writing skills.

Causal Analysis

In this lesson, you will write an essay that examines the causes of a particular problem. Finding the root causes of a problem may require some investigation. For example, your college may be experiencing an enrollment situation common to a number of colleges: the number of women enrollees is growing while the number of men is decreasing. What is causing this somewhat surprising trend? Several potential reasons may be worth investigating: a possible disparity between the number of girls and boys graduating from high school; a significantly higher drop-out rate for high school boys than girls; a larger number of boys than girls entering the work force directly out of high school; a greater emphasis today on girls getting a college education; an expectation among young women that they will have job careers. Some of the reasons may be valid and others may not. It is the writer's job to try and *verify* each potential cause, providing readers with the most reliable information.

To determine the causes of the problem or occurrence you will be writing on, consider these suggestions:

1. **A *cause* contributes directly to the existence of a problem.** In other words, if the cause or causes of the problem were to disappear, the problem wouldn't exist. In determining cause, look for factors without which there would be no problem.

2. **Difficult problems can have multiple causes.** For example, a number of causes contribute to the air pollution problem in the U.S.: industrial emissions, vehicular emissions, wood-burning fireplaces, coal combustion, and acid rain. In addition, some causes may have a greater impact on the problem than others. For the problem that you write on, consider different possible causes and the degree to which each may be responsible for the problem.

3. **Sometimes there is a *correlation* between a particular factor and a problem.** In other words, while a particular factor may not be directly responsible for the problem, it may *contribute* to the problem in some way. For example, many young children who perform poorly in school go without breakfast. Does that mean that if you don't eat breakfast, you will be a poor student? No, but studies have shown a *correlation* between children not eating breakfast and performing poorly in school; not eating breakfast can contribute to poor performance. While a direct cause is the strongest indicator of why a problem exists, you should also consider possible correlations, particularly when the direct causes of a problem are difficult to pin down.

4. **Determine the validity of a possible cause or correlation.** For example, how do we know that burning wood in fireplaces causes air pollution? Air quality studies reveal that in the winter months when people use their fireplaces, the amount of air-

polluting particulates increases. How do we know that there is a correlation between children going without breakfast and doing poorly in school? Studies show that when poor-performing children eat regular nutritional breakfasts for a period of time, their school performance improves. Look for any kind of credible evidence that confirms the validity of a particular cause or correlation.

5. **Avoid speculative causes and coincidences.** If there is no evidence for a possible cause, it may not be valid. For example, some politicians have speculated that Iran is not building nuclear reactors to generate electricity, as it claims, but to create the means to build nuclear weapons. There is no evidence, however, that such a cause exists, but some politicians recommend attacking Iran based on a highly speculative cause. If you can find no evidence to support a particular cause of a problem, you should question its validity.

    A *coincidence*, on the other hand, is a striking chance occurrence of two or more events at one time which indicates no causal or correlational connection. For example, by coincidence, Hurricane Katrina hit New Orleans harder than any other place on the Gulf Coast. To a few religious spokesmen, however, this was not coincidence. The city of New Orleans, a modern-day "Sodom and Gomorrah," had been targeted by God for devastation as punishment for its wicked ways. While most people saw the occurrence for the coincidence that it was, others wanted to attribute a religious cause to it. Coincidences have no causal or correlational value and no place in a causal analysis essay.

Writing Activity 10.1

Determine whether each of the following statements *most probably* indicates a cause, correlation, or coincidence. Remember, a cause means that a factor is responsible, or in part responsible, for the problem or occurrence; a correlation shows a contributing relationship between a particular factor and the problem or occurrence, and a coincidence shows a simultaneous chance occurrence of two or more events with no causal or correlational value.

Examples:

I burned my finger on one of the electric stove burners. (cause)

Jonathan won the lottery on the day he was fired from work. (coincidence)

Amelia studied for the calculus test the morning that she took it rather than the night before, and she got her best grade ever. (correlation)

1. The presidential candidate who spent the most money on campaign ads in Ohio won the largest percentage of electoral votes in the primary election.

2. The presidential candidate who spent the least amount of money on campaign ads in Iowa won the second largest percentage of electoral votes out of five candidates on the ballot.

3. There was a severe snowstorm across Ohio on the day of the election, and the voter turn-out was the smallest of the last four primary elections.

4. In the last ten national primaries, the candidate who won the most electoral votes in Ohio won the presidential nomination for his party.

5. Throughout Ohio, senior citizens who couldn't drive were driven to the polls in vans and buses, and people sixty years and older and made up the largest percentage of voters in the primary election.

6. The candidates receiving the largest number of electoral votes in the last five primary elections in Ohio all stood over six feet tall.

7. The largest voter turn-outs in Ohio came from the state's largest population centers: Cleveland, Columbus, Cincinnati, Toledo, and Akron.

8. The deadline for the return of mail-in ballots was a week earlier than in the last primary election, and the number of mail-in ballots was down 20% from the previous election.

9. The date of the primary election in Ohio was also the date of the Ohio governor's birthday and the opening of a new natural history museum in Cleveland.

10. The two candidates receiving the greatest percentage of votes in the Republican primary election received an overwhelmingly large number of votes from Ohio's most conservative voters, including Tea Party and Christian Coalition members.

Writing Activity 10.2

Read the following paragraphs and identify the direct causes and correlations (contributing factors), making the assumption that the causes and correlations are valid.

High School Students and Steroids

Steroid use among male high school students persists at an alarmingly high level. These students take steroids for different reasons. Some want to get "bulked up" and muscular in a time when muscular physiques are in vogue. Others want to enhance their strength to perform better in sports like football or wrestling. Coaches sometimes turn a blind eye towards steroid use among athletes, which students see as a "green light" to continue taking them. Students also justify taking steroids because some college and professional athletes use them.

Some students take steroids because they are encouraged by their steroid-using friends to try them. Other students who have poor body images and are teased about their obesity or skinny frames take steroids to try and change their lives. Steroids are relatively easy for students to get, and accessibility leads to greater use. In addition, steroid use often flies "below the radar" compared to the attention paid to other drugs that students use. Finally, teenage boys who take steroids usually think little of the negative physical and psychological consequences of steroid use.

Writing Activity 10.3

For any four of the following topics, generate three or four possible causes or correlations (contributing factors), and decide how you might determine the validity of each.

Example:

Topic: The significant increase in the cost of tuition in state-funded colleges

Possible Causes:

   a. The cost of all college's expenses are increasing:: utilities, property taxes, teachers' salaries, building and maintenance costs, etc.
   b. The state funding for colleges has decreased with the economic recession, so the colleges raise tuition to make up the funding gap.
   c. Colleges are receiving less Federal funding for the same reason.
   d. Colleges continue to add administrators to already bloated administrations, increasing the operating costs and driving tuition up. (correlation)
   e. Colleges know that with the demand for a college education, they can increase tuition for students without decreasing enrollment. (correlation)

To determine validity:

   a. Compare costs of college budget items from year to year to validate increases.
   b. Compare state funding level for this year to past years.
   c. Compare Federal funding level this year to past years.
   d. Compare number of administrators today compared to five years ago.
   e. Compare previous tuition increases and impact on enrollment.

Topics:

1. The dramatic world-wide increase in severe weather events (hurricanes, tornadoes, snowstorms, droughts) in recent years.

2. The recent mass protests by citizens in Middle Eastern countries against dictatorial governments.

3. The increase in the U.S. in children's obesity in the past ten years.

4. The highest rate of crime in the U.S. occurring during the summer months.

5. Dentists having the highest rate of suicide among all professions.

6. Seventy percent of pet owners preferring dogs to cats.

Writing Assignment

For this lesson, you will write an essay analyzing the causes of a particular problem or occurrence and draw conclusions based on your analysis. The purpose of your essay, which you will decide on later, may be to provide suggestions for solving a problem, to clear up misconceptions on the causes of a problem or occurrence, or to help readers understand why something - a particular occurrence, phenomena, or incident - has or is taking place.

To help you decide on a topic for your essay, consider these suggestions:

1. **Select a problem or occurrence that has significance to some group of readers.** The readers may be motorists (the terrible condition of the state's major north-south freeway), college students (the recent outbreak of crime on campus), the general public (increasing dangers of drinking tap water), or women (some states passing legislation requiring women to have ultrasounds before abortions are approved). Select a problem or occurrence that would interest or have an impact on some group of readers.

2. **Select a problem that does in fact exist.** For example, some people believe that the crime rate among illegal immigrants in the U.S. is a big problem. However, the facts show that the crime rate among illegal immigrants is significantly lower than for American citizens, the problem being more in some people's minds than in reality. Some people believe that there is a problem with younger girls dressing older than their age. However, what they may not realize is that young girls have always emulated the styles of older girls, and that if there is a problem, it may be in the more provocative clothing that older girls wear today. If necessary, do a "fact check" to make sure that the problem or occurrence you choose actually exists.

3. **Select a problem whose causes are not clearly evident to most people.** For example, we know why in warmer states electric bills go up in the summer (air conditioning) and in colder states, gas bills go up in the winter (house heating). We may not know for sure, however, why the price of gasoline suddenly increases, why college graduates can't find jobs in the fields they majored in, or why the

performance gap between elementary students from lower income and middle-higher income families remains persistent.   Select a problem or occurrence that will help you and your readers better understand why something is happening or has happened.

4.   **You may select a problem from any field - education, health, environment, business, sports, music, politics, medicine, law enforcement, etc. - and at any level: local, state, national, or international.** Choose a problem or occurrence that interests you and whose causes you would like to learn more about.

The following problems and occurrences gives you some idea of the range of possible topics to consider:

The high rate of teenage pregnancy	The escalating price of gasoline
The high cost of college textbooks	The rapidly melting polar ice caps
The high cost of U.S. medical care	Why cities' downtown areas deteriorate
The drop-off in CD music sale	The increase in children's diabetes
The erosion of America's beaches	The destruction of coral reefs around the world
The increasing teen suicide rate	Increasing rate of violent crime among minors
Why marriage rate is dropping	Why students drop out of high school
Why the U.S. middle class is shrinking	Why college students "binge drink"
Why the Soviet Union collapsed	Why the U.S. invaded Iraq in 2003
Why some parents abuse children	Why teenage girls suffer from bulimia
Why kids join gangs	Why asthma is increasing among children
Why college grads can't find jobs	Why many California residents are leaving

Writing Assignment 10.4

Consider a number of problems or occurrences in different fields and then keeping the four topic-selection suggestions in mind, choose a potential topic for your upcoming essay.

Sample topic: Why men and women are marrying less frequently and later in age

Preparation

Once you have selected a topic for your essay, you can begin considering the possible causes of the problem or occurrence, the effects that the problem may have, the conclusions that might you might draw, including possible solutions to the problem, and your writing purpose and primary reading audience for your essay. Each of these prewriting considerations is presented in this section.

Identifying Causes

Identifying the causes of the problem or occurrence is a good starting point in preparing for your draft. You may already have some idea of the causes of the problem but need to do some research to determine their validity and identify other possible causes. For example, a writer who wrote on the erosion of America's coastlines believed that heavy storms over a period of years contributed to the erosion but also that man had a role in it. She needed to do some research to find out if she was right about the effect of storms and to determine exactly how man had contributed to the problem.

To determine the causes of your problem, consider these suggestions.

1. **Make a list of possible causes and correlations (contributing factors).** Write down anything that you think may contribute to the problem.

2. **Do some research to determine the validity of the causes you generated and to find other possible causes.** How do you know if a particular cause or correlation is valid? If experts agree on a particular cause, if observations confirm its existence, if experiments reveal its effect, or if studies confirm its contribution to the problem, it is probably valid. If the same causes come up frequently in different credible sources, they probably exist. The more corroboration you can get from different sources, the more certain you can be that a cause is valid.

3. **Question any cause or correlation for which you can find no evidence.** If something that you thought may be a cause doesn't show up in the research, it probably isn't valid. If you find purported causes in one source that aren't corroborated in other sources, you should question them.

4. **Find the most objective, expert sources to determine the causes.** Question any source that may have a favorable or unfavorable bias towards your topic, and rely on the most expert sources available.

Writing Activity 10.5

Generate some possible causes for your problem. Then do some research to determine the validity of each cause or correlation and to find other possible causes.

Example:

Topic: Why men and women are marrying less frequently and later in age

Possible causes:

> Couples live together without being married.
> There is no stigma to having children without being married.

Young adults whose parents divorced are more wary of getting married.
Young men who impregnate women don't feel a responsibility to marry them.
Couples who marry wait longer, until they are more financially able.
With the job situation, more people can't afford to get married.
Women feel there are fewer and fewer good men available to marry.
Women are more financially independent, not relying on a husband to survive.

Effects

Why should readers care about the problem that you are writing about?   A situation is generally not considered a problem unless it has a negative effect on someone or something. Readers should know what the effects of the problem are and who or what is affected.

For example, why should anyone care about America's eroding coastlines? The writer brought the following concerns to readers: the loss of thousands of homes built along the coastlines, the loss of habitat for millions of coastal birds and other wildlife, the loss of wonderful family beaches, the loss of some of the most beautiful stretches of coastline in the world, and the lost tourist revenue to coastal communities. While the causes of a problem help explain to readers why it exists, its effects may lead them to conclude, "Something needs to be done about it."

In preparing for your draft, it is worthwhile to look into the effects of the problem you are writing about and who or what is effected. For your draft, consider including the most serious or dramatic effects of the problem. Through you research, check the validity of the possible effects as you did the causes.

Writing Activity 10.6

Determine the effects of the problem, how serious each effect is, and who or what is affected.

Example:

Topic: Why men and women are marrying less frequently and later in age

Possible Effects:

There are fewer and fewer traditional families: married couples with children.
More children are living in one-parent households.
More children are being raised by couples who aren't married.
More children are raised in poorer economic situations (single-mother homes).
With couples marrying later, the size of families continues to shrink.
More men and women will never marry.

Drawing Conclusions

After you have presented the causes and effects of a particular problem, you are ready to draw some conclusions for readers. Have you written about a problem that might be solved? Have you written about a situation that isn't going away and that people must adjust to? Have you presented the causes of a particular occurrence to help people understand why it happened? The conclusions that you draw will depend on the type of problem or occurrence that you write about.

To draw conclusions for readers, consider the following suggestions:

1. **Have you presented a problem that has a solution?** If so, present the solution to readers that *addresses its causes*. To eliminate or reduce the size of a problem, some or all of its causes need to be eradicated or their impact reduced. Show how the solution - which may have various components to address different causes or correlations -addresses each cause. For example, to help rebuild America's eroded coastlines, a solution might include bringing in sand to build up beaches; removing the man-made barriers which break up beaches and add to the erosion; and reducing global warming, which produces stronger, more frequent storms.

2. **Have you presented a situation that can't be "solved?"** For example, on the topic of men and women marrying less frequently and later in life, many experts believe that the "traditional family" will never be prevalent again. Therefore, the writer's conclusion may be based on that reality: how do men and women make the best of the situation for themselves and for their children?

3. **Have you presented a particular occurrence to explain why it happened?** For example, if a writer presented the causes of the U.S. invasion of Iraq in 2003, he may draw a cautionary conclusion, suggesting that such questionable causes shouldn't lead to war, or he may suggest that when such causes line up, military action is justified. If you explained why something happened or exists, your conclusion may answer questions such as, "What can we learn from this?" or "What does this mean for the future?" or "How do we adjust or respond to this?"

Writing Activity 10.7

Consider the conclusion(s) you might draw for readers based on the problem or occurrence, its causes and effects. You might offer a solution or solutions to a problem, forecast what the future may hold regarding your topic, explain what we can learn from the problem or occurrence, or suggest how we might adjust to, respond to, or deal with the problem or situation.

Example:

Topic: Why men and women are marrying less frequently and later in age

Possible Conclusion:

> There is no "turning back the clock" to an earlier time when the traditional family was the norm. There is no evidence that the trend towards fewer and later marriages will change. Some young men and women will co-habitate without marrying. A large number of men and women will never get married. Children will continue to grow up in different types of households with single parents, co-habiting parents, married parents and step-parents. Young people growing up must face the reality of a changing marital landscape, not stake their future happiness on getting married, and if they don't marry, finding happiness and satisfaction without it. Above all, no matter what living situation children are raised in, they deserve to have a stable, loving family life.

Audience and Purpose

For your upcoming essay, decide on the most appropriate reading audience: readers whom you would most like to reach, who are most affected by the problem, who can make an impact on the problem, or who need to learn more about the problem. In addition, determine your purpose in writing to them: to engage them in helping to solve a problem, to influence their viewpoint on the problem or occurrence, or to suggest how they might adjust or respond to the problem or situation.

Writing Activity 10.8

Decide on the reading audience and purpose for your upcoming essay.

Example:

Topic: Why men and women are marrying less frequently and later in age

Audience: Primarily young men and women, ages 16-30

Purpose: To enlighten readers on the trend of people marrying less frequently and later in life, how it may affect their lives, and how they might adjust to the changing situation.

Drafting

During your prewriting preparation, you have covered the various elements that are typically found in a causal analysis essay: the problem or occurrence you are writing about, its direct causes and contributing factors (correlations), its effects, who or what is affected, and the conclusion(s) you draw: what can be done to solve or reduce the problem or what we can learn from it. These elements will comprise much of the content of your essay.

Organization

The organization of a causal-analysis essay is rather straightforward: introduce the problem, explain its causes, present its effects, and draw your conclusions. Writers sometimes present the effects of a problem before explaining its causes, first alerting readers to the seriousness of the problem or how it may affect them. Based on your topic, decide whether you think it would be more effective to present the causes or effects of the problem first. You can always reverse the order, upon later evaluation, when you revise your draft.

An organizational outline of your essay may look like this:

1. Problem: What exactly is the problem or occurrence you are writing about?

2. Causes: What are the direct causes of the problem, and what contributing factors (correlations) exist?

3. Effects: What are the main effects of the problem, and what or who is affected?

4. Conclusion: What conclusion can you draw based on your analysis of the problem?

Drafting Guidelines

As you write the first draft of your essay, consider these suggestions:

1. **Introduce your topic in the opening in a manner that creates interest for readers.** Why should they care about this problem? What makes it serious or important enough to write about? How can you best get their attention?

2. **If necessary, provide some explanatory information or definitions to help readers understand the problem clearly.** For example, the writer who wrote about current marriage trends (Writing Activity 10.9) provided statistics in the second paragraph to provide evidence of the trends that she introduced in her opening.

3. **Present the causes of the problem or occurrence, including any evidence of their validity.** For example, cite the agreement of experts, credible studies or experiments, direct observations, or any corroborative evidence that runs through your research sources.

4. **Present the main effects of the problem.** Who or what is affected by the problem, and what are the most serious effects? (You may choose to present the effects *before* the causes if you feel it would be more effective for your particular topic.)

5. **Provide source introductions for all research material.** As in previous essays, always acknowledge the source of your material, paraphrase the majority of research material, and use quotations (" ") for the most striking statements.

6. **Paragraph your draft to delineate each cause and effect clearly.** Change paragraphs as you move to new causes or effects or to different parts of the essay: beginning to middle, middle to ending. Use topic sentences to introduce paragraphs that develop a main idea.

7. **Draw conclusions at the end of the draft, including possible solutions to the problem or what we can learn from it.** Make your purpose clear to readers, helping them understand why you wrote the essay.

Writing Activity 10.9

Read the following first draft "The Future of Marriage," noting how it introduces the topic in the opening two paragraphs, explains the causes in paragraphs three-eight (each beginning with a *topic sentence)*, presents the effects in paragraphs nine and ten, draws conclusions in paragraph eleven, and provides source acknowledgments throughout to introduce research material. Then write the first draft of your essay.

First Draft

The Future of Marriage

(audience: young men and women)

If you have planned for a future that definitely includes being married, you may want to think again. Men and women are marrying later in life and less frequently than at any time in American history. The same trend is also occurring in other countries such as Japan and the Netherlands. The odds of your getting married are smaller today than in any previous time in modern history. What is causing this shift away from marriage, and how will it affect the future, and perhaps your future?

A 2011 Pew Research Center report found that 51% of U.S. adults 18 years and older are married today compared to 72% in 1960, a sizable 21% drop-off rate in the number of married people. That 51% also includes the large number of married couples in their 50's-80's who married in more marriage-friendly times, so the percentage will no doubt continue to drop as these couples inevitably die off. In addition, the average age for brides and grooms is the highest that it has even been: 26.5 for women and 28.7 for men. If you do get married, don't count on it happening much before you are 30.

Why are people marrying less frequently and later in life? First, the stigma of couples living together without being married is a thing of the past, as is the stigma of having children outside of marriage. Millions of Americans co-habitate without marriage, and many of them have children. Some couples eventually get married while others continue co-habitating or go their separate ways. Co-habitation results both in couples waiting later to marry and in fewer marriages.

Attitudes have also changed towards marriage, according to a Gallup survey of young men and women Many of today's marriage-eligible young adults have lived through their parents' divorce, been raised by single parents, been shipped back and forth between mom and dad, or lived with step-parents and step-siblings. They don't have as rosy or as traditional a picture of marriage as earlier generations, and not surprisingly, they often don't view marriage as a lasting, stable life choice and are more reluctant to embrace it.

Women are also not as dependent on marriage as they once were for financial survival or having children, according to a *Woman's Day* article. Women are becoming equal bread-winners with men, able to take care of themselves. If they want to have children, they don't have to be married to have a family. They are less apt to jump at the chance of getting married for the sake of security or having a child as they once were, leading to later and fewer marriages.

According to Gwendolyn Marks, author of books on marriage and family, couples are also getting "smarter" about marrying later, when they both have jobs and are financially able to make it. The struggling young early-20's married couple who lived in the tiny apartment with the wife working to help pay her husband's way through college has been replaced by the late-20's and 30's couple, both of whom are out of college and employed. Women less often sacrifice their college career or put it on hold to help a husband get through school. Today many couples wait on marriage until both partners are out of college and gainfully employed, i.e. in a position to make ends meet comfortably. Sometimes these couples have lived several years together before they officially tie the knot.

There is also the unconfirmed belief among many young people that there are more eligible women out there than men, and that the pool of "marriageable" men, i.e. worth marrying and willing to marry, is in decline. Such beliefs are commonplace in online sites dealing with the travails of single life. Men who buy into this mind-set may feel that it is a "buyer's market," and enjoy the idea of playing the field rather than settling on one woman, relishing the Beach Boys' "Surf City" odds: "Two girls for every guy." There's status in some circles of men in being a "player," and being a player and getting married don't mix. Many women are leery of the player mentality, and a common query from women in young adult online sites is, "Where are all the good men?"

A rather sad factor that has added to the decline in marriage is that among poorer people in America, a majority of women who have children never marry. Sometimes the father remains in the picture but often times he does not. Single mother households are the rule rather than the exception in our inner cities, and unless the employment situation and young men's attitudes change dramatically, poor, unwed mothers will continue to add to the declining marriage statistics.

Is marriage becoming obsolete in America? Apparently despite the declining numbers, most men and women don't believe so. In fact, in survey after survey, the majority of men and women still plan on getting married - someday. The difference today is that there is no rush, and if marriage doesn't come along, it's not the end of the world, particularly for men. There is no reason to believe that the trend towards couples living together without marriage and more single mothers will not continue and perhaps increase.

When it comes to children, common wisdom indicates that a loving, stable, two-parent family is the best environment to be raised in. However, many marriages aren't that loving and stable, and children of married couples are as likely to see their parents divorce as stay together. Single-parent households are on average among the poorest, and single mothers are among the most poorly educated, both of which can negatively affect children. It is no coincidence that children who do poorly in school or have discipline problems often come from single-parent or unstable family situations. The changing marital landscape may have the greatest impact on children, and despite their resiliency, may create problems that could affect them as well our future society.

Young women and men need to face the future with a different mind-set than earlier generations. Marriage is not a given, and many men and women will never get married. Those that do will marry later than at any time in our history. Happiness and success should not be equated with getting a man (or woman) to the altar, and no woman should stake her future on it. Certainly being married and having children is still the dream of many young girls and boys, but there also needs to be alternate happy endings for all of those for whom marriage doesn't happen. After all, marriage is often no story-book ending itself. And we all need to think deeply about how our life circumstances affect the children we may bring into the world. Whether we become single parents, co-habitating parents, married parents, or divorced parents, the welfare of our children needs to come first. And when it comes children, nothing can replace a loving mother and father living under the same roof.

Revision

After writers have completed their first draft, there are often some things they don't discover until they begin the revision process. This isn't surprising since during the drafting process, you are writing your essay one word, one sentence, one paragraph at a time. Once you get the entire draft on paper, it is easier to evaluate how each word fits within a sentence, how each sentence fits within a paragraph, how each paragraph fits within the essay, and how all parts - beginning, middle, ending - fit together.

In evaluating a draft, most writers find some things to revise - an underdeveloped paragraph, some inelegant sentences, an organizational glitch, an uninspired opening - and some things to add - a clarifying example, a fresh idea, some vivid details. For most writers, revision is crucial to creating the essay that they want. As you evaluate your draft, assume that you will find some things to revise, and be open to adding to, deleting from, and changing your draft in any way that you feel with improve it.

Revision Suggestions

To revise your current draft, consider these suggestions:

1. **Read the entire draft to get an overall sense of its strengths and weaknesses.** Reading the draft as a whole, you may find some obvious problem areas that you want to address as well as some strong paragraphs or sections that stand out.

2. **Evaluate the impact of your opening.** Do you get your readers' attention in your first few sentences? Do you introduce the problem clearly and give readers a reason to care about it? Make any changes to strengthen your opening.

3. **Evaluate your explanatory information.** Have you presented any information that explains the problem to readers or that provides evidence of its existence or seriousness? Make sure that readers understand the problem clearly.

4. **Evaluate your causal analysis.** Have you clearly presented each cause or correlation (contributing factor) that is responsible for the problem or occurrence? Do readers understand how each cause is responsible? Have you provided evidence to confirm the validity of each cause (e.g. experts' agreement, studies or experiments, direct observations)? What might you add that will help readers best understand each cause or correlation and its impact?

5. **Evaluate your presentation of effects.** Have you presented the major effects of the problem and shown who or what is most affected? Do readers understand how the effects may relate to them? Are there other effects that you could add? Make any changes that will help readers understand the effects and their seriousness.

6. **Evaluate your organization.** Did presenting the causes (or the effects) first seem the most sensible, effective order? If you reversed the order, what impact might that have on the essay? Are you satisfied with the order in which you presented the individual causes? The individual effects? Are there any sentences or paragraphs that seem out of place that could be moved to a better location?

7. **Evaluate your source acknowledgments.** Do you provide a source introduction for each piece of research material? Do you paraphrase most of the research information and use quotations (" ") for a particularly striking or critical statement?

8. **Evaluate your paragraphing.** Did you present the major causes and effects in separate paragraphs and change paragraphs as you moved from opening to middle to ending? Did you use *topic sentences* to begin paragraphs that develop a main idea?

9. **Evaluate your sentence wording.** Revise sentences to eliminate wordiness, smooth out awkward sentences, clarify vague sentences, replace questionable word choices, and create more structural variety. In addition, check your use of transitional wording (*first, next, finally, in addition, as you can see, therefore, however*), determining whether an added transition here or there would help show relationships between ideas or paragraphs.

10. **Evaluate your conclusion.**   If you presented a solvable problem, do you provide a workable, sensible solution? Do readers understand how they might help solve the problem? If you presented a situation or occurrence that doesn't involve a "solution," do you show readers what can be learned from the situation or how they might adjust or respond to it? What might you change to make the greatest impact on readers and leave them with something to think about?

11. **Evaluate your writing purpose.** Are you clear on your purpose in writing to this audience? Does your draft make your purpose clear to readers? Read your draft with your purpose in mind and make any changes that will help you accomplish it.

Writing Activity 10.10

Read the following first draft "Differences in Longevity." With a partner, come up with revision suggestions that would improve the draft in the following areas:

1.   How might the opening be improved?
2.   Find five sentences whose wording could be improved.
3.   Where might source introductions for research material be needed?
4.   How might the writer revise the ending to make her purpose clearer?
5.   What things does the writer do well in the draft**?**

Differences in Longevity (audience: general public)

Where you live can have a big impact on how long you live. Living in one part of a city could mean you will live ten-to-fifteen years longer than if you live in another part. The disparity between life-spans among different population groups depending on where they live is a problem across the country.

A recent county health department study in Ohio confirms what earlier studies in other parts of the country have found. People living in more affluent areas of a city live considerably longer on average than people living in the poorer areas. Those living in the more affluent areas are predominately white and Asian while those living in the poorer areas are often Hispanic and African-American.

There are a number of reasons that health experts agree upon for people living in poorer areas to die ten-to-fifteen years earlier than those in more affluent areas. Poorer people tend to get health treatment less frequently and often poorer quality health care than more affluent people. Left untreated or undertreated, their health problems tend to get worse and lead to earlier deaths while more affluent people get the help they need to combat their health problems and live considerably longer.

Eating habits also affect people's longevity. Poorer urban areas are full of fast-food restaurants that serve the high-fat fried foods that lead to obesity, high cholesterol, and heart and diabetes problems. More affluent areas have a broader choice of eating options including restaurants serving healthier kinds of food. In addition, poorer people eat the food they can afford, which often means McDonald's chicken nuggets and fries or Burger King's Whopper while more affluent people can eat at the more expensive salad-and-vegetable oriented restaurants such as the Ripe Tomato.

According to asthma expert Dr. Timothy Allen, director of environmental research for the Fulbright Medical Center, environmental factors also can affect a person's longevity. Poorer urban areas tend to be more polluted with nearby factories often emitting potent pollutants. Poorer people suffer from pollution-contributing respiratory ailments and asthma more frequently than people living in more affluent suburbs far from the manufacturing areas of the city. Schools in poorer urban areas also have significantly more "bad air quality" days that keep children off of the playgrounds than in more affluent areas where the pollution isn't as bad. When people live their lives from childhood in a badly polluted area, it is not surprising that that exposure ultimately contributes to how long they live.

Environmental factors can also keep poorer people in their homes, leading to inactive, less healthy lives. Disgusting smells from meat-packing or chemical plants near poorer urban areas can discourage people from getting outside and being more active. In addition, poorer areas are frequently more dangerous with more gang activity and drug trafficking, with people feeling safer inside their homes than walking the neighborhood streets. More affluent urban areas don't have the same environmental problems and people can lead healthier, more active lives.

Stress can also contribute to poor health, according to a recent article in *Time* magazine, and poorer people often live with more stress than more affluent people.

Daily stress can come from living in dangerous urban neighborhoods, from being unemployed or in and out of jobs, from living with nagging, often untreated health problems, from living in poverty, or from living with large numbers of people in small living spaces. More affluent people don't suffer from the same sources of stress, which can lead to longer, healthier lives.

Finally, there is a psychological component to how long people live, according to environmental psychologists. People who feel that they have more to live for often live longer than people whose future appears bleaker. Poorer people often can't look forward to the happy, healthy retirement years that more affluent people can. As people get older, their will to live can play a role in how long they live, and poorer people whose health isn't great or whose life circumstances are grim may lose some of that will to live.

That poorer people don't live as long as more affluent people is not surprising, nor are the causes for the disparity. Improving the situation, however, will require significant changes: reducing urban pollution, providing better, more accessible inner-city health care, providing more and better job opportunities in the inner-cities, ridding neighborhoods of gang-related violence, and providing healthier, affordable eating options in poorer areas. Improving the quality of life in poorer urban areas will no doubt increase the life span of its residents. There is little indication, however, that the problem is receiving much attention at local, state, or national levels.

Writing Activity 10.11

Keeping the revision suggestions in mind, make any changes in your draft that you feel will improve the essay.

Sample Revisions

The Future of Marriage (First four paragraphs revised and a new paragraph added)

If you have planned for a future that definitely includes ~~being married~~ **marriage**, you may want to ~~think again~~ **reconsider**. Men and women are marrying ~~later in life and less frequently~~ **less frequently and later in life** than at any time in American history. The same trend is also occurring in other countries such as Japan and the Netherlands, **according to a 2012 article in _The Economist_**. The odds of your getting married are smaller today than in any previous time. What is causing this shift away from marriage, and how will it affect the future, perhaps including your own ~~future~~?

A 2011 Pew Research Center report found that 51% of U.S. adults 18 years and older are married today compared to 72% in 1960, a ~~sizable~~ 21% drop-off rate in the number of married people. That 51% also includes the large number of ~~married~~ couples in their 50's-80's who married in more marriage-friendly times, so the percentage will no doubt continue to drop ~~as these couples inevitably die off.~~ **Based on that report, the odds of any young adult getting married are roughly 50/50.** In addition, the average age for brides and grooms is the highest that it has ever been: 26.5

for women and 28.7 for men. If you do get married, don't count on it happening much before ~~you are 30~~ **age 30.**

Why are people marrying less frequently and later in life? First, the stigma of couples living together without being married is **gone** ~~a thing of the past~~, as is the stigma of having children outside of marriage. Millions of Americans co-habitate without marriage, and many of them have children. Some couples eventually get married while others continue ~~co-habitating~~ **living together** or go their separate ways. Co-habitation results both in **fewer marriages and in couples waiting later to marry.** ~~couples waiting later to marry and in fewer marriages~~.

Attitudes **towards marriage** have also changed ~~towards marriage~~, according to a Gallup survey of young men and women Many of today's ~~marriage-eligible~~ young adults have lived through their parents' divorce, been raised by single parents, been shipped back and forth between mom and dad, or lived with step-parents and step-siblings. They don't have as rosy or ~~as~~ traditional a picture of marriage as earlier generations. ~~and not surprisingly,~~ **Consequently,** they often don't view marriage as a lasting, stable ~~life choice~~ **relationship** and are more reluctant to embrace it.

A lack of role models is yet another reason why people marry less frequently. Earlier generations of young adults followed in the footsteps of their married parents and their friends' parents. Married parents with children were the norm, and getting married was what you did, often soon out of high school or sometime during college. Today such role models are not as prominent, often replaced by other "role models" such as single parents, unwed couples, or single adults. As the "married with children" role model continues to dwindle, so do the number of marriages.

Writing Activity 10.12

Exchange drafts with a classmate or two and provide some reader feedback, making suggestions that you feel could improve the draft. Based on your classmate's feedback, make any additional changes in your draft that you feel will improve it.

Editing

Drafting, revising and editing your essay are presented as distinctly different steps in the writing process since they have markedly different purposes. You write your draft to get your ideas on paper. You revise your draft to improve its content, wording, and organization. You edit your draft to correct any grammatical or punctuation errors. Revision comes before editing because there is no point in correcting errors in a draft that is still undergoing change.

That said, for most writers, there is some overlap among the drafting, revision, and editing processes. For example, some revision may occur during the drafting process, such as rewording an awkward sentence. Some editing may occur during the revision process when an obvious error pops up. In addition, while you are editing a draft for errors, you sometimes find a few last things you want to revise. There is no problem with such overlaps as long as they don't intrude on the main focus for each step.

Frequently Confused Words

As noted in previous lessons, one proofreading suggestion is to scour your paper for incorrect words resulting from inadvertently using a homonym or similar-sounding word in place of the correct word, such as using "their" or "they're" in place in "there." Most word-processing spell checks don't pick up the incorrect word since it is spelled correctly.

Keep the following list of frequently confused words handy when proofreading your draft for errors.

accept	to take what is offered:	I *accept* your apology.
except	not including:	Everyone attended the lecture *except* Jolinda.
advice	(noun) guidance:	Please take my *advice* and get a check-up.
advise	(verb) to give advice:	I would *advise* you to get a check-up.
affect	(verb) to influence:	You *affect* my thinking on religious issues.
effect	(noun) result of a cause:	What is the *effect* of light on plants?
allowed	permitted:	Smoking is not *allowed* in the hotel.
aloud	audibly; not silently:	Please read the poem *aloud* to the class.
altar	a table for religious offerings:	The *altar* was covered with a white cloth.
alter	to change in appearance:	We need to *alter* the setting for the play.
bare	naked; unadorned:	The cupboard was *bare*.
bear	to withstand:	I cannot *bear* the smell of sour milk.

break	shatter; stop working:	The printer *breaks* down if overused.
brake	to slow or stop:	You need to *brake* your car on that sharp curve.
course	field of study:	What science *course* are you taking?
coarse	rough; vulgar:	Don't use such *coarse* language.
compliment	to praise:	I *complimented* Anastasia on her piano solo.
complement	to go well together:	The carpet and wall colors *complement* each other.
council	an elected body:	The city *council* voted against annexing more land.
counsel	to give advice:	Jonathan *counseled* Beatrice on budgeting her money.
desert	barren, dry region:	*Desert* plants require little water.
dessert	after-dinner sweets:	I love apple pie ala mode for *dessert*.
elicit	to draw out:	It is difficult to *elicit* a response from the mayor.
illicit	forbidden:	The governor had an *illicit* relationship with his secretary.
its	possessive pronoun:	The house lost *its* roof in the tornado.
it's	contraction for "it is:"	*It's* time to start watering the lawn daily.
lead	to take charge:	Please *lead* the way to the aquarium.
led	past tense of "lead:"	The football team *led* until the last quarter.
loose	not tight:	Amanda prefers *loose*-fitting sweaters.
lose	not to win; misplace:	I often *lose* my sunglasses.
new	not existing before:	The book store has a *new* section on biographies.
knew	past tense of "know:"	Ralph *knew* his study habits needed to improve.
principal	primary importance:	A *principal* reason for attending college is to prepare yourself for future employment.
principle	moral value:	Your *principles* set an example for your siblings.
site	area of ground:	That vacant lot is the perfect *site* for a dental office.
sight	something seen:	The *sight* of that fresh water spring was welcome.
cite	reference a source:	Please *cite* your research sources in your essay.
stationary	not moving:	I prefer riding a *stationary* bicycle for exercise.
stationery	writing paper:	I don't like flowery *stationery*.
their	possessive pronoun:	*Their* dorm room is quite large.
there	location; introductory word:	*There* are many ways to cook chicken.
they're	contraction for "they are:"	*They're* considering leasing an apartment.

then	at that time:	I attended morning classes ; *then* I went to work.
than	comparative word: You are much taller *than* your father.	

who's	contraction for "who is:" *Who's* going to the concert tonight?	
whose	possessive pronoun: *Whose* purse was left in the classroom?	

your	possessive pronoun: *Your* car is parked by a fire hydrant.	
you're	contraction for "you are:" *You're* an excellent impersonator.	

Writing Activity 10.13

Proofread the following paragraph, replacing any incorrect words with the correct words.

Example:

For desert, sorbet has fewer calories and less sugar then ice cream.

Corrected:

For *dessert*, sorbet has fewer calories and less sugar *than* ice cream.

The college debate team did very well in the regional competition. There preparation was excellent, clearly much better then some of the teams. Their extemporaneous presentations illicited thunderous applause from the audience, who's responses were usually muted. It was a wonderful site to see the diverse team members - Asian, Latino, Indian, white, and African-American - working together and complementing one another after each performance. The team's principle attribute, however, was their reasoning ability. Time and again they outreasoned there opponents, and the affect on the judge's scores was evident. The eight team members won every debate accept two, and those two were lost by narrow margins. Their advise to future team members who watched the debate was to do your research, prepare diligently, practice mock debates, get along with you're teammates, and have fun.

Writing Activity 10.14

If you could use more proofreading practice, identify and correct the errors in the following paragraphs involving run-on and comma-splice sentences, fragments, comma usage, subject-verb agreement, pronoun-antecedent agreement, misplaced and dangling modifiers, apostrophes in possessives, and comparative and superlative adjectives.

Example:

Only one of the monkey siblings share their food with her brothers and sisters, the rest push away anyone who get close when they are eating.

Corrected:

Only one of the monkey siblings *shares* ~~their~~ *her* food with her brothers and sisters. The rest push away anyone who *gets* close when they are eating.

Contaminated Water

Every year contaminants from agricultural fertilizers and dairy waste finds their way into hundreds of rural family wells. The contaminants seep into underground streams which is the water source for the wells and often makes the water unfit for drinking. While many of the more potent fertilizers have been banned by the state. Todays agricultural fertilizers still retain some contaminating elements if concentrated in large enough quantities. Many of the wells tested by the countys water department exceeds the maximum level of contaminants for drinkable water, as a consequence many rural families must drink nothing but bottled water.

Recently a number of rural residents filed a class-action lawsuit against local farmers they want the farmers to pay for the purification process required to make the contaminated water drinkable. In addition they are seeking an injunction against farmers from using any fertilizer containing the contaminants found in the well water. In the past such lawsuits took years to process providing no timely relief from the problem.

Arguing that their livelihood is dependent on fertilizing their crops, the fertilizers will continue to be used by local farmers. Adding significantly to the problem contaminants from older fertilizers which were potenter than todays fertilizers can remain in water sources for many years thereby mixing with the more current contaminates to produce a toxic brew. The problem of water contamination in large agricultural areas have always existed while the situation is better today than twenty years ago it is still unacceptable to anyone concerned about the quality and safety of their water.

Writing Activity 10.15

Proofread your latest draft for errors and make any needed corrections. Focus in particular on those areas where you are most error prone and on the problem areas covered in the lessons.

Communicating with Readers

When your essay is in "publishable" form, share it with your reading audience or representatives. Your instructor may have some ideas on how to best communicate with readers and perhaps get some feedback. It is worthwhile both to have your essay read and to assess its impact on readers.

Lesson Eleven: Critique Writing

Objective: To write a critique that analyzes and evaluates a particular essay or article.

Audience: Writer's choice

Purpose: Writer's choice

In previous lessons, you wrote essays that presented your own ideas on a topic, sometimes supplemented by research material. Writers also write essays to *critique* the writing of others: analyzing and evaluating the quality of a particular article, book, poem, or essay. A writer may critique an article or book to let readers know whether, in his opinion, it is worth reading; to convince readers of the merits of a writer's viewpoint and her supportive evidence; or to show readers the flaws in a writer's arguments and reasoning so they won't be influenced by them.

While writing a critique may be new to you, analyzing and evaluating the writing of others is not. You have evaluated essay drafts in the text, your classmates' drafts, and the articles that you read during your research. In addition, all of the evaluation and revision you have done on your own drafts helps you evaluate the writing of others. Indirectly, you have been preparing throughout the course for writing a critique.

Critical Reading

Writing a critique involves two tasks: reading and analyzing the essay you are critiquing and writing the critique based on your analysis and evaluation. The first task - reading, analyzing, and evaluating the essay - is perhaps the most important since it provides you with the basic elements of the critique: a summary of the essay's content, your opinion of the essay, and the content evaluation which led to your opinion.

Analyzing and evaluating an essay are different reading functions. When you *analyze* an essay, you examine its content in detail, trying to understand both its meaning and purpose. Once you clearly understand the essay, you can *evaluate* its content and its impact on you as a reader. In critiquing an essay or article, analysis comes before evaluation since you can't fairly or knowledgeably evaluate something until you clearly understand it.

To read, analyze, and evaluate an essay most effectively, consider these suggestions.

1. **Read the essay several times to gain the best understanding.** Reading an essay a second and third time is the best way to get the clearest picture: what every

sentence and paragraph mean, how the parts of the essay fit together, whether there is a logical progression in the presentation of ideas, and what the writer presumably is trying to accomplish.

2. **Clearly identify the topic of the essay.** Does the writer present the topic in a way that makes it understandable to readers? Are any explanations or definitions provided to help readers understand the topic?

3.. **Identify the thesis of the essay: the writer's viewpoint on the topic.** The thesis may be stated in the opening or conclusion or it may be implied, the essay's content clearly revealing the writer's viewpoint. Once you identify the thesis, you can analyze and evaluate its support.

4. **Identify and evaluate the support for the thesis.** Does the essay provide factual evidence? Does it allege certain facts without substantiation? Does it present any opinions as if they were facts? Are the supporting arguments reasonable and sensible? Does it use relevant comparisons to help make its points? Does it provide source introductions for any material that appears "borrowed" from research?

5. **Does the essay omit things that leave questions in your mind?** Does it omit facts that don't support its thesis? Does it ignore major arguments against its thesis? What can you infer, if anything, from what *isn't* included in the essay?

6. **Does the essay reveal any writer *bias* on the topic?** Is it obvious in the essay that the writer is biased in favor or against the topic, not showing any objectivity or consideration for opposing viewpoints? If such bias is apparent, how does it affect you as a reader?

7. **Does the essay contain any *logical fallacies?*** Essays often contain logical fallacies - defective or fallacious arguments - intended to influence readers. The next section will cover logical fallacies in some detail.

8. **Is the purpose of the essay clear, and how well is it accomplished?** Does the essay make the desired impact on you as a reader?

9. **What is the overall impact of the essay?** What effect does it have on you and why?

10. **How well written is the essay?** Are its ideas clearly presented? Are its sentences well worded? Is its organization effective? Are its opening and conclusion strong? Does the writing quality of the essay enhance or detract from your reading experience?

11. **Evaluate the essay objectively.**   Readers sometimes let their own viewpoints or biases influence their evaluation of an essay, favoring writings whose viewpoint they agree with. Try your best to evaluate an essay objectively on its merits, not letting your own opinions on the topic color your thinking.

Logical Fallacies

In trying to persuade readers, writers sometimes write things that are simply not true, that are irrelevant, that are not reasonable or logical, or that try to appeal to the "heart" rather than the mind. *Logical fallacies* - faulty arguments that tend to obscure rather than reveal the truth - can influence readers who don't recognize their flaws. The following logical fallacies are among the most common that you may come across in your reading.

1. **Hasty generalization: Making a general assumption from limited experience or a small sampling of evidence.**
    For example, if you are bitten by a cat and make the assumption, "Cats are vicious animals," you have made an erroneous assumption based on a single experience. If you watch one college basketball game and conclude, "Our college team has terrible shooters," you have based your assumption on too small a sampling of games. The problem with hasty generalizations is that they are often wrong, leading readers to false conclusions.

2. **Slippery slope: Claiming that a particular occurrence will ultimately produce dire consequences when there is no evidence to support the claim.**
    For example, when the U.S. went into a deep recession in 2008, some prognosticators claimed that the recession would lead to the downfall of America as a great power. When the Federal government put a national health care program into law, some detractors claimed that this was the first step in the government taking over private industries and "socializing" America. Neither claim was substantiated by evidence and both have been proven wrong. In your reading, question any prediction that seems ludicrously extreme and has no basis in fact.

3. **False cause: Assuming a cause/effect relationship that doesn't exist.**
    For example, on the day that a state tax increase went into effect, six large companies declared bankruptcy. A newspaper editorialist claimed that the tax increase caused the companies to declare bankruptcy when in reality, there was no connection, the bankruptcies resulting from the prolonged recession.   In your reading, if a cause-and-effect relationship seems questionable to you or isn't proved in any way, question its validity.

4. **Overgeneralization: Assuming a consensus of opinion that doesn't exist.**
    For example, when someone writes, "*All women* agree that child rearing is the hardest job there is," or "*Everyone* agrees that Federal taxes are too high, " or "*No*

one in his right mind would support the proposed tuition increase," he is guilty of overgeneralizing. Writers overgeneralize to make readers think that *everyone* supports their viewpoint, which is seldom the case.

5. **Ad hominem: Attacking the person rather than his position on the issue.**
   For example, the position of a congressman who supported a cut in the military budget was attacked in a "letter to the editor" because the congressman never served in the armed forces: "Congressman Brown never served his country in the military, so it is not surprising that he wants to cut military spending." Rather than argue against a cut in military spending, the writer attacked the person and ignored the issue.

6. **Red herring: Getting off of the subject to mislead readers or distract them from the real issue.**
   For example, a writer who opposed stricter gun control laws argued that politicians were trying to cut military spending, which would weaken the country's national defense. The introduction of cuts in military spending was a *red herring*, having nothing to do with the issue of gun control. Be aware when a writer gets off on a tangent, and question her motive.

7. **Either-or fallacy: Erroneously assuming only two choices are available.**
   For example, when someone writes, "Either we tax the wealthy at a higher rate or continue to see the national deficit increase," he is committing the either-or fallacy because there are more than two options available, such as reducing government spending, taxing all Americans at a higher rate, or improving the economy to produce greater tax revenues. A writer commits the either-or fallacy to give readers only two options - the one favored by the writer and a less appealing one - when other options exist.

8. **Appeal to popularity: Assuming the "rightness" of a position on an issue because of its popularity.**
   For example, some proponents of the death penalty use the argument that a vast majority of Americans polled support the death penalty. Politicians who want the U.S. military to leave Afghanistan argue that popular support for the war is at an all-time low. That the majority of people agree on something doesn't necessarily make it fair or right; at one time in history, for example, most Americans supported slavery. Question any "popular appeal" argument, evaluating the writer's viewpoint on the evidence presented, not the popularity of the position.

9. **Name calling: Using emotionally charged language to influence readers.**
   For example, opponents of the national health care law refer to it derisively as "Obamacare." Some Democrats label Republican conservatives as "right-wing extremists" while some Republicans label Democrats as "bleeding-heart liberals." Such loaded language encourages an emotional response from readers rather than a rationale analysis of issues and positions.

Writing Activity 11.1

The following paragraphs contain examples of the logical fallacies presented. Identify each fallacy, the writer's probable intent in using it, and how you respond to it as a reader.

The Cost of Textbooks

It is obvious to every student that the price of textbooks in the college bookstore is excessively high. If the prices continue to increase, they will drive a majority of students out of college. Either the college needs to lower the prices of their textbooks or an alternative off-campus bookstore needs to be established to give students a less expensive option. Even college instructors agree that the price of textbooks at the bookstore is too high, making it an undisputable fact.

   The bookstore manager, who sets the price of textbooks, is paid an excellent salary, so she is not going to support reducing the prices. In addition, the price of paperback novels in the bookstore is twenty-to-thirty percent higher than at the Barnes and Noble bookstore downtown. Given the price of textbooks at our college bookstore, it is obvious that overpriced textbooks are a problem at most colleges. Colleges sometimes see a decrease in revenue from lower enrollment or less funding from the state, so they sell textbooks at outrageous prices to make up the revenue loss. Students are particularly frustrated because despite repeatedly voicing their concerns, they see no effort by the cowardly college administration or the lazy board of trustees members to improve the situation.

Writing Activity 11.2

Read, analyze, and evaluate the following essay by applying the critical reading suggestions presented. Based on your evaluation, draw a conclusion on the effectiveness of the essay and be prepared to discuss how you reached your conclusion.

Capping Campaign Spending for County Supervisor Candidates

In the 2010 Corona County Board of Supervisor's race, supervisor candidate Loreen Demeter spent over $500,000 on her campaign, far outspending the rest of the candidates. With the money, Demeter filled the airways and local television networks with political ads, sent out glossy campaign mailers to the majority of registered voters, and inundated the county with posters. The outcome of the election was predictable: a landslide victory for Ms. Demeter.

   With the $500,000, a campaign-spending record for county supervisor candidates, Demeter was able to "buy" the election. In most county elections, where the candidates are seldom well-known by voters, the candidate who gets his or her name out to the public most frequently usually wins. $500,000 buys a tremendous amount of name recognition, far more than the other candidates could afford, and most voters cast their ballots for the name they recognized.

Based on records from the County Elections Office, in the last five supervisorial elections, the candidate who spent the most money on his or her campaign won the election. Ms. Demeter's victory was just the latest example of how candidates who outspend their opponents can buy local elections. Money spent should not be the main criteria for a person getting elected to office, and a ceiling needs to be placed on the amount that any candidate can spend on a campaign.

With the current system, people who don't have a lot of money or access to wealthy donors don't stand a chance of being elected. Therefore, many people who may have an interest in running for supervisor stay on the sidelines. These are people who may best understand the problems and needs of the majority of County residents, who, like themselves, aren't that well-to-do. Some of the best candidates may be the ones who never run for office. Eventually, only wealthy candidates will run for office, and the Board of Supervisors will become an oligarchy of the rich.

In addition, some of the big-spending candidates clearly have political aspirations beyond the Board of Supervisors. Of the five candidates elected to the Board over the past twelve years, only one remains on the Board, the other four moving on to higher elected positions in the state. Do we want to elect supervisors who view their election as a springboard to higher office or supervisors who truly care about the County and want to serve its residents for a period of years?

Putting a ceiling on campaign spending would put the campaign focus where it belongs: on the qualities and qualifications of the candidates. More emphasis would be placed on local newspaper interviews with each candidate and on candidates' debates on local public radio and television stations. In addition, the hardest-working candidates who walk the precincts and put in the time would have the advantage rather than the candidates with the most money. A cap on campaign spending would provide the greatest assurance that the most qualified, capable candidates for the job would have the best chance to win.

A further problem with the wealthiest candidates winning the elections is that once in office, people tend to take care of their own. Once elected, wealthy supervisors are not going to do anything to upset the large landowners, agri-business magnates, and developers, who are often their biggest supporters. In addition, wealthy supervisors will most often side with management, not County workers, when it comes to bargaining salaries and benefits or laying off employees in the face of budget problems. While the majority of County residents fall within the middle and lower-middle class economically, wealthy supervisors will be more concerned with keeping the upper-class residents happy, their kind of people.

Putting a ceiling of $25,000 on campaign spending for supervisorial elections would go a long ways towards leveling the playing field for all candidates. Any candidate who is really interested in the office should be able to garner enough support to raise $25,000. With today's system, where the biggest-spending candidate usually wins, that elected candidate may be the best person for the job or the worst. There is no correlation between buying a campaign with big money and being a good supervisor. However, with all candidates spending a maximum of $25,000, the chances of electing the best candidates year in and year out are much better, with a candidate's qualifications and qualities being more important than how much money he or she has.

Please sign a petition to place a spending-limit initiative for supervisorial races on the next county election ballot. 50,000 signatures are required to qualify the initiative, not a difficult number to reach given the importance of electing good county supervisors and the inequity of the current system. If you believe that candidates should be judged on their qualifications and not elected based on the amount of campaign money they spend, please support the spending-limit initiative.

Writing Assignment

For this lesson, you will write an essay critiquing an essay or article of your choosing. You may find the essay or article online, in the newspaper, in a periodical, or in a collection of essays. To select an essay to critique, consider these suggestions:

1. **Select an essay on a topic that interests you.** The topic may be from any field - politics, the environment, education, sports, music, medicine, children's issues, law enforcement - and on the local, state, national, or international level.

2. **Select an essay on a topic on which people's opinions differ.** Make sure that there are differing viewpoints on the topic from the one expressed in the essay.

3. **Select an essay with a clear thesis.** A main part of your critique is to evaluate the supportive evidence for the essay's thesis, so make sure that the writer expresses (or implies) a definite viewpoint in the essay.

4. **Select an essay that would be of interest to some group of readers.** When you consider an essay, think of a reading audience that would have an interest in the topic or be affected by it in some way.

Writing Assignment 11.3

Read several essays or articles on different topics and select an essay for your critique keeping in mind the essay-selection suggestions.

Sample topic:

Essay to critique: "Gun Control Doesn't Work"
                     by Christie Snyder, *Discerning the Times Digest*

Preparation

A major part of preparing to write a critique, of course, is to read, analyze, and evaluate the essay that you are critiquing. As suggested earlier in the lesson, you may want to read the essay several times to understand it best and see how its different parts fit together. The better you understand the essay, the more assuredly you can critique it.

Since you already evaluated an essay earlier in the lesson, you have some idea on how to proceed with your current essay. In preparing for your critique, consider the following questions:

1. What is the topic of the essay, and what is the essay's thesis (viewpoint)?

2. What are the main supportive points for the thesis, and what evidence, if any, is provided to substantiate each point?

3. How valid or believable is each supporting point and why?

4. What problems, if any, does the essay have (e.g. unsubstantiated facts, opinions presented as facts, poorly reasoned arguments, logical fallacies)? How do they affect the impact of the essay?

5. What, if anything, does the essay leave out of importance? Are major opposing arguments ignored? Are some obvious facts not presented? Do some points need further clarification?

5. What are the strengths of the essay: the supportive evidence (facts, comparisons, examples, statistics, studies, etc) you find most effective or influential?

6. Based on your evaluation, what is your overall impression of the essay: the degree to which the essay supports its thesis convincingly?

7. What do you think the purpose of the essay is, and how well did the writer accomplish her purpose?

Writing Activity 11.4

Write out or think through your responses to the seven previous questions.

Thesis

Like most essays, a critique usually has a thesis expressing the writer's viewpoint on the essay or article being critiqued. Your thesis expresses your overall opinion of the essay: how convincingly it supported its thesis and the resulting impact on you as a reader. Your evaluation of the essay takes into account both its strengths and weaknesses, which may lead to a favorable, unfavorable, or mixed overall response.

To consider your thesis for the essay you are critiquing, answer these questions:

1. Based on your evaluation, what is your overall impression of the essay? How convincingly did the essay present and support its thesis? Your thesis is an expression of this overall impression.

2. What were the main aspects of the essay from which you formed this impression?

Writing Activity 11.5

Based on your evaluation, generate a potential thesis statement for your essay.

Sample thesis:

Essay :   Gun Control Doesn't Work

Thesis: While the article raises some questions on the effectiveness of gun control, based on the evidence presented, I'm not convinced that gun control doesn't work.

Thesis Support

In supporting your thesis in an essay, you answer the question, "What are your reasons for believing as you do?" In other words, what was it about the essay you critiqued that led you to your concluding opinion? How well you reveal the strengths or deficiencies of the main points in support of the essay's thesis will largely determine the readers' response to your thesis.

To support the thesis of your essay most effectively, consider these suggestions:

1. **Present and evaluate each supporting point the critiqued essay uses to validate its thesis.**   Most of your critique involves presenting and responding to the major points of the essay. Evaluate each argument in a way that is consistent with your thesis.

2   **In evaluating the essay, include both its strengths and weaknesses.**   While you may have an overall favorable impression of the essay, there may be some weaknesses to point out. While you may have a less favorable impression, it may have some strengths to reveal. You can provide an honest assessment of the essay, including both its strengths and weaknesses, without compromising your thesis.

3. **Don't "cherry pick" the material you evaluate from the essay.** Sometimes a critique writer will only present certain aspects of an essay that support her favorable or unfavorable opinion, leaving out relevant material that may not conform to her viewpoint. A fair evaluation of an essay takes into account everything within it. A critique that evaluates only selective material may leave readers with an inaccurate and slanted portrayal.

Writing Activity 11.6

Identify and evaluate the major arguments presented in the critiqued essay to support its thesis.

Audience and Purpose

As with most of your essays, your critique is intended for a particular audience and written for a purpose of your choice. Your reading audience and writing purpose will influence how you write the critique.

To decide on an audience and purpose for your critique, consider the following suggestions:

1. **Who would be interested in the topic of the essay you are critiquing?** Who might be affected by it or need to learn more about it?

2. **What should you keep in mind about your audience as you write your critique?** How knowledgeable are they on the topic? What is their probable viewpoint? How may they be affected by the topic?

3. **What might your purpose be for writing to this particular audience?** To recommend that they read the article? To suggest they not waste their time reading it? To show the good sense or fairness of an article's thesis and arguments? To expose the specious reasoning and fallacious information in an article? To educate readers on the topic? To get them to take action?

Writing Activity 11.7

Decide on a tentative audience and purpose for your critique.

Sample audience and purpose:

Essay to critique: Gun Control Doesn't Work

Reading audience: General public

Purpose: To point out the flaws in the essay's gun-control arguments so that readers aren't influenced by them.

Drafting

Writing a critique is somewhat different from the essay writing you have done during the course. In a critique, you present enough of the content of the critiqued essay for readers to gain a good understanding. In supporting your thesis, you present and evaluate the arguments that the essay makes in support of *its* thesis. Rather than creating your own essay content, you are responding to the content of another essay.

Critique writing also has its similarities to your previous writing. You are still presenting and supporting a thesis based on your evaluation of the topic; introducing your topic in the opening; presenting the supportive points for your thesis in the middle paragraphs; reinforcing your thesis in the conclusion, and writing to a reading audience for a particular purpose. With so much familiar ground to cover, writing the critique will not seem that foreign.

Writing a Critique

Since you may not have written a critique, this section provides a basic "how to" for critique writing. You will find the organization of a critique quite straightforward and sensible for presenting and evaluating the content of the critiqued essay.

To write the first draft of your critique, consider these suggestions:

1. **In your opening, introduce the topic of the critiqued essay, the essay's viewpoint (thesis) on the topic, and your *own* thesis: your overall impression of the essay.** From your opening, readers should know the topic of the critiqued essay, what the writer believes about the topic, and how convincingly you feel the essay supported its thesis.

2. **If readers may need further explanation to understand the topic clearly, include the explanatory material after the opening.** For example, if the topic of the critiqued essay is "The Burgeoning Federal Debt," readers may need some explanation of what comprises the "Federal Debt" and what its size is.

3. **Present and evaluate the main arguments that the critiqued essay uses to support its thesis, keeping your thesis in mind.** The major content of the critiqued essay should be presented and evaluated in the middle paragraphs.

4. **Conclude your essay in a way that reinforces your thesis and writing purpose.** What thoughts do you most want to leave readers with regarding the critiqued essay?

5. **Don't let "topic bias" influence your critique.** Your task is to evaluate the essay's content *objectively*, basing your viewpoint on the quality of the essay rather than your own opinion on the topic.

6. **Keep in mind that your readers have probably not read the essay you are critiquing.** Whatever they learn about the essay, they learn from your critique. Present them with a clear and accurate picture.

Writing Activity 11.8

To gain a better understanding of critique writing, read the following two sample critiques as well as the original article that precedes each critique. Note the opening of the critiques, their thesis statements, their presentation and evaluation of the essay's content, and the conclusions they draw in the ending.

Gun Control Doesn't Work
by Christie Snyder

Anyone familiar with statistical analysis knows that statistics can be twisted to say almost anything. Take for example the number of deaths caused by medical mishaps: 120,000 per year in the U.S. which has approximately 700,000 physicians. That's 171 deaths per year per doctor each year. Compare that with the number of gun owners, which is around 80,000,000, with 1,500 accidental gun deaths each year. That means that the number of accidental, gun related deaths each year per gun owner is .0000188. Nevertheless, it would be ludicrous to say that doctors are 9,000 times more dangerous than gun owners. The comparison between gun owners and physicians just makes no sense. So let's look at some statistics that really do make sense.

Advocates of gun control want us to believe that banning private gun ownership will reduce violent crime. In 1996, in the wake of a mass shooting, the Australian government seized more than 640,000 guns from its citizens. According to the Australian Bureau of Statistics, in the next two years, armed robbery rose by 73%, unarmed robbery by 28%, kidnaping by 38%, assault by 17% and manslaughter by 29%.

Following the trend from down under, the government in the U.K. also imposed new gun controls after a mass shooting. Again violent crime did not decrease. According to the U.S. Justice Department Bureau of Justice Statistics, although the rates of murder and rape are higher in the U.S., England has surpassed us in its rate of robberies, assaults, burglaries and motor vehicle thefts. And the English crime rate has been rising while the U.S. rate has been falling. In 1998 the mugging rate in England was 40% higher than in the U.S.; furthermore, assault and burglary rates were nearly 100% higher in England than in the United States.

Another rate that will strike terror in the heart of women is the rate of hot burglaries, which are burglaries that take place when people are home. I think one of my worst nightmares would be to wake up in the dead of night to find an intruder in my room. Yet, most criminals in this country know that breaking in with people home is a good way to get shot. In fact, if someone were to break into my home when we are home, that is exactly what will happen. The hot burglary rate in the U.S. is 13%. However, in countries with strict gun control, such as England and Canada, the hot burglary rate is closer to

50%. The criminals know that their victims, having been rendered helpless by their governments, cannot defend themselves.

If the facts show that gun control legislation does not lower crime rates, then why is there such a push to take guns away from law abiding people? What happened to our Constitutional right to bear arms? The founding fathers knew that a well-armed citizenry would not easily be taken over by a tyrannical government. Those pushing for a global government are keenly aware of this fact as well. To control a people, first you must disarm them.

U.S. Code Title 22 section 2551, which was passed as Public Law 87-297 by President Kennedy in 1961, lays out the plan to completely disarm both citizens and governments of the world. Section 2552 defines disarmament this way: "Identification, verification, inspection, limitation, control, reduction, or elimination, of armed forces and armaments of all kinds under international agreement including the necessary steps taken under such an agreement to establish an effective system of international control, or to create and strengthen international organizations for the maintenance of peace."

Every president since Kennedy has worked to implement this agenda. The United States has been systematically emasculating its military for more than a decade. The Russians and Chinese are supposed to be reducing their military in the same manner, but as DTT has previously reported, that is just not happening. The final outcome of this plan is that the armies of the world will be centrally controlled, becoming a global force, and that only the military will be armed. Our national sovereignty has been traitorously undermined.

Gun control finds its greatest success in keeping guns out of the hands of ordinary, law abiding citizens. The government will always be armed. And the criminal mind will always find a means of acquiring weapons. That will leave you and me stuck somewhere in the middle between criminal corruption and government tyranny. It's getting harder and harder to tell the difference.

Critique of "Gun Control Doesn't Work" (first draft)

(audience: general public)

Kristie Snyder's article "Gun Control Doesn't Work" contends that banning private gun ownership not only wouldn't lead to less violent crime in America, it would make the situation worse. While the article raises some questions as to the effectiveness of gun control, based on the evidence presented, I'm far from convinced that she is right.

Snyder's opening paragraph, the longest of the article, presents statistics comparing the relatively high rate of medical mishaps causing death per physician in the U.S. to the relative low rate of accidental gun deaths per gun owner. She concludes that the comparison obviously makes no sense, which I agree with, so why lead the article with it? Then in the next paragraphs she proceeds to use statistics to make her case against gun control after admitting in the first paragraph that "Statistics can be twisted to say almost anything." So she weakens her case from the start.

The article does present some statistics to consider carefully. In 1996, after a mass murder in Australia, the article says that the government "seized" more than 640,000 guns from its citizens. In the next two years, armed robbery, unarmed robbery, kidnaping, assault, and manslaughter all rose at an alarming rate. Questions, however, arise. Does 640,000 guns represent a large or small percentage of the guns that citizens owned? Is Australia a "gun-toting" country like the United States or is gun ownership much lower, like in the U.K.? The fact is, while the United States has the highest murder rate of any industrial nation, Australia has among the lowest. Did the seizure of 640,000 guns change that in any way?

The article goes on to say that when the U.K. imposed stronger gun control laws, violent crime did not decrease. However, the article did admit that the rates of murder and rape are higher in the U.S. than in England, although it failed to admit that they are overwhelmingly higher. The article then contended that the mugging, assault, and burglary rates were higher in England than in the U.S. although it provided no evidence to support that claim nor concluded that the stronger gun control laws had anything to do with it.

Snyder next contends that the "hot" burglary rate, burglaries occurring when people are home, is higher in Canada and England than in the U.S., 13% in the U.S. compared to closer to 50% in Canada and England. 13% of what? 50% of what? Does she mean that 13% of American households are broken into while 50% of Canadian and U.K. households are broken into during the same time period? Without knowing, the statistics remain highly suspect, and since there is no source cited for the statistics, they may have come from an NRA publication or pulled from thin air.

The article next takes a prolonged detour into the paranoid world of anti-government conspiracy theory, which both hurts the author's credibility and weakens the article. The real reason that the government wants to disarm its citizenry, according to the article, is so that we cannot defend ourselves against a well-armed, tyrannical government, meaning our own. Then it goes on to contradict itself and claim that the U.S. has been "systematically emasculating its military," and that our national sovereignty has been "traitorously undermined." There is no evidence presented to support this claim, and given that the U.S. is the strongest military power in the world, it makes little sense. Moreover, U.S. military strength has nothing to do with the gun control issue, an obvious red herring. In addition, I know of no one who is fearful of a tyrannical American government imposing its will on an unarmed citizenry. Finally, what evidence is there that the U.S. government wants to take away people's guns? I've seen no legislation to support that contention.

Would greater gun control make the U.S. a more dangerous place to live? The essay doesn't convince me. First, it leaves questions unanswered. Since the U.S. is by far the most violent country in the industrialized world, and since most violent crimes are caused by hand guns, what is the author's solution to reducing the murder rate in the country? In addition, what has happened in states like Massachusetts that have enacted stricter gun control laws? If Massachusetts has been unsuccessful, I would guess that would have been included in the article. The article also weakens its statistical arguments by citing conditions in Canada, the U.K., and Australia, three countries with much lower violent crime and gun ownership rates than the U.S. The fact is, the U.S. would gladly trade its violent crime rate with any of those countries, where hand gun ownership is rare compared to the U.S.

Finally, the article lost me when it swerved off on its anti-government tirade that has nothing to do with today's gun control issue in the U.S. An admitted gun-toter herself,

Snyder ends her article in a manner that only the most paranoid readers would embrace. I question that the essay would influence anyone other than those whose beliefs on gun ownership mirrored the author's.

"Snubbing the Kyoto Protocal"
by Cynthia Watts

The Kyoto Protocol is a world=wide agreement entered into by most countries of the world to work together to decrease global warming and its negative effects. Championed by the Clinton administration through environmental spokesperson Vice= President Al Gore, it was rejected by former President Bush, whose administration refused to participate.

Scientists have agreed for years that our atmosphere is getting warmer due to man-made pollutants that form a blanket in the atmosphere and don't allow heat to escape as it naturally would. How else could we account for the fact that the polar icecaps are melting at an unprecedented rate, that the oceans' waters are warming and rising as a result, and that the majority of the hottest days in recorded history have occurred in the past ten years?

Should we care that our atmosphere is warming? Definitely. Rising oceans can result in the displacement of millions of people whose oceanside communities and farmlands would be permanently flooded. Changes in climate can negatively affect agriculture across the world where crops depend on the natural climate of the area. Overheating the planet could destroy millions of acres of farmland.

Global warming is also warming the currents that run through the oceans, which is paradoxically resulting in colder temperatures in places such as Northern Europe, where the warmer currents meet the colder northern waters, resulting in increased rain and snowfall. Global warming is also being viewed as the possible culprit behind the exceptional climatological upheavals we've seen in recent years, such as the devastating 2003 tsunami in Japan and Hurricane Katrina, one of three powerful hurricanes that have pounded the Gulf of Mexico in the last three years.

Whether global warming is responsible for every climatological problem we are facing is beside the point. There is enough evidence of its negative impact to convince most of the nations of the world to band together to do something about it. Then why on earth did former President Bush thumb his nose at the Kyoto Protocol and send the message to other countries that the United States isn't going to cooperate in combating global warming? Why did the Bush administration turn its back on a world=wide anti=pollution effort that the Clinton administration embraced?

The chief cause of global warming is the millions of tons of hydrocarbons pumped into the atmosphere by the emissions of automobiles and heavy industries. Reversing global warming would require governmental regulation of the auto, coal, and oil industries that Bush wasn't willing to commit to. He claimed that such regulation would hurt the U.S. economy, but in reality, he didn't want to offend the industry magnates that helped put him in the White House. In addition, how can you regulate and police the very industry that you and your family are a major part of: big oil? The fox, unfortunately, was guarding the henhouse.

It is unconscionable for the Bush administration not to have supported the Kyoto Protocol and take a leadership role in combating global warming and its disastrous environmental effects. Bush's response to critics was similar to his response to worldwide criticism of the Iraqi war: we are right and the world is wrong. When it comes to global warming, the world has it right and the Bush administration had it dead wrong.

Why Americans weren't in an uproar over Bush's environmental position on global warming probably lies in the fact that the very worst results of global warming lie in the future. We tend not to worry about environmental issues until the situation becomes dire, like the terrible pollution of America's lakes and rivers in the 1980's. But if we do nothing about global warming now, we may be leaving our children and grandchildren with an environmental catastrophe of hideous proportions.

Perhaps the crowning blow for the Bush administration was a meeting of six former heads of the Federal EPA (Environmental Protection Agency), five of whom served under Republican presidents, who unanimously stated that global warming was a serious issue and the Bush administration was not doing enough to combat it. Their purpose was obvious: to get Bush to change course dramatically on global warming. Unfortunately, he didn't listen to environmental experts, he listened to the big polluters who wrote his campaign checks: the auto, coal, and oil industry magnates. If Americans don't get angry over this environmental outrage, nothing is going to change. And the planet will keep getting hotter and hotter.

Critique of "The Kyoto Protocol"

(audience: general public)

The article "Snubbing the Kyoto Protocol" is an indictment of former President Bush's administration for not supporting the Kyoto Protocol, an agreement among most nations to reduce global warming and its negative impacts. While the Clinton administration supported the Kyoto Protocol and played a leadership role in combating global warming, the Bush administration virtually ignored the problem and didn't cooperate with the participating nations, according to author Cynthia Watts. The essay presents a good case for the dangers of global warming, but I wonder if Americans really care enough to get involved.

Why would anyone not support a world=wide effort to reduce global warming, Watts questions. She provides evidence of global warming such as melting icecaps, warming, rising ocean waters, and abrupt climatological changes, and possible future effects: the flooding of farmlands and oceanside communities world wide, the negative impact of climate changes on agriculture, perhaps even the disastrous natural disasters such as tsunamis and hurricanes that have been occurring at an alarming rate. While Watts expects us to accept her evidence and the effects of global warming without presenting any real proof, enough has been written on the topic in recent years to substantiate what she says. It is difficult not to agree with her assessment that global warming is a problem that needs addressing.

To explain why President Bush didn't support the Kyoto Protocol, Watts offers two reasons. First, Bush didn't want to regulate the industries such as coal and oil that emit a lot of the hydrocarbons into the atmosphere that cause global warming. These industry leaders were big Bush contributors, claims Watts, and he and his family are a part of big oil themselves. Second, Bush claimed that it would hurt the economy to move too fast on global warming. Watts doesn't explain her reasoning.

The article doesn't provide support for the assertion of Bush's relationship with the coal and oil industries, but with the Bush family in the oil business, it's not hard to believe. Watts also expects readers to accept that these industries are major global warming polluters without providing evidence, but their contribution wouldn't be surprising. If reducing global warming would hurt the U.S. economy, I'd like to know how and to what extent, but even then, what's more important: today's economy or the environmental future of our planet?

Watts's best evidence against the Bush administration's position is that six former heads of the Environmental Protection Agency, five of them serving under Republican presidents, stated together publicly that global warming was a serious problem and that the Bush administration wasn't doing enough. It's difficult not to believe these experts, and at least five of them aren't playing partisan politics. In addition, why would most of the nations of the world band together through the Kyoto Protocol to fight global warming if it wasn't a serious problem?

While I agree with the article that global warming is a problem and that former President Bush's position on the issue was terrible, I'm afraid I'm one of those Americans that Watts mentions in her essay: the ones who don't get too excited until the effects of global warming are at our doorstep. But will it be too late by then to change course? I too want our government to take an outspoken leadership role against global warming, but I suspect that won't happen until the American public embraces the issue. Unfortunately, I'm not enraged enough to do much, but that's not Watts's fault. While her essay probably wouldn't rouse many Americans to action, I'm not sure what she could have said that would.

Writing Activity 11.9

With a classmate or two, evaluate the two critiques, determining how convincingly and objectively the writers responded to the main points of each article. Then write the first draft of your critique, keeping in mind the six suggestions for critique writing.

Revision

Evaluating your critique for possible revisions is similar to previous draft evaluations you have done: assessing the effectiveness of your opening, thesis support, conclusion, organization, paragraphing, and sentence wording. The new considerations for a critique draft include evaluating how accurately you have presented the critiqued essay's content, how effectively you have responded to its main points, and whether you have presented an objective evaluation despite your viewpoint on the topic.

Revision Suggestions

As you revise your draft, consider these suggestions:

1. **Reread the essay you critiqued and then your draft to make sure that the draft accurately reflects your viewpoint: the overall impression the essay made on you.** If your perspective changes in any way, revise your draft to reflect your change in viewpoint. If your viewpoint remains unchanged, make any revisions to ensure that all parts of your essay coincide with your viewpoint (thesis).

2. **Evaluate your opening.** Do you present the topic of the essay you critiqued and its thesis? Do you present the thesis of the critique: your overall impression of the essay? Do you create reader interest by showing the importance of the topic, how it may affect readers, or why they should be concerned about it? Make any revisions that would strengthen your opening.

3. **Evaluate how accurately you present the content of the critiqued essay.** Do readers understand what the essay is about, the writer's viewpoint in the essay, the main points that support her viewpoint, and the essay's probable intent? What revisions might you make to help readers understand the essay better or to provide a more accurate or complete picture of it?

4. **Evaluate your assessment of each of the essay's main supporting points.** Do readers understand how you feel about each point and why? Do your responses support your thesis? Do you respond to all of the essay's primary arguments rather than just those that may further your purpose? Do you point out any strengths or weaknesses in the essay in ways that don't compromise your thesis? Do you try not to let your own opinion on the topic influence your evaluation?

5. **Evaluate your conclusion.** Does your ending reinforce your thesis in some manner? Do readers understand your purpose in critiquing this particular essay? Does it leave them with something new to think about? Make any changes that

will strengthen your conclusion and its impact on readers.

6. **Evaluate your paragraphing.** Do you change paragraphs as you move to different parts of the essay: opening to middle, middle to ending? Do you present and evaluate the main points of the critiqued essay in separate paragraphs? Do you use topic sentences to introduce the main idea of each paragraph? Are there any overly long paragraphs that need dividing or short, successive paragraphs that need combining or developing further? Make any paragraphing revisions that will help readers move through the paper with the greatest understanding.

7. **Evaluate your organization.** Do you present the main points of the critiqued essay in the most effective order? Are there any paragraphs or sentences that would fit more logically or effectively in a different location? Make any changes in the draft that will improve its organization.

8. **Evaluate your sentence wording.** Revise sentences to eliminate wordiness, smooth out awkward sentences, replace questionable word choices, and create structural variety. Check your use of transitional wording (*first, second, in addition, finally, as you can see, however, therefore*) and add any transitions that will help tie paragraphs together and show relationships among ideas.

9. **Evaluate how well you accomplished your purpose.** Read each part of the draft with your audience and purpose in mind, and make any changes that will further your purpose for your particular audience.

Writing Activity 11.10

Revise your draft keeping in mind the revision suggestions presented.

Sample revisions:

"Why Gun Control Doesn't Work" (final three paragraphs)

 The article next takes a prolonged detour into the paranoid world of anti-government conspiracy theory, which ~~both~~ hurts the author's credibility and weakens the article. The real reason that the government wants to disarm its citizenry, according to the article, is so that we cannot defend ourselves against a well-armed, tyrannical government, meaning our own. Then it goes on to contradict itself and claim that the U.S. has been "systematically emasculating its military," and that our national sovereignty has been "traitorously undermined." There is no evidence presented to support this **outrageous** claim, and given that the U.S. is the strongest military power in the world, it makes little sense. Moreover, the entire anti-government tirade **is an obvious red herring,** ~~has~~ **having** nothing to do with the gun control issue~~, an obvious red herring~~. In addition, **is any rational person** ~~I know of no one in their right mind~~

~~who is~~ fearful of a tyrannical American government imposing its will on an unarmed citizenry? Finally, what evidence is there that the U.S. government wants to take away people's guns? I've seen no Federal legislation to support that contention.

Would greater gun control make the U.S. a more dangerous place to live? This article doesn't convince me, **and I'm just as inclined to believe that it would make it a safer place.** First, ~~it~~ **the article** leaves **too many** questions in my mind unanswered. Since the U.S. is by far the most violent country in the industrialized world, and since most violent crimes are caused by hand guns, what is the author's solution to reducing the murder rate in the country? Second, what has happened in states like Massachusetts that have enacted stricter gun control laws? If Massachusetts has been unsuccessful, ~~I would guess~~ **wouldn't** that ~~would~~ have been included that in the article? The article also weakens its statistical arguments by citing conditions in Canada, the U.K., and Australia, three countries with much lower violent crime and gun ownership rates than the U.S. The fact is, the U.S. would gladly trade its violent crime rate with any of those countries, where hand gun ownership is ~~rare compared to the U.S.~~ **is less common.**

Finally, the article lost me, **and I would assume most readers,** when it swerved off **in the end** on its anti-government tirade that has nothing to do with today's gun control issue in the U.S. An admitted gun-toter herself, Snyder ends her article in a manner that **I believe** only the most paranoid readers ~~would~~ **might** embrace. ~~I question~~ **doubt** that the essay would influence anyone ~~other than those~~ whose beliefs on gun ownership **didn't** mirror the author's. **The article is a prime example of the questionable, misguided thinking of many people who oppose any type of gun control in the U.S.**

Writing Activity 11.11

Exchange your revised draft with a classmate or two to get some reader feedback. Based on the feedback, make any further changes in your draft that you feel would improve it.

Editing

The last step in getting your critique in final form is to proofread it for errors. Even the most experienced writers often find some inadvertent errors in their drafts. Those errors most often reveal themselves when you shift your focus from content to correctness in the editing phase.

In this lesson, you are introduced to another editing consideration: the correct use of quotation marks. In your latest draft, you may have quoted from the essay that you critiqued, so you can apply what you learn when you proofread your draft. Proper quotation punctuation will also be useful when you write a research paper in your final lesson.

Punctuating Quotations

You are already familiar with the basic punctuation of quotations, which you have used in previous essays. This section will focus primarily on the situations that may be less familiar to you.

To punctuate quotations correctly, follow these rules:

1. **Introduce the speaker, put a comma after the speaker introduction, put quotation marks (" ") around the spoken words, capitalize the first word of the quotation, and put the second quotation mark outside of the ending punctuation:**

   According to biologist Rene Wright, "Many endangered species are losing much of their natural habitats at an alarming rate."

2. **If the speaker introduction follows the quote, put a comma at the end of the quotation and a period at the end of the sentence:**

   "Prepare yourself for a very challenging final exam," warned Dr. Valencia, my sociology instructor.

3. **When you begin a quotation mid-sentence rather than at its beginning, don't capitalize the first word of the quotation and don't put a comma after the speaker introduction:**

   Defense attorney Marcus McBride argued that his client "wasn't even in the state when the robbery was committed."

4. **If a second quoted sentence by the same speaker follows the speaker introduction, put a period after the speaker introduction, capitalize the first**

word of the second quoted sentence, and put quotation marks around the sentence:

"The margin of error in Gallup polling results is relatively insignificant," said pollster Adam Ferrer. "People who dismiss such polls due to their margin of error usually don't like the results."

5. **If two quoted sentences follow in succession, put quotation marks only at the beginning of the first sentence and the end of the second sentence:**

Freda exclaimed loudly, "The shower water is freezing cold. The pilot on the hot water heater must have gone out!"

6. **If the same quoted sentence *continues* after the speaker introduction, put a comma after the speaker introduction and quotation marks around the second half of the sentence, but don't capitalize the first word:**

"I don't believe for a second," said the college lacrosse coach, "that you never played lacrosse in your life."

7. **Don't use quotation marks with an *indirect quotation.* which refers to what the speaker said without quoting her.**

Indirect: Child nutritionist Melanie Sinclair believes that healthy eating habits can dramatically reduce the frequency of childhood obesity in the U.S.

Direct: Child nutritionist Melanie Sinclair stated, "Healthy eating habits can significantly reduce the rate of childhood obesity in the U.S."

Writing Activity 11.12

Punctuate quotations in the following sentences correctly, including inserting quotation marks, commas, periods, and capital letters. Don't insert quotation marks in sentences that aren't direct quotations.

Example:

Noted zoologist Amy Kang stated most traditional zoos don't provide enough space for animals to live normally, often resulting in their depression, inactivity, and destructive behavior.

Noted zoologist Amy Kang stated, "Most traditional zoos don't provide enough space for animals to live normally, often resulting in depression and destructive behavior."

1. According to behavioral psychologist Alicia Juarez, the impact of color on people's moods and behavior is significant.

2. Employees are most productive in muted-colored settings said Juarez and their moods are more genial.

3. Juarez said that bright colors can make employees more irritable and negatively affect their productivity. (Quote begins with "can.")

4. Ralph Imu, general manager for Freitas Electric, agrees. We painted all of our walls and ceiling light blues and greens, said Imu employees seem more relaxed and attentive, and we get fewer worker complaints.

5. Schools have picked up on the correlation between color and behavior. We paint all of our classrooms pastel colors said Assistant Superintendent Beatrice Grice of the Bedford Unified Schools bright colors clearly make students more excitable and less focused on their work.

6. Results of experiments conducted by the University of Toronto behavioral psychology department confirm the impact of color on students.

7. In our experiments, students who took tests in pastel-colored rooms performed better than students who were tested in brightly colored rooms said University of Toronto department chair Alex Fertig when we questioned them, students in the brightly colored rooms were aware of their surroundings while the other students were not.

8. Many doctors and dentists have long known what the color experts now confirm. I've been painting my office walls light blue for twenty years said Dr. Candice Goodfellow which has a calming effect on my patients. I tried a bright blue for a while and could notice the difference in their anxiety level.

Writing Activity 11.13

Check the use of quotations in your current draft to make sure you have punctuated them correctly.

Writing Activity 11.14

If you could use more editing practice, proofread the following paragraphs and correct any errors involving run-on or comma-splice sentences, fragments, comma usage, subject-verb agreement, pronoun-antecedent agreement, colons, semi-colons, or dashes, dangling or misplaced modifiers, comparative and superlative adjectives, apostrophes in possessives and contractions, or frequently confused words (e.g. there/they're/their, know/no, affect/effect, it's/its).

Economic Gridlock

Ideas on how to "fix" the economy and create jobs in a recessionary period varies greatly. Some economists favor cutting government spending and lowering taxes. While others support increased government spending to stimulate the economy. Most Republicans believe that only the private sector can create jobs therefore they support reducing regulations and taxes on businesses. On the other hand most Democrats believe that the government should also be involved in job creation primarily through government-funded programs to rebuild the countrys aging infrastructure.

With Democrats and Republicans at odds on the best ways to stimulate the economy gridlock in the Senate and House of Representatives occur regularly and little gets done. Creating frustration and anger among many Americans. While people remain out of work and the economy continues to contract politicians often seem more interested in maintaining there idealogical purity then working together to solve the nations problems. A compromise solution lowering business taxes and creating infrastructure jobs seem reasonable but no one in Washington appears to look beyond their own narrow political interests.

Writing Activity 11.15

Proofread your draft for errors, focusing in particular on your personal error tendencies and the types of errors presented in the text, and make the necessary corrections.

Communicating with Readers

When you complete the final, error-free draft of your essay, find the most accessible way to share it with your reading audience or representatives. Your instructor may have some ideas on how to get the essay into readers' hands and get some feedback.

Lesson Twelve: Research Writing

Objective: To write a thesis-centered research paper following the MLA style format.

Audience: Writer's choice

Purpose: Writer's choice

Your final, culminating writing assignment is to write a research paper following a widely accepted format familiar to most readers. The MLA (Modern Language Association) style format is most commonly used in colleges for research writing. The MLA format is popular because it is easy for writers to use and for readers to follow. The main purpose of a research-paper format is to acknowledge clearly to readers the sources of the research material used, and the MLA format does that in a sensible, logical way.

Since you have already incorporated research material into previous essays, you have experience researching topics, using research material to support your thesis, acknowledging sources, and using paraphrasing and quotations to present the material. This experience will serve you well in writing the research paper. The main differences with your upcoming paper include relying more exclusively on research material to support your thesis, incorporating parenthetical references to acknowledge sources, and providing a "works cited" bibliography.

Parenthetical References

As with your previous essays, any time that you incorporate research material into a paper, you acknowledge its source. Source references let readers know where the material came from, lending it credibility and distinguishing it from your own ideas and responses. When a writer correctly acknowledges sources, readers always know when the information is "borrowed" from research and when it comes from the writer herself.

Following the MLA format, you will use *parenthetical references* in your research paper to acknowledge sources. More complete bibliographical information for each source will appear in the "Works Cited" section at the end of the paper. To reference your sources correctly, follow these guidelines:

1. **Include a parenthetical reference at the end of the research material to acknowledge your source.**

A. Include the author's last name and the page number of the material, if available:

Hand guns cause over 90% of homicides in the U.S. (Witherow 11).

B. If the author is anonymous, include the title of the article and page number.

Animals continue to evolve to survive in changing environments ("How Animals Evolve" 8-9).

Children raised in threatening environments often become more timid, less trusting adults ("The Psychology of Fear" 131).

C. If page numbers aren't available, as with some online articles, include the author's name, or if anonymous, the title of the article:

In some teen sub-cultures, there is no stigma attached to becoming pregnant ("Proud, Pregnant Teens").

Proponents of universal health care insist that the requirement for all Americans to have health insurance is essential (Vasquez).

D. If the research material includes several consecutive sentences, put the parenthetical reference at the end of the last sentence:

The housing bubble that burst in 2008 and led to the nation-wide recession also had an upside. Housing prices had become ridiculously high, and the recession created a "correction" which dropped housing values dramatically. While this didn't please current homeowners, it allowed millions of future home buyers into the market that could have never afforded the higher prices (Corminger 32).

2. **While source introductions aren't required along with parenthetical references, they can still be used, particularly if the source lends credibility to the material (e.g. a renown expert, an esteemed periodical, an influential study).**

A. If you include the author in the source introduction, put only the page number of the article or book in parentheses:

According to Harvard historian Dr. Evan Grayson, accounts of historical events are often colored by the perspective of the writer (32).

B. If the author is anonymous and you include the title of the article or book in the source introduction, put only the page number in parentheses:

According to the recent *Times* article "The Fast-Fading Euro," the European monetary system is in free-fall due to the debt crisis in Greece and Portugal (17).

C. If you introduce the author or title of the article in the source introduction and there is no page number (e.g. online article), do not include a parenthetical reference:

Children's book author Gwendolyn Mathers believes that young children want to read books that deal with real-life problems.

D. If you reference a particular study, experiment, or poll found in an article or book, provide a parenthetical reference that includes the author of the article or book, or, if anonymous, the title of the article or book and the page number:

An experiment conducted by the Mayo Research Clinic revealed that mice who are given chemotherapy for cancer eventually build a resistance to the treatment (Wright 12-13).

E. Always provide a source introduction as well as a parenthetical reference when you quote from a source:

According to marine biologist Glenda Wu, "The damage that man has done to the marine ecosystem cannot be undone in a few short years," (3).

As noted in the *Art First* 2012 journal, "Art is considered a mainstay in the educational curriculum of many countries and a supplemental diversion in U.S. education," (18).

F. Always use a source introduction when you incorporate information from a personal interview:

According to archaeologist Willard Smeds of Norfolk University, findings in African caves confirm that man was using fire for heat over one million years ago (Smeds).

Writing Activity 12.1

For practice using parenthetical references, write a sentence that includes a parenthetical reference for each of the following pieces of research material based on the source information provided. Paraphrase the material unless instructed to use it as a quotation. You will also be asked to include a source introduction for some sentences.

Examples:

Georgia was first settled by former English convicts who worked for years as indentured servants to gain their freedom.
By George Strait, "Our Earliest Settlers," page 3

(Do not include source introduction)

English prisoners were the first settlers of Georgia, working for years as indentured servants before gaining their freedom (Strait 3).

Urban renewal projects have resulted in remarkable turnarounds for blighted urban areas long resistant to improvement.
Mercy Montanez, *Solutions to Urban Decay,* page 36

(Include source introduction)

In her recent book *Solutions to Urban Decay*, Mary Montanez says that long-time areas of urban blight have benefitted greatly from urban renewal projects (36).

1. U.S. dependence on foreign oil has contributed to our government coddling Middle Eastern dictators intolerant of democratic principles.
   Molly Kinkcaid, *U.S. Middle Eastern Policy*, page 112

   (Do not include source introduction)

2. While the majority of college football, basketball, and baseball players aspire to a career in the professional ranks, only a small minority ever make it.
   "Making the Grade: Educating Our College Athletes" (online article, no page numbers, anonymous author)

   (Do not include source introduction)

3. Refined white sugar is a major culprit in the problem of childhood obesity.
   Rachel Marquez, nutritionist, "Obesity in Children," *Today* magazine, page 14

   (Include source introduction)

4. America's thirty-year "War on Drugs" has not produced the desired effects. Drug use in the U.S. is higher today than when the "war" began, and the flow of illicit drugs into the country has not decreased. Clearly a different approach needs to be tried to alter the drug-taking habit of millions of Americans.
   Clarence Collins, "End the Drug War," *Time* magazine, page 47

(Do not include source introduction)

5. Pet owners continue to allow their pets to breed while millions of unwanted dogs
    and cats are euthanized annually in animal shelters.
    Mark Kato, "The Silent Epidemic of Unwanted Animals," *The Atlantic*, page 12

    (Use as a quotation, which requires a source introduction)

Paraphrasing, Quoting, and Responding

A research paper consists of two intermingled sources of information: the research
material, presented through paraphrasing and quotations, and the writer's own thoughts
and responses. A writer distinguishes between the two by providing source references
for all research material; anything that isn't referenced in the paper comes from the
writer.

How a writer mixes paraphrasing, quotations, and personal input in a research paper
contributes significantly to its effectiveness. To incorporate paraphrasing, quoting,
and your own ideas into a paper most effectively, consider these suggestions:

1. **Paraphrase the majority of the research material that you incorporate.** When
    you paraphrase the research material, your own writing "voice" dominates the
    paper. It doesn't read like a compilation of other writer's voices. While
    presenting the research material in your own words, you can retain key words from
    the material that would not be easily or effectively paraphrased.

2. **Use an occasional quotation to highlight a particularly important or striking
    statement.** Quote from your most credible sources: a noted expert on the topic, a
    renown physician, sociologist, or scholar, or a highly regarded periodical or
    journal. Reserve your quotes for statements whose exact wording will make the
    greatest impact on readers.

3. **Intersperse your own responses and thoughts throughout the paper.** Respond
    to the research material or add your own ideas as you cover different aspects of the
    topic. Your comments show readers that you are in control of the paper,
    knowledgeable on the topic, and using the research to further your writing purpose
    rather than just presenting information.

4. **Clearly distinguish the research material from your own thoughts and
    responses.** Make sure that readers always know when you are presenting research
    material or sharing your own ideas. Provide parenthetical references for all
    research material, whether paraphrased or quoted.

Writing Activity 12.2

Read the following excerpts from a sample research paper, noting how the writer mixes paraphrasing, quotations, and her own thoughts and comments and provides parenthetical references for all research material. (The writer's own comments are italicized for your easy identification.)

Young Girls and Puberty

A study conducted by researchers at the Lincoln Medical Center reveals that American girls are going through puberty at earlier ages. The study found that thirty years ago the average age of the onset of puberty in girls was 13.2 years while today it is 11.8 years, a statistically significant difference (Faris 37). It is also not uncommon for girls to go into puberty as early as 8 or 9 years of age ("Growing Up Too Fast: Little Girls and Puberty" 4).

Some medical experts have speculated that the earlier onset of puberty is a natural evolutionary trend, and others have cited the regular exposure to chemicals in the environment (Faris 39). In March of 2011, the journal *Pediatrics* revealed a study in which a significant correlation was found between rates of obesity among young girls and early puberty ("Earlier Puberty Among Girls: Should Parents be Worried?"). *Of the possible causes, the link between obesity and early puberty seems the strongest. Many young girls, and much of America's population, are overweight compared to thirty years ago. Even casual observation reveals that most young girls who have gone through puberty are on the heavier side.*

The earlier onset of puberty is a cause for concern. No doubt it can be embarrassing for a 9 or 10 year old girl to be developing breasts and having to deal with menstruation. Early puberty seems like an assault on childhood, which may have a disturbing emotional impact on young girls. In addition, according to biologist Sandra Steingraber, "The data indicates that if you get your first period before age 12, your risk of breast cancer is 50 percent high than if you get it at age 16. For every year we could delay a girl's first menstrual period, we could prevent thousands of breast cancers," (Austin 1). *Certainly no one wishes for their daughter to go through puberty at an early age, but parents need to be aware of the possibility.*

If obesity is the leading cause of early puberty in girls, the solution to the problem is obvious: don't let your child become overweight. Of course some children have a greater natural propensity for being heavier than others, but according to child nutritionist Wendy Wang, most obesity is caused by overeating, by the soda, hamburger, and fries fast-food diet that too many children are raised on, and by a lack of exercise (Wang 4). In addition, says Steingraber, there is "an especially strong connection between obesity in younger children, ages 2 through 5, and the early onset of puberty," (Austin 2).

Clearly, parents need to monitor their children's eating and exercise habits from an early age. If a child does go through puberty at a young age, parents need to do everything possible to help the child through the transition and provide the emotional support that may be needed. Whether or not she goes through early puberty, a child is still a child.

Writing Activity 12.3

To practice paraphrasing, quoting, and presenting your own thoughts and responses in a research paper, incorporate material from the following three sources in a short paper, organizing the material to present it most effectively. Provide parenthetical references for all research material, paraphrase most of the material, use at least one quotation, and include some of your own thoughts and responses. Then exchange papers with classmates to see how they incorporated the research material in their papers.

Topic: College loan debt for senior citizens

> Surprisingly, over 15% of outstanding college loan debt is owed by senior citizens over 55 years of age. Some of this debt continues to haunt seniors from their undergraduate years thirty or more years ago. Others took out loans when they returned to school later in life to prepare for a career change. Still others co-signed on their children's or grandchildren's loans and have assumed the payments.
> Ancel Branch, "Seniors Paying College Loans," *Nation*, page 10

> With the current recession adding to the problem of seniors trying to pay off large college loans, President Obama eased the repayment requirements for Federal loans. Borrowers can now pay 10% of their income for 20 years, at which time the loan is forgiven. This sliding payment scale based on income will help the many senior citizens whose incomes have shrunk dramatically in retirement.
> "President Eases College Loan Payment Requirements," *StarTribune* online newspaper, page 2

> Is a college education worth the lifetime debt created by large student loans? That is a question many senior citizens, who are currently saddled with 15% of the the outstanding college loan debt, are asking themselves. The last thing that they envisioned while attending college was that college loan payments would plague them in their "golden years." Those who had to file bankruptcy as a result of the recession discovered a sobering truth: bankruptcy does not erase Federal loan debt.
> Margaret Singh, "Still Paying on Your College Loan?" *AARP* magazine

Works Cited

The parenthetical references within a research paper direct readers to the "Works Cited" section at the end, which provides the bibliographical information for readers to access the referenced sources if they choose. Each "Works Cited" entry begins with the author's name or the article title appearing in a parenthetical reference. To provide the correct bibliographical information for each source in the "Works Cited" section, follow these guidelines:

1. **List the entries in alphabetical order, beginning either with the last name of the author, or, if the author is anonymous, the title of the article or book.**

2. **Double space between "Works Cited" entries, and single space between lines in an entry that runs more than one line, indenting subsequent lines five spaces.**

3. **Include the following information for each entry:**

book: author, title, publishing location, publisher, date of publication:

Monroe, Claire. *The Darkest Dawn.* Cambridge: Camden Press, 1999.

article (periodical or newspaper)

author, title of article, name of magazine or newspaper, volume number, date, page numbers of article:

Ormand, Greg. "Who Cares about the Environment?" *Harpers* Vol. XXIII 4 August 2001: 12-13.

article (online)

author (if provided), title of article, name of organization and website, location of organization, date, date site accessed, website address:

Wu, Dr. Stanley. "Treatments for Squamous Cell Cancer." International Cancer Foundation. New York, New York. *Med.Web.* 3 November 2001. May 2008 http://InternationalCancerFoundation.com.

article (author anonymous)**:**

If the author is anonymous, begin the entry with the title of the article, followed by the appropriate periodical, newspaper, or online information:

"Speculators Driving Up Cost of Oil." *Newsweek* 3 September 2011: 30-37.

interview

author, personal interview, date of interview:

Gamez, Dr. Roberta. Personal interview. 3 December 2011

When you do the "Works Cited" section at the end of your research paper, refer to this section as well as the "Works Cited" section at the end of the research paper "Teen Smoking" in Writing Activity 12.9 to help you provide the correct bibliographical information for each of your entries.

Writing Assignment

In this final lesson, you write a research paper using a number of sources to develop your topic and support your thesis. Other than relying more heavily on the research and using more sources, your paper will be similar to previous essays where you incorporated research material. To help you decide on a topic for your paper, consider these suggestions:

1.   **For your topic, you may either select a particular issue or problem to write about.** Select a topic that interests you, that you would like to learn more about, and that may interest a particular group of readers or a more general audience.

2.   **Select a topic for which you can find research material from different sources.** Consider a few possible topics, eliminating those that have little available research information.

3.   **Select a topic for which you can find factual information.** Avoid topics for which factual information is scarce or doesn't exist.

4.   **Select a topic that you can develop in a five-to-eight page double-spaced paper.** (Your instructor may set different length parameters.) For example, while you might write a book on "Eliminating Cancer in the Next Twenty Years," you could probably cover a topic such as "New Alternative Breast Cancer Treatments" effectively in a research paper.

5.   **Select a topic that is serious and substantial enough to warrant your research efforts and your readers' time and attention.** Choose an issue or problem that is current or ongoing and that readers should be aware of.

6.   **Consider topics from a range of fields: education, politics, the environment, health care, law enforcement, foreign policy, children's issues, economic issues, college issues, etc.** Identify issues and problems in different areas before narrowing your choices.

Writing Activity 12.4

Consider a few possible topics for your research paper, check out the available research, and then select a topic that is researchable and that interests you the most.

Sample topic: Teen smoking

Rationale: I know that smoking is still a big problem because a lot of students where I went to high school smoke, including some of my friends. Looking online and in a periodical index at the library, I found a lot of articles on teen smoking written in recent years, so I think there is plenty of information available.

Preparation

In preparing for your paper, the first step is doing your topic research. If you are writing about a problem, you will learn more about the problem, its causes and effects, and possible solutions. If you are writing about an issue, you will find differing viewpoints and evaluate the supportive evidence for each viewpoint. Based on your research, you will eventually arrive at a thesis which you will support in your paper with your research material. In addition, you will be considering the best reading audience for your paper - the people who would be most interested in or most affected by the topic - and your purpose in writing to them.

Researching Your Topic

To research your topic effectively and glean the most relevant research information, consider these suggestions:

1.   **Cast a wide net with your research, checking on a number of potential sources.** Some sources will prove valuable for your paper, some will have little or no useful information, and some may be too dated to be relevant. If you find ten sources on your topic, half of them may prove useful.

2.   **Check the credibility of each source.** Use sources that you believe to provide reliable information, whether they are online sources, periodicals, journals, newspapers, or books. Look for information from experts on your topic, people that readers would tend to believe. Be suspicious of sources that may have a bias towards your topic and consequently provide unreliable or questionable information.

3.   **Before you begin your research, determine what you want to find out**

about your topic. Are you trying to understand your topic better? Are you looking for the causes and effects of a problem? Are you looking for the evidence that supports a particular viewpoint on the topic? In evaluating the relevance of the research information, it helps to know in advance what you are looking for while also being open to ideas you hadn't considered.

4. **As you read from your sources, write down everything that may be relevant to your paper.** If you are writing about an issue that people's opinions differ on, include arguments from different viewpoints. If you are writing about a problem, include possible causes, effects, who or what is affected, and possible solutions. Keep your sources separate, which is most easily done on note cards, and include the bibliographical information for each source that you will include in the "Works Cited" section of your paper.

5. **Don't over-rely on one or two sources.** If you only use one or two primary sources for most of your information, readers may assume that you didn't research your topic thoroughly, that you are only using sources that fit your thesis, or that you are providing too narrow a perspective on the topic. The most effective research papers usually include several sources, providing readers with a comprehensive view of the topic.

6. **Consider interviewing local experts on your topic.** Information that you obtain from interviews is acceptable in research papers. If there are credible local experts on your topic - college professors, law enforcement officials, physicians - they may provide you with some valuable information.

7. **As you research your topic, look for the different types of development you used in writing your previous essays.** Look for factual information and evidence, relevant comparisons, credible statistics, reliable studies or experiments, strong examples, striking description and detail, and insightful analysis.

Writing Activity 12.5

Begin researching your topic, checking on a variety of sources (e.g. online, newspapers, periodicals, journals, books, interviews). A college librarian can help you locate periodical and newspaper bibliographies of articles on your topic. Take notes as you read through your sources, keep the sources separate, include the bibliography information for each source (e.g. author, title of article, periodical, volume, date, page numbers), and maintain the exact wording for any statements that you may quote in your paper. Use the most credible and current sources you can find.

If you are writing about a problem, find information on the seriousness of the problem, its causes, its effects, who or what is affected, and possible solutions. If you are writing about an issue on which people's opinions differ, find the differing viewpoints, the reasons (arguments) in support of each viewpoint, and the validating evidence for each reason.

Thesis

As you researched your paper, no doubt you drew some conclusions and made some judgments on the information you found. When you conclude your research, read over your findings to see whether those initial conclusions and judgments are confirmed. Based on all of your research, come up with a potential thesis statement: your viewpoint on the topic that your evaluation of the research led to and that it most strongly supports. Your thesis will influence how you incorporate the research material into your paper, the information that you include, the purpose(s) that you use the information for, and what you want to convince readers of.

If you are writing about an issue, your thesis will reflect your viewpoint on the issue based on your analysis and evaluation of the research. If you are writing about a problem, your thesis will reflect your viewpoint on the problem. Is it a serious problem that most people aren't aware of? Is it a problem whose solution needs the support of readers? Does the problem have a devastating impact on children? Your viewpoint should reflect what you want readers to keep in mind about the problem as they read.

Writing Activity 12.6

Generate a potential thesis statement for your paper, one that reflects your viewpoint and is best supported by the research.

Sample thesis statement:

Topic: Teen smoking

Thesis: Teenage smoking continues to be a serious problem throughout the country, one which has disastrous effects on the long-term health of millions of American teens.

Thesis Support

Once you have decided on your thesis, take a closer look at your research material to see how you can best use it in your paper. If you are writing an issue-oriented paper, look for the following elements in your research:

1. Information that explains or clarifies the issue.

2. Information that reveals the seriousness of the issue: why readers should care.

3.   Differing viewpoints on the issue.

4.   Reasons (arguments) in support of each viewpoint.

5.   Projections (speculation) on what the future may hold for the issue if one or another viewpoints prevails (i.e. what may happen if the U.S. enacts stricter gun control laws, and what may happen if it doesn't).

6.   Evidence to validate each reason (e.g. factual information, comparisons, examples, statistics, studies, etc.).

If you are writing about a problem, look for the following elements:

1.   An explanation of exactly what the problem is.

2.   Causes of the problem, and evidence of the validity of each cause.

3.   Effects of the problem, and evidence of the validity of each effect.

4.   The people or things affected by the problem.

5.   Possible solution(s) to the problem.

As you read through the research material considering different elements to include in the paper, you may find some "holes" or weaknesses in your research: not enough evidence in support of a particular viewpoint, no clear explanation of the problem, no comparative information to support the thesis, a lack of examples to help readers understand a particular point, or insufficient information on the effects of a problem. Your analysis of the research material may send you back to the Internet or library to find more information.   This is not uncommon since it is difficult to evaluate the information until you have compiled and read through your research notes.

Writing Activity 12.7

Read through your research material identifying the elements for an issue or problem-oriented paper, as well as other pertinent information. Determine what material you may include in your paper and how you might use it. If you find holes or weaknesses in your material, do some additional research.

Audience and Purpose

By now, you no doubt have a pretty good idea of the best audience for your paper based on its topic, whether it be a specific group of readers or a more general audience.

To decide on the best audience for your paper and your purpose in writing to them, consider these questions:

1. **Who is most affected by the issue or problem?** What group of people need to be most aware of the problem and perhaps take some action or change some behavior?

2. **Who could have an impact on the issue or problem?** For example, if the problem or issue involves children, what group of people could help reduce or solve the problem?

3. **Whose minds would you like to change on the issue or problem?** If a resolution to a problem or issue involves changing some people's minds, whose minds need changing?

4. **Who could benefit most from reading the paper?** For example, older readers might benefit from reading a paper on investment scams targeting senior citizens, or expectant mothers might benefit from reading a paper on coping with post partum depression.

5. **Why would you write to this particular audience: your writing purpose?** Do you want readers to change their behavior, take a particular action (e.g. vote for a particular candidate, support a particular initiative, or write the local board of trustees), become more aware of a particular problem or issue, or reconsider their viewpoint?

Writing Activity 12.8

Decide on the best primary audience for your paper and your purpose in writing to them.

Sample audience and purpose:

Topic: Teen Smoking

Audience: Teenagers and parents of teens

Purpose: To alert teens and parents to the short-term and long-term effects of teenage smoking and to show them ways to quit.

Drafting

When you have completed your research, evaluated your findings, and decided on a thesis, you are ready to write the first draft. Following the MLA research paper format should not be that difficult, and your research material will fill most of your paper. Your biggest challenge is incorporating the research material and including your own thoughts and responses in ways that most convincingly support your thesis.

As you begin writing your draft, consider the following suggestions.

1. **Introduce the topic in your opening and include your thesis statement.** Create interest for readers, stressing the seriousness of the topic. Include your thesis statement so that readers have a sense of what lies ahead. Your opening may be somewhat longer than in your previous essays, balanced with the greater length of the paper.

2. **Provide any explanatory information needed to help readers understand the topic.** For example, someone writing on post partum depression would need to explain what it is. Someone writing on investment scams targeting seniors would need to show the types of scams to be aware of. Someone writing on the electoral college would need to explain how it works. Given your topic and audience, decide what readers need to know and provide the information.

3. **If you are writing an issue-oriented paper, present your thesis support and address opposing arguments in the middle paragraphs.** Begin by presenting your supportive evidence, relying primarily on research material. Include any factual evidence, comparisons, statistics, studies, or examples to support your thesis. Then respond to one or two opposing arguments as in previous essays.

4. **If you are writing a problem-oriented paper, present the causes and effects of the problem, including who or what is affected, in the middle paragraphs.** Decide whether it would be most effective to present the causes or the effects first. Which order would have the greatest impact on readers and help further your writing purpose?

5. **Include your own thoughts and responses along with the research material.** Your writer's "voice" should be evident throughout the paper, commenting on the research material and adding your own thoughts on the topic. Your comments should help support your thesis, further your writing purpose, and reveal your understanding of the topic and the research material.

6. **Provide parenthetical references at the end of each piece of research material presented.** Paraphrase most of the material, and include an occasional quotation of an especially important or striking statement. Use some source introductions (According to Dr. Joseph Saenz, A ten-year Alzheimer study presented in

Scientific Journal) along with parenthetical references to highlight particularly credible or impressive sources and with all quotations.

7. **Conclude your paper in a way that reinforces your thesis and writing purpose.** If you are writing a problem-oriented paper, present the solution(s) to the problem. If you are writing an issue-oriented paper, you might summarize the supportive evidence, introduce a final compelling piece of evidence, or speculate on the future of the topic. Keep the length of your conclusion balanced with the overall length of the paper, and leave readers with something to think about.

Writing Activity 12.9

Read the following first draft of "Teen Smoking," noting its opening, thesis statement, incorporation of research material, parenthetical references, source introductions, writer's thoughts and responses, conclusion, and "Works Cited" section. Then write the first draft of your paper, including a "Works Cited" section at the end.

Teen Smoking (first draft)

Audience: teenagers and parents

A 2005 study by the Center for Disease Control and Prevention (CDC), a Federal agency under the Department of Health and Human Services, found that nearly one in four high school students reported smoking in the last month. The study found an increase in teen smoking compared to a 2003 study when one in five students reported smoking ("Teen Smoking: Statistics and Prevention"). More recent studies show no decline in the number of teens who smoke despite everything that is known about the long-term health effects of smoking. Teenage smoking continues to be a serious problem throughout the country, one which has disastrous effects on the long-term health of millions of American teens.

Teens smoke for a number of reasons. Some feel insecure in social situations, and puffing on a cigarette seems to help them cope. Teens smoke because of peer pressure, wanting to fit in with their smoking friends. Teens are also more apt to smoke if their parents smoke or other older people that they admire ("Why Teens Smoke"). According to Denise Witmar in the article "Why Do Teens Start to Smoke," "They are drawn to the 'forbidden' lure of smoking that also attracts teens to drinking and marijuana use," (Witmar 1). Some teens also smoke because they think they look "cool" with a cigarette dangling from their mouth, a defiant gesture against adult authority.

Smoking can also produce pleasurable feelings and reduce stress. Nicotine in cigarettes activates the brain circuitry that enhances feelings of pleasure in cigarette smokers, and since the pleasurable feelings wear off within seconds of the last drag on a cigarette, smokers are quick to light up the next cigarette ("Nicotine"). Nicotine in cigarettes is also a strongly addictive drug which can hook cigarette smokers early in their usage and make it a difficult habit to break.

Some teen smokers argue inaccurately that smoking for a year or two and then quitting will have no effect on their long-term health, so why not enjoy smoking? In fact, teen smoking can have serious and immediate effects on the body since there is still some physical development taking place during these formative years. Teen smoking can cause a great deal of coughing, shortness of breath, poor lung function, respiratory problems, circulatory and hearing problems, and of course, addiction ("Effects of Teen Smoking").

Many teens also argue that they plan on quitting smoking after a year or two, which they can do easily. However, while most teens plan on quitting, over 60% are still smoking seven to nine years later, destroying the teen myth that it is easy to stop smoking ("Effects of Teen Smoking"). Finally, many teens simply ignore the long-term health effects of smoking, disinterested in what the distant future may hold for them, or are negatively fatalistic about their futures, particularly if they are among the high percentage of teen smokers from lower socio-economic backgrounds ("Teen Smoking: Statistics and Prevention").

The harmful effects of cigarette smoking are well known. One in two lifetime smokers will die from their habit, and many of these smokers begin in their teens. Tar coats the lungs of smokers and causes cancer. Men and women who smoke are ten times more likely to die from lung cancer than non-smokers ("Harmful Effects of Smoking Cigarettes"). Smoking is also associated with cancers of the mouth, pharynx, larynx, esophagus, stomach, pancreas, cervix, kidney, ureter, and bladder ("Nicotine").

Heart disease and strokes are also more common among smokers, and smoking causes one in five deaths from heart disease. In younger people, three out of four deaths from heart disease are caused by smoking. Emphysema is a common smoker's disease that slowly rots your lungs, leading to a long downward spiral ending in death. Cigarette smoking during pregnancy increases the risk of low birth weight, prematurity, spontaneous abortion, and perinatal mortality, referred to as the fetal tobacco syndrome ("Harmful Effects of Smoking Cigarettes"). Finally, smokers are not only ruining their own health, they are contributing to the bad health of those around them who suffer from second-hand smoke inhalation, which can lead to all of the problems that beset smokers. Some people make the argument that smoking around children is a form of child abuse, knowingly endangering the children's lives by subjecting them to second-hand smoke.

Knowing all of the horribly harmful effects of cigarette smoking is important for any teen smoker or potential smoker, and this knowledge will get some smokers to quit and others not to start. However, given that this information has been around for decades, the health message has not by itself gotten enough teens to stop smoking or never start. There has to be a greater attempt to address the root causes of smoking for most teens.

According to an online Mayo Clinic article, "Teens must be made more aware of the immediate negative effects of smoking, which may resonate more strongly than the later-life health issues they may to brush aside," ("Teen Smoking: How to Help Your Teen Quit"). For example, smoking gives you bad breath, stinky clothes and hair, yellow teeth and fingernails, a pale, unhealthy look, premature wrinkles, and a hacking cough, and saps your energy for sports and other activities ("Teen Smoking: How to

Help Your Teen Quit").

Most teens do care about their appearance and the image they project, and if they understand that bad breath, stinky clothes, yellow teeth and wrinkles aren't cool, they may think twice about smoking. They also need to have the courage to quit something that their friends are doing, which may be easier said than done. Going along with their particular crowd is the way that most teens handle high school peer pressure, and it takes a lot of courage to swim against the tide. Any teen who faces rejection or ridicule from his or her "friends" for quitting smoking knows one thing: they aren't really your friends, and you are threatening their comfortable status quo.

Finally, teens who want to quit smoking need to know that they are dealing with a highly addictive drug and that quitting may take great willpower. If it didn't, the millions of smokers who confess that smoking is a dirty, unhealthy habit they would like to break would quit. However, according to the article "How Can I Quit Smoking?", there are some proven strategies that help teens kick the smoking habit:

- **Put it in writing.** Teens who are successful at quitting smoking often put in writing that they want to quit and why. Putting it in writing makes the goal more real and binding.

- **Get support.** Teens who quit smoking often are supported by friends and family. If this support isn't available, consider joining a support group either online or in person.

- **Set a quit date.** Set a date when you are going to quit and let friends and family know. Mark the date on your calendar and stick to it ("How Can I Quit Smoking?" 1)

- **Throw away your cigarettes, along with ashtrays and lighters**.

- **Wash all your clothes.** Get the smoke smell out of all of your clothes and if you smoke in your car, have it cleaned out too.

- **Think about your triggers.** Be aware of situations and times when you typically smoke - things that "trigger" your smoking - and avoid these situations as much as possible.

- **Substitute something else for cigarettes.** You are used to having a cigarette in your hand and mouth, so substitute other things: gum, lollipops, tooth picks, mints ("How Can I Quit Smoking?" 2)

- **Expect some withdrawal symptoms.** If you have smoked regularly, expect some nicotine withdrawal symptoms such as headaches, depression, sore throat, or the "munchies." These symptoms will pass, so be patient.

- **Keep yourself busy.** The more distracted you are with activity, the less likely you'll be to crave cigarettes.

- **Quit gradually**. While some people have success quitting "cold turkey," many others are successful by reducing the number of cigarettes they smoke daily until they get down to zero.

- **Use a nicotine replacement if necessary**. If you find that none of these strategies is working, you might talk to your doctor about treatments. Using a nicotine replacement, such as gum, patches, inhalers, or nasal sprays, can be very helpful. Sprays and inhalers are available by prescription only, and it's important to see your doctor before buying the patch and gum over the counter so that he or she can help you find the solution that will work best for you ("How Can I Quit Smoking?" 3)

- **If you slip up, don't give up.** If you slip up, it doesn't mean you've failed. You are overcoming a deadly, addictive habit, and you might suffer some lapses. The key is not to give up: the one thing that everyone who kicks the habit has in common ("How Can I Quit Smoking?" 4).

Smoking is a deadly, dirty, addictive habit that harms anyone who smokes, and 90% of life-long smokers begin in their teens ("The Tragedy of Teen Smoking"). If you begin smoking in your teens, there is a great likelihood that you will die well before your time from a horrible smoking-induced disease. The longer you smoke as a teen, the greater your addiction to nicotine and the greater the chance you will continue smoking.

Smoking isn't a cool or adult thing to do. Most adults who smoke wish they had never started. Smoking is, in fact, a stupid thing to do, ruining your health and creating a drug addiction. It takes courage to stop smoking when your peers smoke, but if you stop smoking, you may get others to stop also and get others not to start in the first place.

Quitting smoking may not be easy, but there are strategies that have worked for millions of former smokers that can work for you. The small nicotine-induced pleasure you may get from smoking is nothing compared to the life-long damage you are doing to yourself, including drug addiction. Many former smokers say that the best day of their lives was when they kicked the habit. That day could be yours, and the sooner you quit, the easier it will be.

Works Cited

"Effects of Teen Smoking." *TeenSmoking.us*.
    http://www.teensmoking.us/content/effects-teen-smoking.html.

"Harmful Effects of Smoking Cigarettes/" *QuitSmokingStop.com*.
    http://www.quit-smoking-stop.com/harmful-smoking-effects.htlm.

"How Can I Quit Smoking?" *KidsHealth.Org.*
  Http://kidshealth.org/teen/drug_alcohol/tobacco/quit_smoking.html.

"Nicotine." *HomeDrugTestingKit.com.*
  http://www.homedrugtestingkit.com/nicotine.html.

"Teen Smoking: How to Help Your Teen Quit." *MayoClinic.com.*
  http://www.mayoclinic.com/health/teen-smoking/tn00016.

"Teen Smoking: Statistics and Prevention." Help for Troubled Teens.
  FamilyFirstAid.org. http://www.familyfirstaid.org/teen-smoking.htlm.

"The Tragedy of Teen Smoking." *TeenHelp.com.*
  http://www.teenhelp.com/teen-health/teen-smoking-statistics.htlm.

Witmer, Denise. "Why Do Teens Start to Smoke?" *About.com.*
  http://parentingteens.about.com/od/tobaccouse/f/teen_smoking4.htm.

"Why Teens Smoke." Teen Health. *ThinkQuest.org.*
  http://library.thinkquest.org/10991/teen18.html.

Revision

Once you have completed your first draft, you can evaluate the entire paper to see how everything fits together. With longer papers, writers sometimes run into organizational problems, lose their writing focus, or discover some imbalances in content: spending too much time on one aspect or too little on another. Such problems can be remedied during the revision process.

   To revise your draft most effectively, consider these suggestions.

1. **Read your entire draft a couple times, looking for any problems that need attention: a paragraph that seems out of place, a weakly argued point, the need for a clarifying example, the omission of a parenthetical reference, a paragraph that strays off the topic.** Make note of problem areas that need some attention.

2. **Check your opening.** Is your topic clearly and interestingly presented? Is your thesis statement obvious? Does your opening engage your readers' interest so they will want to read further?

3. **Check your explanatory information.** Do you explain everything that readers need to know to understand your topic?

4. **If you wrote a problem-oriented paper, check your causes and effects.** Do you provide evidence to validate your causes? Are they presented in the most effective order? Are the major effects of the problem clearly presented in the most effective order?

5. **If you wrote an issue-oriented paper, check the supportive points for your thesis and your responses to opposing arguments.** Have you presented the strongest supportive arguments for your thesis and provided evidence to validate each argument? Have you provided factual and comparative information and used examples to help make your points? Have you addressed the major opposing arguments to your thesis in the most effective manner for your readers?

6. **Check your personal input in the paper: your responses to the research material and your thoughts on the topic.** Have you responded to the research material in ways that support your thesis and further your writing purpose? Have you included your own thoughts on the topic, making the paper more than a compilation of research material? Is your writer's "voice" evident throughout the draft?

7. **Check your draft's adherence to the MLA style format.** Have you provided a parenthetical reference at the end of each piece of research material? Have you included some source introductions for your most distinguished or credible

sources? Have you paraphrased most of the research material and used an occasional quotation for a particularly striking or important statement? Can readers always distinguish the research material from your own thoughts and responses?

8. **Check the overall organization of your draft.** Are there any paragraphs or sentences that would fit better in a different location? Does each paragraph follow logically from the previous paragraph?

9. **Check your paragraphing.** Do you change paragraphs as you move to a different point, idea, or aspect of your draft? Are there any overly long paragraphs that could be divided or short paragraphs that could be combined or developed further? Does your paragraphing make the content most understandable for readers?

10. **Check your sentence wording.** Revise sentences to eliminate wordiness, smooth out awkward phrasing, replace questionable word choices, clarify vaguely worded sentences, or vary your sentence structures. In addition, check your use of transitional wording to tie paragraphs together and show relationships between thoughts.

11. **Check your conclusion.** If you wrote a problem-oriented paper, do you present the most viable solution(s) to the problem? If you wrote an issue-oriented paper, do you reinforce your thesis in an effective manner? Does your conclusion clarify your writing purpose for readers? Does it leave them with something to think about?

12. **Read your draft with your audience and purpose in mind.** What might you change, add, or delete to make a stronger impact on readers and further your writing purpose?

13. **Check your "Works Cited" section.** Make sure that you have listed all sources alphabetically and provided the appropriate bibliographical information for each entry.

Writing Activity 12.10

Keeping the revision suggestions in mind, revise your draft and make changes to improve your paper. Then exchange drafts with a classmate to get some feedback, and make any further revisions that are warranted.

Sample revisions

Teen Smoking (first four paragraphs)

Given the media emphasis on drug use among teens, cigarette smoking receives less attention. However, a 2005 study by the Center for Disease Control and Prevention (CDC), a Federal agency under the Department of Health and Human Services, found that nearly one in four high school students reported smoking in the last month. The study found an increase in teen smoking compared to a 2003 study when one in five students reported smoking, **and** ~~("Teen Smoking: Statistics and Prevention").~~ more recent studies show no decline in the number of teens who smoke **("Teen Smoking: Statistics and Prevention").** **D**espite everything that is known about the ~~long-term~~ **negative** health effects of smoking, teenage smoking continues to be a serious problem ~~throughout the country~~ **in the U.S., with** ~~one which has~~ disastrous effects ~~on the long-term health of~~ **for** millions of American teens.

Why do teenagers continue to smoke in record numbers? ~~Teens smoke for~~ **There are** a ~~number of~~ **several** reasons. Some feel insecure in social situations, and puffing on a cigarette seems to help them cope. Teens smoke because of peer pressure, wanting to fit in with their smoking friends. ~~Teens~~ **They** are more apt to smoke if their parents smoke or other older people that they admire ("Why Teens Smoke"). According to Denise Witmar in the article "Why Do Teens Start to Smoke," "They are drawn to the 'forbidden' lure of smoking that also attracts teens to drinking and marijuana use," (Witmar 1). Some teens also smoke because they think they look "cool" with a cigarette dangling from their mouth, a defiant gesture against adult authority.

Smoking can also produce pleasurable feelings and reduce stress. **According to the article "Nicotine" on the *Home Drug Testing* website,** "Nicotine in cigarettes activates the brain circuitry that enhances feelings of pleasure in cigarette smokers, and since the pleasurable feelings wear off within seconds of the last drag on a cigarette, smokers are quick to light up the next cigarette," ("Nicotine"). Nicotine ~~in cigarettes~~ is also a strongly addictive drug which can hook **teen** ~~cigarette~~ smokers ~~early in their usage~~ and make it a difficult habit to break.

Some teen smokers argue ~~inaccurately~~ that smoking for a year or two and then quitting will have no effect on their ~~long-term~~ health, so why not enjoy smoking? In fact, teen smoking can have serious and immediate effects on the body since there is still ~~some~~ physical development ~~taking place~~ **occurring** during ~~these formative~~ **the teen** years. Teen smoking can cause ~~a great deal of~~ **chronic** coughing, shortness of breath, poor lung function, respiratory problems, circulatory and hearing problems, and of course, **nicotine** addiction ("Effects of Teen Smoking"). **Teens begin experiencing firsthand the physical damage caused by smoking that is most often associated with adult smokers.**

Editing

In editing a research paper, there is one additional consideration: making sure that your parenthetical references and "Works Cited" entries are punctuated correctly. The following guidelines will help you do that.

Punctuation: MLA Format

Check to make sure your source references include the following:

1. Quotation marks (" ") around the title of articles.

2. The titles of books, periodicals, newspapers, and online sites in italics.

3. No comma between the author's last name and the page number in parenthetical references (Krantz 13).

4. When the author is anonymous, no comma between the title of the article and the page number in parenthetical references ("Disappearing Rainforests" 8).

5. A source introduction for all quoted material: According to climatologist Eugene Wu, "Global warming is a fact, not a theory," (Wu 118).

6. To punctuate "Works Cited" entries correctly:

   A. Put a period after the author's name, the title of the article, the title of the book, the name of a website, and the end of the entry.

   B.. Put a colon (:) after the location of the publisher for a book: St. Louis: Herbert Stone and Company.

   C. Put a comma after the name of the publishing company of a book, followed by the date of publication: Herbert Stone and Company, 2007.

   D. Put a colon after the date of an article, followed by the page numbers of the article: 4 August 2008: 23-26.

   E. Write dates of articles in the following manner: 6 August 2010.

Writing Activity 12.11

Check your parenthetical references and "Works Cited" entries to make sure they are punctuated correctly.

Writing Activity 12.12

Proofread your paper and correct any errors that you find. Focus in particular on the types of errors you are most prone to make and on the common problems covered in the text: run-on and comma-splice sentences, fragments, subject-verb agreement, pronoun-antecedent agreement, comparative and superlative adjectives, comma usage, colon, semi-colon, and dash usage, apostrophes in contractions and possessives, dangling and misplaced modifiers, and frequently confused words (e.g. there/their/they're, know/no, affect/effect, its/it's, etc.).

Communicating with Readers

Sharing the research paper with your reading audience or representatives may take some thought and help from your instructor. Because of its length, a research paper is not as easily disseminated as a shorter essay. Talk with your instructor about the possibility of putting the paper in college or high school libraries, of distributing electronic copies, or of posting the paper on a website or on Facebook. Of course, you can also provide copies for classmates.

Index